"The Bible is a book about Jesus. The disciples walking to Emmaus after the resurrection discovered this as Christ himself walked along with them and explained how the Old Testament pointed to the Savior. This book is the first in an important series by Nancy Guthrie, and it spotlights how Jesus can be seen in the book of Genesis. I recommend this—and the entire series—to you."

Alistair Begg, Senior Pastor, Parkside Church, Chagrin Falls, Ohio

"The perfect blend of biblical scholarship and heartfelt passion, Guthrie guides us through Genesis, helping us discover for ourselves God's magnificent plan of redemption. Her steps are sure, and her grasp of the Scriptures is breathtaking. Above all, God's unfailing love, grace, and sovereignty shine forth from every page. A brilliant start to a very promising series."

Liz Curtis Higgs, New York Times best-selling author of *Mine Is the Night* and *Bad Girls of the Bible*

"It's not hyperbole to say, 'It's about time.' While there are good books out there telling pastors how to preach Christ from all the Scriptures, there have been very few Bible studies for laypeople—especially for women—along these lines. Nancy Guthrie does an amazing job of helping us to fit the pieces of the biblical puzzle together, with Christ at the center."

Michael Horton, Professor of Systematic Theology and Apologetics, Westminster Seminary California

"Nancy takes us by the hand and the heart on an exegetical excursion to see Christ in the Old Testament . . . the beauty of Guthrie's writing is that you are certain she has met him there first."

Jean F. Larroux III, Senior Pastor, Southwood Presbyterian Church, PCA, Huntsville, Alabama

"Every leader of small-group ministries knows the difficult task of finding good material—material that causes participants to think carefully while striking a chord in the heart; material that challenges the mature Christian, while gently leading those younger in the faith into deeper truths; material that digs into the Bible and applies its treasures to our everyday lives. *The Promised One* manages to do it all! A meaningful, 10-week Bible study with thought-provoking questions and solid teaching, and a peek at what is still to come. I am delighted to offer this to the women in my church and look forward to the remaining books in this series."

Jean Bronson, Director of Women's Ministries, Kirk of the Hills Presbyterian Church, St. Louis, Missouri

"An excellent resource for the church. Nancy explains biblical connections in a way that will be helpful to new believers as well as those steeped in the faith. I wish I had these resources years ago."

> **Wendy Alsup,** author, *Practical Theology for Women* and *By His Wounds You Are Healed*

"There are many great Christian books, but not many great Bible studies. Nancy is a master of getting the Word of God into the mouths, hearts, and lives of her students. I cannot wait to share this study with my people."

> **Donna Dobbs,** Christian Education Director, First Presbyterian Church, Jackson, Mississippi

"Many of us have grown up in the church learning and reciting one Bible story after the other, but how many of us can clearly connect those stories with clarity and understanding of the grand drama? *The Promised One* will lead this generation to clearly recognize that the Bible is God's purposeful story—an amazing unfolding of his promised provision through Jesus. I pray your eyes and mind will joyfully recognize him as the Promised One, making your heart burn with a deeper and more passionate love for the Savior!"

> **Jennifer Adamson,** Director of Women's Ministries, First Baptist Orlando, Orlando, Florida

"Do you ever wish you could have listened to the conversation Jesus had with his friends on the road to Emmaus? Luke tells us that Jesus started with Moses and walked his way through the Bible and explained to them the things concerning himself in all the Scriptures. Nancy has done us all a great service by carefully and precisely unpacking the teachings regarding our Savior in the Old Testament. My experience with this book has been rich and has deepened my love for the Word and for Jesus. I am in debt to my sister for this treasure of a study!"

> **David Arthur,** Executive Vice President, Precept Ministries International; coauthor, *Desiring God's Own Heart: A Study on Samuel*

"Because the stories of Genesis are so familiar to many, it can be easy to think we don't need to study it again. But *The Promised One* enables us to read all of the familiar stories with fresh eyes so that God's redemptive purposes through Christ from the very beginning become clear. I look forward to putting this study in the hands of the women at my church!"

> **Julie Wesselman,** Women's Ministry Director, Desert Springs Church, Albuquerque, New Mexico

"After nearly a decade of serving women in the church, I have to say that finding Bible study curriculum that compels women to fall in love with God's Word is perhaps one of the most challenging aspects of this job. Promotions for women's materials fill my mailbox and my inbox daily, yet rarely have I found a curriculum so well written. *The Promised One* is full of truth, humility, and grace. Nancy leads us to the Scriptures where we find there to be one story, that of our Lord Jesus. I am so grateful for this series, and I am certain it will help women come to know Christ better."

> **Kari Stainback,** Director of Women's Ministries, Park Cities Presbyterian Church, Dallas, Texas

"Is there a need for another study guide on Genesis? In a word, *yes*. And this is the book. Nancy Guthrie sets a new standard by being truly Christ-centered, starting with Jesus's fulfillment of the entire Old Testament and maintaining that focus throughout the guide. Having read three of her previous books, and the Christ-centered nature of them, I expected the same top-notch quality. I was not disappointed. The proven format of personal study, teaching chapter, and group discussion highlights Christ as the center of Genesis. Do you want to study or teach Genesis? Then this book is for you. Guthrie has provided a valuable resource for the church."

> **Rev. Richard P. Shields,** President, American Lutheran Theological Seminary

"At last! Real living water from Scripture that enables us, together, to behold the Lord Jesus in his glory—this is what nourishes and matures the soul! The expositions in Genesis, the development in Scripture, the fulfillment in our Lord Jesus Christ, and then the bridge to application to now and to the blessings yet to come when all meets the final consummation in glory. So well done. I pray that Nancy's book, as well as the series, ignites a fire that blazes from here to the Third World and strengthens all Christians everywhere to come alive in our testimony of Jesus."

> **Thaddeus Barnum,** Senior Pastor, Church of the Apostles, Fairfield, Connecticut; author, *Never Silent*

**Other books in the
Seeing Jesus in the Old Testament series:**

*The Lamb of God: Seeing Jesus in Exodus, Leviticus, Numbers,
      and Deuteronomy*

The Son of David: Seeing Jesus in the Historial Books

The Wisdom of God: Seeing Jesus in the Psalms and Wisdom Books

The Word of the Lord: Seeing Jesus in the Prophets

The Promised One

Seeing Jesus in Genesis

(A 10-Week Bible Study)

nancy guthrie

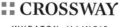

:: CROSSWAY

WHEATON, ILLINOIS

The Promised One: Seeing Jesus in Genesis (A 10-Week Bible Study)

Copyright © 2011 by Nancy Guthrie

Published by Crossway
   1300 Crescent Street
   Wheaton, Illinois 60187

Cover design: Amy Bristow

Cover photo: Bridgeman Art Library

First printing 2011

Printed in the United States of America

Unless otherwise indicated, Scripture quotations are from the ESV® Bible (*The Holy Bible, English Standard Version®*), copyright © 2001 by Crossway. Used by permission. All rights reserved.

Scripture references marked NLT are from *The Holy Bible, New Living Translation*, copyright © 1996, 2004. Used by permission of Tyndale House Publishers, Inc., Wheaton, Ill., 60189. All rights reserved.

All emphases in Scripture quotations have been added by the author.

Trade paperback ISBN: 978-1-4335-2625-1
PDF ISBN: 978-1-4335-2628-2
Mobipocket ISBN: 978-1-4335-2627-5
ePub ISBN: 978-1-4335-2628-2

Library of Congress Cataloging-in-Publication Data

Guthrie, Nancy.
 The promised one : seeing Jesus in Genesis : a 10-week Bible
study / Nancy Guthrie.
  p. cm.
 Includes index.
 ISBN 978-1-4335-2625-1 (tp)
 1. Bible O.T. Genesis—Textbooks. 2. Typology (Theology)—
Textbooks. 3. Bible. N.T.—Relation to the Old Testament—
Textbooks. 4. Bible. O.T. Genesis—Criticism, interpretation,
etc.—Textbooks. 5. Christian women—Religious life—Textbooks.
I. Title.
BS1239.G88   2011
222'.11064—dc22   2011001937

Crossway is a publishing ministry of Good News Publishers.

VP		24	23	22	21	20	19	18	17	16	15	14
21	20	19	18	17	16	14	13	12	11	10	9	8

Contents

Before We Get Started

A Note from Nancy

Welcome to *The Promised One: Seeing Jesus in Genesis*. I'm so glad you have committed to set time aside to look into God's Word along with me through this book. I'm praying that you will make fresh discoveries about God and what he is doing in the world and in your life as you work your way through this study over the weeks to come.

As we open up Genesis, we're not simply looking to increase our Bible knowledge; we want to see Jesus. We want this study to enlarge our understanding and correct our misunderstandings about who he is and what his gospel is all about. Usually we don't turn to the Old Testament to see Jesus. Instead, we turn to the Gospels in the New Testament. Yet Jesus said to the Jewish religious leaders at one point: "You search the Scriptures because you think they give you eternal life. But the Scriptures point to me!" (John 5:39). And, of course, the Scriptures he was talking about are the books of the Old Testament. Jesus himself made it clear that we can search the Old Testament Scriptures and find him there. This study is uniquely designed to help you to look into the wonder of the first book of the Old Testament—Genesis—and see how it prepares for and points to Christ.

There are three essentials parts to this study. The first is the personal time you will spend reading your Bible, seeking to strengthen your grip on its truths as you work your way through the questions provided in the Personal Bible Study section of each week's lesson. This will be the easiest part to skip. But nothing is more important than reading and studying God's Word, expecting that he will meet you as you do.

As you work on the Personal Bible Study, don't become frustrated if you can't come up with an answer to every question, or if you're not sure what the question is getting at. I am hoping that the questions will get you into the passage and get you thinking it through in a fresh way. The goal is not necessarily to record all of the "right" answers but to interact with the passage and grow in your understanding. Certainly some answers to your lingering questions will become clearer as you read the Teaching Chapter and as you discuss the passage with your group.

You will notice that several of the questions have a ⏱ beside them. If there are weeks when you feel you just cannot give enough time to the study to complete all the questions, completing the ⏱ questions will give you a foundation for understanding the Teaching Chapter and equip you to take part in the group discussion.

The second part of each lesson is the Teaching Chapter, in which I seek to explain and apply the passage we are studying. At the end of each chapter is a short piece that will turn your attention to how what we've just studied in Genesis gives us insight into what is still to come when Christ returns. One woman who worked through the study called this part "dessert," and I do hope it will be a sweet reminder to you of our future hope. If you would like to purchase a DVD of the Teaching Chapters, go to http://www.SeeingJesusInTheOldTestament.com.

The third part of each week's lesson is the time you spend with your group sharing your lives together and discussing what you've learned and what you're still trying to understand and apply. A discussion guide is included at the end of each week's lesson. You may want to follow it exactly, working through each question as written. Or you may just want to use the guide as an idea-starter for your discussion.

Each aspect is important—laying the foundation, building on it, and sealing it in. We all have different learning styles, so one aspect of the study will likely have more impact on you than another, but all three together will help you to truly "own" the truths in this study so that they can become a part of you as you seek to know your covenant God in deeper ways.

I've put the sections of this study together in a way that offers flexibility for how you can use it and flexibility in how you can schedule your time working through it. If you are going to use it for a ten-week group study, you will want to read the Teaching Chapter in week 1, "The Road to Emmaus," before the first meeting. (There is no Personal Bible

Study section for the first week.) From then on, each week, participants will want to come to the group time having completed the Personal Bible Study section of the next week's lesson as well as having read the Teaching Chapter. You may want to put a star beside questions in the Personal Bible Study that you want to be sure to bring up in the discussion and underline key passages in the chapter that are meaningful to you. During your time together each week, you will use the Discussion Guide to discuss the big ideas of the week's lesson.

There is a great deal of material here, and you may want to take your time with it, giving more time to discuss its foundational truths, allowing it to sink in. To expand the study over twenty weeks, you would break each week into two parts, spending one week on the Personal Bible Study section, either doing it on your own and discussing your answers when you meet or actually working through the questions together when you meet. Then group members will read the chapter on their own over the next week and use the discussion guide to discuss the big ideas of the lesson the following week.

If you are leading a group study, we would like to provide you with some resources that have been developed specifically for this study. We hope that these resources will increase your confidence in leading the group. To request those helps, go to http://www.SeeingJesusInTheOldTestament.com

I would love to hear how your study is going, so please go to http://www.nancyguthrie.com sometime and send me a message. I am praying, as you see Jesus in a fresh way over the coming weeks through the book of Genesis, that your love for him will go deeper and that your longing for him to come again will grow stronger.

—*Nancy Guthrie*

The Road to Emmaus

Luke 24

The Beginning in Light of the Ending

Have you ever seen the movie *The Sixth Sense*? It's the one with Bruce Willis and Haley Joel Osment, who whispers through trembling little lips, "I see dead people." I know; it's a strange movie. Honestly, it is not my kind of movie. When I first saw the previews for it, I wrote it off as out of my preferred realm of reality. But my husband, David, said it was one of his favorite movies of all time, and so when it was finally free on TV, for the sake of marital harmony and togetherness, I watched it with him. And I have to say, I came to understand his appreciation for it. If you haven't seen it, go rent it this weekend and see for yourself what I mean. No spoiler alert needed here; I won't tell you how it turns out.

Suffice it to say that *The Sixth Sense* is one of those movies that, when you come to the end, you immediately think, *Okay, I need to watch that again.* That's because something so significant is revealed at the end of the movie that you realize this knowledge will change everything you thought you were seeing and understanding throughout the entire movie as you watched it the first time. You want to watch it a second time with the knowledge of what was hinted at but not revealed until the end. It's like when you get to the end of a whodunit, and you are so surprised by who did it that you want to watch it again to look for the clues you missed.

So why am I starting a book about Genesis talking about the movie *The Sixth Sense*? Because it illustrates why we want to start our study of Genesis at the end of Jesus's earthly ministry. Something is revealed

15

in a final scene of Jesus's life that makes us want to go back to the very beginning of God's story and read it again in light of what we know now. Now that we've seen clearly what was hinted at but hidden, we want to start at the beginning and trace the story, looking for what we missed the first time because we didn't even know to look for it.

So today we begin at the end, and next week we'll continue at the beginning! We start at the end because it was at the end of his earthly ministry that Jesus himself made clear to his disciples that the whole story of the Old Testament, beginning in Genesis, had always been all about him.

Seeing Jesus

Let's look at the final chapter of Luke's Gospel, Luke 24. The chapter begins with several women going to Jesus's tomb. Even though Jesus had repeatedly told his disciples that he was going to "suffer many things and be rejected by the elders and chief priests and scribes, and be killed, and on the third day be raised" (Luke 9:22), when the women saw that his body was gone and reported it to the apostles, reminding them that he had said he would rise, the apostles didn't believe them.

Right after Luke records this finding at the tomb, he tells us about two of Jesus's followers who were walking to the village of Emmaus. Likely they were walking home after traveling to Jerusalem for Passover. After witnessing what happened to Jesus in Jerusalem, they were confused and sad and disappointed that the one they thought had come to save them had been humiliated and crucified, and, in their estimation, soundly defeated by the political and religious establishment.

As they walked and talked, Jesus came alongside and walked with them. I don't know why they didn't recognize him except that Luke tells us "their eyes were kept from recognizing him" (Luke 24:16). Evidently God purposefully wanted to keep them from recognizing Jesus, perhaps so that they would not become so caught up in him actually being alive that they would not be able to think through what he had to teach them. Jesus asked them what they were talking about, and they explained that they were talking about Jesus of Nazareth, a man who was a prophet mighty in deed and word before God and all the people, and how our chief priests and rulers delivered him up to be condemned to death, and crucified him. But we had hoped that he was the one to redeem Israel. Yes, and besides all this, it is now the third day since these things happened. Moreover, some women of our company amazed us. They were at the tomb early in the morning, and when they did not find his body, they came back saying that they had even seen a vision of angels, who said that he was alive. Some of those who were with us went to the tomb and found it just as the women had said, but him they did not see. (Luke 24:19–24)

"We had hoped that he was the one to redeem Israel," they said, with obvious disappointment. They thought they had understood who Jesus was and what he came to do. But because they actually misunderstood who he was and what he came to do, they completely missed him!

Do you think you have Jesus figured out? Have you, at times, found yourself profoundly disappointed because Jesus has not done what you expected him to do?

Sometimes, when we think we've got Jesus all figured out, we simply can't hear or can't see that our understanding is distorted or diminished. And sometimes we think we have Jesus figured out when really all we've done is create in our own minds the Jesus we want, the Jesus we can be comfortable with. We read the Bible and take what we want, shaping for ourselves a Jesus who is passionate about what we are passionate about, and skeptical about we are skeptical about, condemning what we want to condemn.

Some who would say they have Jesus figured out have settled on a Jesus who was primarily an agent of change in the social and religious system he entered into, while others have settled on Jesus primarily as one who taught people to be loving and accepting and tolerant or simply good citizens of the world.

> *As I see Jesus more clearly, he shows me my false assumptions.*

Isn't it interesting that we feel free to take so much liberty with defining who Jesus is and what he came to accomplish?

Have you ever had someone sum you up? You know what I mean—they took a little bit of what they know about you and made some leaps and assumptions and proceeded to declare something like, "You are one of those creative types who can never be anywhere on time or do things the same old way," or, "I can tell that you are the kind of person who would never try something so adventuresome." And have you sometimes thought to yourself, "What are you talking about? That's not who I am! That is not what is important to me! Who do you think you are to define me?"

Where We Must Look to See Jesus

Jesus is about to tell these two followers where to look if they want to truly see and understand who Jesus is. But he seems a little frustrated—the kind of frustration a parent has with a child who has been told something a thousand times, and yet it seems the child has never truly listened:

> He said to them, "O foolish ones, and slow of heart to believe all that the prophets have spoken! Was it not necessary that the Christ should suffer these things and enter into his glory?" (Luke 24:25–26)

These followers had heard Jesus teach and witnessed him perform healings and challenge the Pharisees, and ultimately they had seen him carry his cross to Calvary. But more than that, they had spent years as children studying the Torah under the Rabbi and years in the temple listening as the scrolls were opened and read from. Jesus was saying that if they had really listened to what the prophets wrote, and if they had gone beyond listening to examining it, processing it, and truly believing it, they could have understood that the one God had promised to send to them would save them through suffering, because that truth is interwoven into the entirety of the Old Testament.

Jesus was saying that they should have understood that his crucifixion didn't negate his identity as the Messiah but confirmed it, because the death of the Messiah was predicted in the Old Testament. In fact, each portion of the Old Testament anticipates Christ's suffering and glory in its own way. In our study of Genesis we will see that the very first promise in the Old Testament of an "offspring," or descendant of Eve, points directly to his suffering. God said that the Serpent will "bruise his heel" (Gen. 3:15). So, from the first time a Savior was promised in the Old Testament, it was clear that this Savior would suffer.

But it is not just specific promises or prophecies that point to Jesus's suffering. More profoundly, the whole of the Old Testament was designed by God to provide a context within which we can understand the necessity of the suffering and the certainty of the glorification of Christ. In fact, without the Old Testament foundation of fall, curse, law, sacrifice, temple, priesthood, and salvation, then the cross, resurrection, and glorification of Christ would make little sense.

So Jesus said that if they had really taken in and believed what the Old Testament prophets said, they would have seen and understood that indeed he was the one they had hoped for who would redeem Israel—they would have understood that this redemption would be accomplished not through strength but through weakness, not by a conquering king but by a suffering servant.

Jesus was not content, however, to leave these followers with just this generalized pointer to what all the prophets had said. Luke writes:

> And beginning with Moses and all the Prophets, he interpreted to them in all the Scriptures the things concerning himself. (Luke 24:27)

Take this in and think it through. To explain to these followers who he was and why he had to die, Jesus did not start with his birth, or his sermon on the mountain, or his wrangling with the Pharisees, or the plot against him facilitated by Judas. Jesus opened up Genesis and Exodus and Leviticus and Psalms and Hosea and Isaiah and all the way to Malachi, showing them, "This is who I am . . . this is why I came . . . this is the curse I came to bear . . . this is the mercy I came to show . . . I am the blessing God promised . . . I am the sacrifice God provided."

As Jesus worked his way through the writings of Moses and the prophets, he didn't merely point out specific prophecies that he fulfilled, which is what my understanding of how the Old Testament points to Christ has been limited to for most of my life (i.e., that he would be born in Bethlehem and that he would enter Jerusalem riding on a donkey). And he didn't use Old Testament characters or situations as examples to instruct the two disciples on how to live the life of faith, which is how many of us have always heard the Old Testament taught.

It is doubtful that he turned to the story of Noah and began teaching them that they needed to obey God even when it meant going against the crowd. More likely he turned to the story of Noah, the one whose name means rest, and said, "Hide yourself in me like Noah and his family hid themselves inside the ark and were saved from the judgment." He didn't turn to the story of Abraham offering Isaac and tell these disciples that they needed to be willing to give up what is most precious to them for their God. Instead, perhaps he said something like, "See how this father was willing to offer up his only son as a sacrifice? Can you see that this is what my Father did when I was lifted up on the cross?" He didn't turn to the story of Joseph to teach them that they should flee temptation. More likely he said something like, "Remember how Joseph became the one person that everyone in the world came to for food in the famine? That's me. I am the bread of life, the one to whom all men and women must come to find life."

Jesus didn't work his way through Genesis to point out what we must do for God, but to help us to see clearly what God has done for us through Christ.

As we read the Old Testament, we don't want to merely make observations about the behavior of the godly and godless and then try harder to be like the godly and less like the godless. Instead, we must realize that there are no true heroes in the Old Testament. No one is perfectly and persistently pleasing to God—the judges aren't strong enough, the kings aren't good enough, the prophets aren't clear enough, and the priests aren't pure enough.

The Old Testament serves to point out our cavernous need for a better law keeper, a better judge, a better prophet, a better priest, a better king. Jesus must have looked Cleopus and his companion in the eyes that day, and said, "That's me. I'm the one the whole of the Old Testament points to. I'm the one God intended to send all along."

The Old Testament is an uncompleted story, a promise waiting for its fulfillment. And Jesus is that fulfillment. It must have been amazing to sit with Jesus himself, like those two disciples did, and hear him clearly make the connections. I wish Luke had written a run-down of exactly what Jesus said, because I would like to know! But the fact that this conversation was not recorded for us does not mean we cannot discover these connections ourselves. They are there to be found in the pages of the Old Testament for all who will invest in looking for them. That's what we will do in this study of Genesis.

What It Will Take to See Jesus

As Jesus walked and talked with these followers, they must have been amazed at how he had so much of the Torah committed to memory and such a thorough grasp on its meaning—especially in the ways it pointed to the Christ. It served to make them hungry for more, so when they got to Emmaus, they asked him to stay with them. Then Luke records:

> *As I see Jesus more clearly, he answers my stubborn questions.*

> When he was at table with them, he took the bread and blessed and broke it and gave it to them. And their eyes were opened, and they recognized him. (Luke 24:30–31)

As Jesus took the bread, blessed it and broke it, perhaps they recognized him because they had been there on the hillside when Jesus did the same thing and fed five thousand people (Luke 9:16), or perhaps they had been there a few nights before when he did the same thing in the upper room with his disciples (Luke 22:19). But it seems to be more than that. This seems to be a work of God done in their hearts and minds. Their eyes could see him. Their hearts burned as they listened to him work his way through the Old Testament.

Isn't this what we want? We don't want to read little bits of Scripture and take away an inspirational thought. We don't want to pluck out Scriptures that make us feel good regardless of whether we're reading them in context. We want to understand the big picture of what God has done and is doing in the world. But more than that, we want our hearts to burn in recognition that this is not just a story outside of us, but a story God is accomplishing in us through Christ!

God, open our eyes to see Jesus!

Make our hearts burn in your presence!

We do not want to settle for dry doctrine or factual knowledge about the Bible. We want the Word of God to do its work in us, burning away the impurities in our hearts; we want sparks of new insights to fly; we want the flames of our passion for God to be fanned into a raging fire. We want our hearts to melt at the beauty of Christ.

How will this happen? We will go to the Old Testament and read it through gospel eyes. We will ask God to open our eyes to see Jesus, to give us the ability to recognize him in the people, the promises, the stories, the symbols, and the shadows of the Old Testament.

Evidently this is exactly what happened to the disciples. A few days after his conversation with the two followers on their way to Emmaus, Jesus appeared to the rest of the disciples and said to them:

> These are my words that I spoke to you while I was still with you, that everything written about me in the Law of Moses and the Prophets and the Psalms must be fulfilled. (Luke 24:44)

Then, once again, he did what he had done a few days before:

> Then he opened their minds to understand the Scriptures. (Luke 24:45)

First he opened their eyes to see him and made their hearts burn as they listened to him, and then he opened their minds to understand the Old Testament. That's what we want. We want our eyes to be opened to see Jesus in the Old Testament. We want our hearts to burn as this revelation kindles in us a fresh passion for Jesus. And we want our minds to be opened so that we understand the Scriptures. We want to see God's plan to save sinners through Jesus Christ in all of its vast wonder. We don't want to settle for our disjointed collection of Old Testament Bible story knowledge and all the tips on trusting God that came with it. We want to see the big picture of God's salvation and truly understand this glorious mystery now revealed.

How We Will Come to Understand Jesus

It becomes evident in the book of Acts that after Jesus opened the minds of the disciples to understand the Old Testament Scriptures, they did indeed grasp the big picture of why Jesus came, died, and rose from the dead. They finally saw his coming in context of God's unfolding plan of redemption. And throughout the apostles' sermons recorded in Acts,

> *As I see Jesus more clearly, he melts my hardened heart.*

we discover that they presented the gospel of Jesus—not beginning with his birth or with his teachings or with his death but beginning in the Old Testament.

In Acts 2 Peter said that King David wrote about Jesus in the Psalms. In Acts 3 he said to the Jews in the temple, "I know that you acted in ignorance, as did also your rulers. But . . . God foretold by the mouth of all the prophets . . . that his Christ would suffer. . . . And all the prophets who have spoken, from Samuel and those who came after him, also proclaimed these days" (vv. 17–18, 24). In Acts 4:11, before the council Peter said, quoting Psalm 118, "This Jesus is the stone that was rejected by you, the builders, which has become the cornerstone." This continues through Acts and the rest of the New Testament, which teach us how to read and understand the entire Old Testament with gospel eyes.

As we study Genesis through the lens of the revelation of Jesus Christ, it will do two things. First, we'll understand the significance of aspects of the salvation story in the Old Testament that made little sense to us before. Looking through the lens of how the promises of God were fulfilled in Christ will add meaning and fullness to our understanding of the story and setting in which the promises were made.

Second, not only will studying Genesis in light of Christ help us to understand Genesis more clearly, but it will also enable us to see Christ more clearly. It will reshape our perspective about his person and purpose as we explore the need he came to address and the promises he came to fulfill.

We will not study simply to accumulate knowledge. That's what the Pharisees did. Jesus said to them:

> You search the Scriptures because you think that in them you have eternal
> life; and it is they that bear witness about me, yet you refuse to come to me
> that you may have life. (John 5:39–40)

We will study so that we will *not* refuse to come, so that we will see that
we *must* come to him to have life.

When we hear Jesus say that the Scriptures "bear witness of me,"
we realize that the Bible is not primarily about what God wants *us* to
do—even though that is what most people think the Bible is about. If
you have ever heard any of those man-on-the-street kinds of interviews
with people asking what the Bible is about, you will hear over and over
that the Bible tells people how to live. Most people see the Bible as a
"guidebook for life." But Jesus is saying here that the Bible is not primarily about *what* God wants us to do but about *who* God wants us to see.
And it is Jesus we are going to see as we study Genesis together.

- As we gaze into the wonder of creation, we will see Jesus as the light
  that was in the world before there was a sun or moon.
- As we agonize with Adam and Eve over the curse that came after
  the fall, we'll see Jesus as the promised offspring who will crush the
  head of the serpent.
- In the terror of the flood, we'll see Jesus as the ark of safety in whom
  we are saved in the storm of God's judgment.
- In the story of the tower of Babel, we will see that we do not need to
  build a tower to get to God, because Jesus is God come down to us.
- When we walk alongside Abraham, we'll see that it is Jesus's righteousness that was credited to him because he believed God.
- When we walk up the mountain with Abraham and Isaac, we'll see that
  they point us toward the Father's provision of a once-for-all sacrifice—
  his own beloved Son.
- As we feel the intensity of Jacob's wrestling in the dark to gain a
  blessing for himself, we'll see One who wrestled with God in the dark
  of the garden of Gethsemane so that he might gain a blessing for us.
- As we look with Joseph into the faces of the brothers who sought
  to kill him, we'll see the One who also could have said to those who
  nailed him to the cross: "You meant evil against me, but God meant

it for good, to bring it about that many people should be kept alive"
(Gen. 50:20).

~ And as we see Jacob's sons become the leaders of the twelve tribes
through whom God intends to bless the whole world, we will see the
One through whom that blessing will come, the Lion of the tribe of
Judah, before whom people from all tribes and people and languages
will one day bow.

It is going to be wonderful to discover together where to look for
Jesus, how to see Jesus and understand Jesus. But I have to tell you that
all of that is worthless, and ultimately harmful, if it does not ultimately
lead you to embrace Jesus. That was the problem with the Pharisees.
They studied the Old Testament, but they refused to come to the one
the Old Testament pointed to. Their grip on religious tradition and their
own righteousness was too tight to take hold of Christ.

I am praying for you, that you will not be like the Pharisees who
refused to come to Jesus but like these disciples whose eyes were
opened to a clearer view of Jesus, whose hearts burned with a more
passionate love for Jesus, and whose minds were opened to a deeper
understanding of Jesus.

How Genesis Points to What Is Yet to Come: "Your Kingdom Come"

When the two followers on the road to Emmaus said, "But we had hoped
that he was the one to redeem Israel" (Luke 24:21), they reveal that they
had placed their hope in God's promises of a great redeemer, a great deliverer who would come. And they were exactly right about what God had
promised and what this redeemer would do. But they were confused about
the timing and means by which the Messiah would redeem his own.

The kingdom of God on earth as it is in heaven is the goal of God's
work in history. What Old Testament saints and those who were closest
to Jesus expected was that his kingdom would come in a singular event—
that Messiah would come to save and judge all at the same time. But the

restoration of God's kingdom is a progressive event. While it has been established and inaugurated, it has not yet been consummated. The day is yet to come when Jesus will come again, and the new heaven and the new earth will become the place where God's redeemed people will live under God's perfect rule.

As we begin our study of Genesis, we discover that the first book in the Bible is not only the source for understanding how history began; it provides picture after picture about what we can expect in the future, when God's unfolding story of redemption culminates in the new heaven and the new earth described in the last book of the Bible, Revelation. So as we study Genesis each week, we will look not only for what it has to tell us about Christ's ministry in his first coming but also about Christ's victory that is still ahead in his second coming.

Genesis begins with the creation of the kingdom of God in the garden of Eden, where Adam and Eve lived in willing obedience to God's word and rule. But a rival regime established a beachhead in God's kingdom. The rest of the Bible is the story of God's restoration of a people to be the willing subjects of his perfect rule living in a perfect environment.

When God promised Abraham that his descendants would possess the Promised Land and be the people of God under his authority, he was describing his kingdom. When he rescued Israel out of captivity in Egypt, it was so he could bring them into the place where the kingdom would be established. But while Israel's kings revealed many aspects of the nature of the kingdom of God, these human kings inevitably failed to measure up. The prophets continued to direct the eyes of Israel to a great future day when the perfect and everlasting kingdom of God would be revealed.

This is what all the Jewish disciples had grown up focused on and longing for. And when they began to follow Jesus they heard him say, "The time promised by God has come at last! . . . The Kingdom of God is near! Repent of your sins and believe the Good News!" (Mark 1:15 NLT). They anticipated that all the prophecies about the restored kingdom would become reality then and there at the first coming of Jesus. But it will be in his second coming when the kingdom of God on earth as it is in heaven will be consummated. The consummation of the kingdom—when we will know God fully and by sight, whom we now know only by faith—is still to come. "When Christ, who is your life, is revealed to the whole world, you will share in all his glory" (Col. 3:4 NLT).

Discussion Guide

The Road to Emmaus

LUKE 24

Getting the Discussion Going

1. Some of us grew up going to Sunday school and getting the Old Testament in bits and pieces by learning stories, while perhaps understanding very little about how they fit into the big-picture story of the Bible. Others of us grew up without the benefit of being taught the Bible. Would each of you tell some of what you remember thinking about the Bible from your childhood?

Getting to the Heart of It

2. Try to take yourself back to the days following the death and resurrection of Christ. Imagine that you were one of those disciples whom we read about walking on the road to Emmaus. What have you just seen and heard and experienced in Jerusalem? What questions are in your mind and what concerns are in your heart?

3. Likely these disciples had grown up being taught the Torah and were well-versed in the stories of Genesis. What do you think it must have been like to realize that there was something they had missed and to have Jesus take them through the Old Testament revealing how it pointed to him?

4. On the last page of the chapter you read (pages 24–25), there was a list of snapshots of how we are going to see Jesus in this study of

Genesis. Turn to that page and look at that list. Which one is most intriguing to you and why?

5. Jesus said that the Pharisees studied the Scriptures intently, thinking that their knowledge of the Scriptures and tedious law keeping would put them in good stead with God. But there was Jesus standing in front of them, and they rejected him. He infuriated, offended, and threatened their power, so they had him killed. How do we keep from being like those Pharisees as we study the Scriptures?

Getting Personal

6. In Luke 24 we read that Jesus "opened their minds" to understand the Scripture (v. 45). As we begin the study of Genesis, would you share with the group why you are here? What do you hope to gain from the investment you will make in this study over the coming weeks? How do you want to be different after you complete it?

Getting How It Fits into the Big Picture

7. Throughout this study, we will be seeking to grasp how the passage we're studying fits into the bigger story of God's plan for redemption. And each week, the Teaching Chapter will be followed with a short piece on how the beginning of God's story in Genesis points to the end of God's story, when Christ returns. When he comes again, everything will be restored and renewed, and we will begin an eternity in his presence, ruling and reigning with him in the new heaven and the new earth. But right now we're living in an in-between time. Christ has accomplished everything necessary to usher in that day, but he said that only the Father knows when that day will be. This will be the culmination of all that Genesis and the rest of the Bible has pointed us toward. This is where human history is headed, and yet some of us rarely think about it or long for that day when the Promised One comes a second time. As we close our first time together, let's pray that God will use this study of the beginning of his story to implant in us a greater longing for the end of the story—when we will one day enjoy the Promised One in the way he has always intended for us.

Week 2

Creation

Genesis 1:1–2:3

Personal Bible Study

Creation

GENESIS 1:1–2:3

1. In Genesis 1:1, where we read, "God created . . . ," the name of God is in its plural form, *Elohim*, and the verb used for "created" is singular. In Genesis 1:26 we read, "Then God said, 'Let *us* make man in our image, after our likeness.'" This is the first revelation in Scripture that God is one being in three persons—Father, Son, and Holy Spirit. They were all there, active in creation. God the Father spoke the creative words to bring the universe into being. God the Son, the eternal Word of God, carried out these creative decrees. And the Holy Spirit manifested God's immediate presence in his creation. How do these passages add to that understanding?

∼ Genesis 1:2

∼ John 1:1–3

∼ Colossians 1:15–16

∼ Hebrews 1:2

2. What do the following passages from outside of Genesis add to our understanding of *why* or *for what purpose* God created the world and formed humanity?

～ Psalm 19:1–2

～ Isaiah 43:7

～ Romans 1:20

3. In Genesis 1:2, we read that the world was "without form and void, and darkness was over the face of the deep." It is as if God had created all of the raw materials and they were there, waiting to be shaped and developed into a world that would be inhabitable for humans. In the following verses we discover how God addressed the formlessness, emptiness, and darkness. Using the chart below, work your way through Genesis 1:3–2:3 noting what God did on each day of creation (begin each answer with a verb).

Verse	God's Action	Day of Creation
Gen. 1:1		—
Gen. 1:2		—
Gen. 1:3		Day 1
Gen. 1:4		Day 1
Gen. 1:5		Day 1

Gen. 1:6–8		Day 2
Gen. 1:9–10		Day 3
Gen. 1:11–12		Day 3
Gen. 1:14–16		Day 4
Gen. 1:17		Day 4
Gen. 1:20–21		Day 5
Gen. 1:22		Day 5
Gen. 1:25		Day 6
Gen. 1:27		Day 6
Gen. 1:28		Day 6
Gen. 1:29–30		Day 6
Gen. 1:31		Day 6
Gen. 2:2		Day 7
Gen. 2:3		Day 7

4. Genesis 1:26 says that we were made in the image of God, which means that we are *like God*, and that we were made to *represent God*. The

Westminster Shorter Catechism says in answer to the question, "What is God?": "God is a spirit, infinite, eternal, and unchangeable, in His being, wisdom, power, holiness, justice, goodness and truth." How does this help us to understand some of the ways Adam and Eve were made in God's likeness, and yet not exactly like him?

5. What does Genesis 1:26–28 reveal about what mankind was to do as a representative of God?

6. In the ancient world, a king would place images of himself (statues) in far-off provinces. The images of the king told everyone that these provinces were part of the king's domain. How might this picture be why God made human beings in his image and placed us on this earth?

7. One of the key words in Genesis 1 is "good." It appears seven times, and the seventh time it's intensified to "very good." Think about this for a minute. When God's word went out and formed and filled creation, God saw it and deemed that it was good. What does this tell you about God, about the world, and about yourself?

~ About God:

~ About the world:

~ About myself:

8. When Adam and Eve sinned, the image of God in them became distorted, but it was not lost completely. And when we come to the New Testament we discover that redemption in Christ means that we can progressively grow in our likeness of God.

What can be restored in the "new self" according to Colossians 3:10 and Ephesians 4:24?

How does this happen according to 2 Corinthians 3:18?

When will this work of God be complete according to 1 John 3:2?

9. In practical terms, how can we experience the newness that comes from the power of God's word—his written Word—according to these verses?

~ Romans 12:2

~ Colossians 3:16

~ Hebrews 4:12–13

10. If you have a desire for the newness that only comes as the Word of God accomplishes its work in your life, write out your commitment to this study of Genesis. How much time will you give to it? When will you schedule that time? How will you respond to the Word as it speaks to you? In what way(s) do you want it to make you new?

11. How does the Genesis account of creation point to Christ? The New Testament passages in the chart below will help us see the connections. As we do this exercise and those like it in subsequent lessons, we'll discover that the Old Testament points to Christ in a number of different ways. In some passages we'll see the presence of the pre-incarnate Christ. We'll see problems that only he will solve, promises that only he will fulfill, and needs that only he can meet. We'll discover informative parallels between Christ and various people, symbols, and events, as well as significant contrasts that will help us to understand significant aspects of the person and work of Christ. We'll see connections to Christ's life and teaching as well as themes and patterns that paint a picture for us of God's saving work through Christ. Most significantly, we'll see evidence of God's sovereign control of history that assures us that history is proceeding according to a divine plan.

In Genesis 1, we see that God prepared our planet to become the home of man and, above all, the scene of his supreme revelation of redemption through Jesus Christ. As we consider how pleasing mankind was to God in man's original state, how God's blessing made him fruitful and gave his life purpose and meaning, we can also see how the God-man, Jesus Christ, perfectly fulfilled what God originally intended for mankind, and how Christ has done what is necessary to restore mankind to be even better than the original design and destiny.

Using the chart below, look up the passages about Christ in the second column and state the connection to the creation account. Your answers don't need to be wordy. Some connections will be obvious and some more complex. See the example in the first block.

Creation	Christ
"In the beginning, God created." (Gen. 1:1)	Ps. 33:6; John 1:1–3 *Jesus was the Word going out at creation and doing the work of creation.*
"The Spirit of God was hovering." (Gen. 1:2)	Luke 1:34–35

"And God said . . . " (Gen. 1:3, 6, 9, 11, 14, 20, 24, 28, 29)	John 1:1; 1 Pet. 1:20–23
"And there was light." (Gen. 1:3)	Isa. 9:2; John 8:12; Rev. 21:23–24
"Let us make man in our image, after our likeness." (Gen. 1:26)	Col. 1:15; Heb. 1:3
"Let them have dominion." (Gen. 1:26)	Eph. 1:21–22; Rev. 5:9–10
"And God blessed them. And God said to them, 'Be fruitful and multiply.'" (Gen. 1:28)	Luke 1:42; John 12:24; 15:16
"Fill the earth." (Gen. 1:28)	Matt. 28:18–20
"Subdue it." (Gen. 1:28)	Heb. 2:5–9
"It was very good." (Gen. 1:31)	Matt. 3:17
"God blessed the seventh day and made it holy, because on it God rested from all his work that he had done in creation." (Gen. 2:3)	Isa. 11:10; Matt. 11:28

Teaching Chapter

All Things New

The mechanic had told us that the transmission of my twelve-year-old car was about to go out, and fortunately the car was in our driveway when it happened. We made a deal with the mechanic, who said he wanted to use it for parts, and so his tow truck driver came and hauled it away.

A few days later, we stopped by a small used-car lot and began our search for a replacement. And there, in the middle of the lot filled with sensible sedans, was a cherry red, two-seater, rag-top convertible sports car. I saw it catch David's eye and suggested the possibility that I could begin driving his car and we could get that car for him. But he said that would be "too extravagant . . . impractical . . . no, we couldn't do that."

A couple of days later David went to the dentist about a front bottom tooth that was bothering him and was surprised to hear from the dentist that the tooth was going to need to be pulled. "The reason this tooth is having problems is that you never had your wisdom teeth out, and they are putting pressure on your other teeth, so you're going to need to have your four wisdom teeth pulled too, and get braces." David was then sent over to see the orthodontist, and called me when he left there, saying, "If, at age forty-five, I'm going to be missing one of my front teeth and wearing braces for a year and a half, *I think I'm gonna need that car.*"

So we got the cool car, and it transformed David's commute from a dreaded drudgery to a daily vacation. A few months later we were in the garage, and he said to me, "You know what I love about this car?

Even though we bought it used, it is so pristine. It still has that new-car smell."

Later that summer David was gone on a business trip, and I decided it was a beautiful day to drive his convertible with that top down. Now, I knew we had the "no eating or drinking" rule in the car due to its light tan upholstery, and I really had no intention of actually consuming the cherry limeade I stopped to get from Sonic while in the car—honest. I merely planned to transport the luscious beverage to consume at home.

There was a cup holder between the seats of the car, and as I pulled away, I put the Styrofoam cup into the cup holder. But I forgot that my cell phone, with its antenna on top, was already in the cup holder. And suddenly I realized that the antenna had punched a hole in the bottom of the cup, where all the cherry syrup had collected. Pink goo was spewing all over the interior of the car!

As soon as I got home, heart beating out of my chest, I called my friend Bonita, who knows how to clean anything and everything, and she said, "OxiClean!" So I got the OxiClean and began wiping and scrubbing to get rid of the pink that seemed to have worked its way into every crevice of the car's interior. But pretty soon I realized that not only was the pink not coming out, but my desperate scrubbing was having its own impact, making those areas of the interior look like they'd been scrubbed way too vigorously.

I was sick. Should I just keep quiet, hoping David wouldn't notice that pristine had become pink, and risk offending him that I had done this and not even told him? Or should I just fess up and come clean about what he was bound to notice anyway? How was I going to break it to him that his car was no longer like new?

We love new, don't we? A new restaurant or recipe to try for dinner, a new lawnmower to replace the old clunker, a new outfit, a fresh layer of mulch on the flowerbed. But nothing stays new for long in this world, does it? Everything gets old; everything breaks down. Over time, everything and everyone becomes spotted and stained.

Is there any hope, in this world where everything gets old, to actually become new? More significantly, is there any hope for those of us whose lives are marked by deteriorating health, broken relationships, and destructive habits to be given a fresh start, a new perspective, a virtual reset button on life?

We find the answer by beginning at the beginning of God's story in Genesis 1, when everything was new.

The Eternal Word

> In the beginning, God created the heavens and the earth. (Gen. 1:1)

There is a matter-of-factness to this poetic account Moses wrote for the children of Israel about the beginning of everything. Certainly it was not written to answer our modern-day questions about the process or timing of how the earth came to be or about the origins and existence of God. His existence and his creative work are a given.

When we read that God "created," the Bible uses a word reserved for something done only by God. It's not talking about something being made or formed from existing material but the creation of something from nothing. When you or I "create" something—like a meal or a work of art—we use preexisting material. But only God creates something from nothing. In the creation of the heavens and the earth, he created not just *something*, but *all there is*, using only one tool—his word, the revelation of his will. He willed creation to be and spoke it into being. But initially it was a mass of unformed matter.

> The earth was without form and void, and darkness was over the face of the deep. (Gen. 1:2)

The earth God spoke into being was initially a wasteland, uninhabitable, where nothing could live. But there was hope for something good to come out of this dark, unformed emptiness, as we read in the same verse:

> And the Spirit of God was hovering over the face of the waters. (Gen. 1:2)

The Spirit of God was hovering, or fluttering, over the collection of raw material with creative power. Something was getting ready to happen as the Spirit hovered, waiting for God to give the command.

The word *spirit* in Hebrew also means "breath." God's creative breath, which hovered over the water, would come forth as speech—the Word of God.

The Eternal Word Illumined the Darkness

> And God said, "Let there be light," and there was light. (Gen. 1:3)

There it is! God's powerful word went out, and a brilliant light eradicated the darkness. But this was not speaking the sun into being. It wasn't until the fourth day of creation that "God made the two great lights—the greater light to rule the day and the lesser light to rule the night—and the stars." (Gen. 1:16). So there was light in the world even though there was no sun in the sky.

The Eternal Word Ordered the Chaos

Just as the word of God illumined the darkness, God's word went out bringing order to the unformed matter. On days one, two, and three of creation, we read that what had been formless was shaped into something good and beautiful. By separating light from darkness and calling the light "day" and the darkness "night," God brought order to time. By separating the waters from the expanse, God brought order to his environment. And gathering the waters so that dry ground appeared, God brought order to his earth. God also established himself as ruler over his creation simply by naming the things in it, because the one who has the right to name has the right to rule.

> God called the light Day, and the darkness he called Night. . . . God called the expanse Heaven. . . . God called the dry land Earth, and the waters that were gathered together he called Seas. (Gen. 1:5, 8, 10)

By separating the waters from the waters, God made space for an inhabitable earth, where plants and trees can grow and animals and human beings can live.

Warmed by light and robed in blue sky and bordered by sparkling seas, the earth began to take shape. What was originally a wasteland became a well-ordered cosmos that God deemed "very good."

The Eternal Word Filled the Emptiness

God's word also went out to fill the void. Just as the earth's chaos was remedied as God's word did its forming work in days one, two, and three, so was the earth's void addressed by the word's filling work on days four, five, and six.

> And God said, "Let the earth sprout vegetation, plants yielding seed, and fruit trees bearing fruit in which is their seed, each according to its kind, on the earth." And it was so. The earth brought forth vegetation, plants yielding seed according to their own kinds, and trees bearing fruit in which is their seed, each according to its kind. (Gen. 1:11–12)

From there God filled the waters with living creatures, and the skies with flying birds, and the earth with livestock and creeping things, and beasts of the earth according to their kinds.

God formed this world and then he filled it with the light of the sun and moon and stars and furnished it with trees and plants and creatures in the waters and the skies and on the land. But God was not nearly done with his creative work. In fact, he was about to do his crowning work of creation.

God Breathed into Man the Breath of Life

The final creative act on day six of creation began with this divine deliberation between Father, Son, and Holy Spirit:

> Then God said, "Let us make man in our image, after our likeness."
> (Gen. 1:26)

Rather than being created "according to their kind," as the animals had been, man was created one of a kind. If he had a kind at all, it was according to God's kind. He was made in the image and likeness of God. This is the highest honor God could bestow upon this creature, the greatest destiny to which he could call him—to reflect his own image.

Rather than *ex nihilo*, created out of nothing, as all the rest of creation came into being, the creation of man was *de novo*, that is, God started with inorganic matter into which he then breathed life.

> The LORD God formed the man of dust from the ground and breathed
> into his nostrils the breath of life, and the man became a living creature.
> (Gen. 2:7)

God chose the most lowly and humble matter possible—dust from
the ground—and infused it with the most significant and glorious
of all substances—the breath of God.
Though we are made of dust, we are
more than dust. We are also spirit
because God breathed into us some
of his very own breath. In fact we
are still dependent on God for every
breath. In Job we read, "If he should

*My life began anew
on the day the Spirit
breathed newness
into my lifeless soul.*

set his heart to it and gather to himself his spirit and his breath, all flesh
would perish together, and man would return to dust" (Job 34:14–15).

God created humanity in his own likeness with a magnificent destiny in mind. From Genesis we learn that we were made in God's image
so that we might be God's representatives in his creation to do what he
had done: the creative work of forming and filling and the administra-
tive work of naming and subduing.

> "And let them have dominion over the fish of the sea and over the birds of
> the heavens and over the livestock and over all the earth and over every
> creeping thing that creeps on the earth." So God created man in his own
> image, in the image of God he created him; male and female he created
> them. And God blessed them. And God said to them, "Be fruitful and mul-
> tiply and fill the earth and subdue it and have dominion over the fish of
> the sea and over the birds of the heavens and over every living thing that
> moves on the earth." (Gen. 1:26–28)

God gave Adam and Eve the blessing of fruitfulness and the task of
ruling over all the creatures he had made. Just as God worked, bringing
order to his creation, those made in his image are to work, bringing
order to the creation by cultivating the earth and exercising dominion
over the animals. This was not a license for exploitation but a calling to
servanthood to maintain this world where those made in God's image
could be at home.

Here, at the beginning of God's story, we see the picture of the kingdom of God as God created it originally and the way God intends for it to be into eternity—God's people (originally Adam and Eve, later the children of Israel, and ultimately the church) living in God's place (originally the garden of Eden, later the Promised Land, and ultimately the new heaven and new earth) under God's rule (the word of God expressed originally in God's instructions to Adam and Eve, later in the Ten Commandments, and most fully in the person of Jesus). The rest of the Bible is the story of God's work to restore his original creation to all he intends for it to be forever. In Genesis 1 we discover the meaning and purpose for which each of us was created—to bear the image of God and fulfill the destiny he has given to us—to be like him, to be with him, and to rule with him.

The Eternal Word Rested

Though the creation and calling of man is the crowning work of creation, it is certainly not the climax of the account of creation. Mankind is not the reason for God's creation of the heavens and the earth. Humans are not the focus of the creation story. The glory of God is at the heart of creation. We were created to glorify the creator and enjoy him forever. And God established this by setting a pattern for humanity: to set aside one day for worship.

> Thus the heavens and the earth were finished, and all the host of them. And on the seventh day God finished his work that he had done, and he rested on the seventh day from all his work that he had done. So God blessed the seventh day and made it holy, because on it God rested from all his work that he had done in creation. (Gen. 2:1–3)

God did not rest because he was tired. He rested so that those made in his image would share in his rest through worship. He rested so that he could turn Adam and Eve's attention from the creation to the Creator. In a sense God was saying to Adam and Eve and all humanity, "Come and rest in who I am and what I have accomplished. Enjoy with me the goodness of all I have made." This was to establish a rhythm of engagement with the world through work and then thankful enjoyment of the world through worship.

This is the account of creation. It starts with "In the beginning, God created the heavens and the earth," and the rest of Genesis 1 and 2 expounds on that creative work.

The Living Word

It is no accident that the first words in the Gospel of John are exactly the same as the first words in the book of Genesis. John harkens back to Moses's account of creation and draws back the curtain a little farther to reveal more to us about our Creator. Interestingly, John didn't begin his Gospel with the story of the birth of Jesus, as Matthew and Luke did. John wanted his readers to understand that Jesus existed long before he was born as a human baby. Jesus existed as God and with God before the creation of the world:

> In the beginning was the Word, and the Word was with God, and the Word was God. He was in the beginning with God. All things were made through him, and without him was not any thing made that was made. (John 1:1–3)

John helps us to see something about creation, something that was there but hidden in the shadows in Genesis 1. He helps us to see that the pre-incarnate Jesus was there at creation, not as a bystander but as the one through whom God made everything. John tells us that Jesus is the *logos*, the outward expression of all God is. So every time we read the phrase "and God said . . . " in the first chapter of Genesis, we now know that it was the pre-incarnate Christ, the eternal Word of God, who went about accomplishing God's creative plans and directions. Paul's words to the Colossians help us to see the scope of Christ's creative work:

> For by him all things were created, in heaven and on earth, visible and invisible, whether thrones or dominions or rulers or authorities—all things were created through him and for him. (Col. 1:16)

If everything was created not only *through* him but *for* him, that means everything in creation exists for Jesus. Nothing in the universe was created or exists for its own sake but exists to make the glory of the triune God more fully known.

Jesus is not only the agent of creation but is also the sustainer of creation. Hebrews tells us that Jesus "upholds the universe by the word of his power" (Heb. 1:3). He who created the universe in the beginning also sustains and directs his creation moment by moment even now. The reason the physical laws of the universe operate in a consistent and predictable manner is that Christ ordered and blessed it and sustains it just by saying it is so.

From John we also discover how there was light in the world even before God set the sun and the moon in the sky. John identified the source of this light in a poetic tribute:

> In him was life, and the life was the light of men. The light shines in the darkness, and the darkness has not overcome it. . . . The true light, which enlightens everyone, was coming into the world. He was in the world, and the world was made through him, yet the world did not know him. (John 1:4–5, 9–10)

Jesus, the true light since before the beginning, is no mere reflector of the sun's light; he is the one who called the sun into being.

But John had much more to tell his readers about the Word than simply about his work in creation. The good news of the gospel is that the agent of creation, the Eternal Word spoken by God, became the Living Word, the incarnation of God.

> And the Word became flesh and dwelt among us, and we have seen his glory, glory as of the only Son from the Father, full of grace and truth. (John 1:14)

What a wonder! The Eternal Word who made the world entered into his world as one of us. Christ coming into the world was like a new sun rising on a new creation. The true light shone into the darkness of ignorance and resistance and legalism and unbelief. Jesus penetrated the darkness of the world by his very presence, making it clear that he is the light that has illumined the darkness since creation, and that to be alienated from him is to be lost in the darkness.

When we read the Gospels, we see him doing the same thing he did at creation—illuminating the darkness, ordering the chaos, filling the emptiness, revealing the image of God, inviting us into rest. Think through some snapshots from the Gospels with me:

My life is made new day by day as God's Word reshapes me, fills me, and floods my life with his light.

~ Jesus stood in the temple and shouted for all to hear, "I am the light of the world. Whoever follows me will not walk in darkness, but will have the light of life" (John 8:12). Jesus, the living word, illumines the darkness of this world.

~ Jesus stood on the stern of a boat quickly filling with water in the chaos of a storm that arose on the Sea of Galilee, and he rebuked the wind and said to the sea, "Peace! Be Still!" (Mark 4:39). Jesus, the living word, brings order to the disorder of the world.

~ Jesus celebrated at the marriage of a young couple and filled the embarrassed host's jars with wine (John 2:1–12). He stood on a hillside teaching and, using a young boy's lunch of bread and fish, filled the stomachs of a large crowd (John 6:1–14). He stood on the shore and called out to the tired fishermen to throw their nets on the other side of the boat, and their nets filled with fish (Luke 5:1–11). He told a woman at a well that he would fill her life with living water (John 4:7–42). Jesus fills the emptiness of the world.

~ Jesus sat with Nicodemus in the middle of night, telling him, "'You must be born again.' The wind blows where it wishes, and you hear its sound, but you do not know where it comes from or where it goes. So it is with everyone who is born of the Spirit" (John 3:7–8). Just as God breathed life into a human formed of dust at creation, Jesus breathes new life by his Spirit into men and women made of dust, making us into new creations.

~ While no one has ever seen God, John writes that Jesus "has made him known" (John 1:18). While we are made in God's likeness, Jesus is the "exact imprint of his nature" (Heb. 1:3). Jesus shows us the glory of what it means to be in the image of God.

~ Speaking to the crowd weighed down by trying to work their way into being acceptable to God, Jesus offered an invitation: "Come to me, all who labor and are heavy laden, and I will give you rest" (Matt. 11:28). Just as God invited Adam and Eve to rest with him, so Jesus invites all to rest in him.

So we see that as Jesus walked on this earth, he did what he had done at creation—forming, filling, illumining, revealing, offering rest. But he did even more than that. Jesus did something he had covenanted with God the Father and the Holy Spirit to do even before the world was made. Jesus, the agent of creation, became Jesus, the author of salvation, not by exerting his creative power but by offering himself to be crushed in weakness.

~ The Light of the world entered not only into the darkness of this rebellious world but into the pit of darkness itself so that you and I can live in the light.

~ The Prince of Peace entered not only into this corrupt cosmos but also into the wasteland of death so that you and I can know peace.

~ The Treasure of heaven emptied himself of the privileges of deity so that he might fill our lives with all the privileges of being God's own children.

~ The Holy One of God took on the likeness of sinful flesh. The one who made us in God's image became marred by my sin and your sin so that we can be "transformed into the same image from one degree of glory to another" (2 Cor. 3:18).

~ On the cross, Jesus experienced the infinite restlessness you and I deserve because of our rebellion toward God so that we can enjoy his all-encompassing rest in relationship with God.

This is the gospel of the Eternal Word who became the Living Word. And whether or not you've ever heard it before, now you have heard the word of Christ. And what matters more than anything else in this life is your response to this eternal, living word. John tells us that people in his day responded to the Living Word in two very different ways.

> He came to his own, and his own people did not receive him. But to all who did receive him, who believed in his name, he gave the right to become children of God, who were born, not of blood nor of the will of the flesh nor of the will of man, but of God. (John 1:11–13)

Some did not receive him. But others did—and they were born of God, made new by God. Isn't this what you want? Isn't this the real, life-generating newness you crave?

This is what Jesus was talking about when he told Nicodemus that he had to be born a second time. To be "born again" is to experience a second genesis. It is a new beginning, a fresh start in life. Through an instantaneous act of regeneration, a person is changed from a spiritually dead human being into a spiritually alive human being.

> If anyone is in Christ, he is a new creation. The old has passed away; behold, the new has come. (2 Cor. 5:17)

But how does this happen? Just as we had nothing to do with being born the first time, neither is it in our power to be born a second time. The Spirit must hover over the void in our lives just as he hovered over the dark waters at creation. The Word must go out, shining the light of the gospel of Christ into the darkness of our lives so that we can see his true beauty and worth. And when that Spirit breathes new life into our very being, and when that Word convinces us of who he is and what he accomplished for us on the cross, we receive this Living Word. And we are made new.

This newness is not just a do-it-yourself, fix-it-up project to create a "better you." It is not merely taking on a new outlook, or determining to make a fresh start. This work of the Spirit makes us into a genuinely new creation. The Spirit unites us to Christ, taking that which belongs to him and making it increasingly ours day by day. We experience what the prophet Ezekiel said God has always intended to do:

I will give you a new heart, and a new spirit I will put within you. And I
will remove the heart of stone from your flesh and give you a heart of flesh.
(Ezek. 36:26)

The Spirit and the Word do their work turning a heart that is lifeless
and hard into a heart that beats with the very heartbeat of God—a heart
of flesh that is touched by what touches God's heart, broken by what
breaks his heart, and passionate about what is pleasing to him.

A New Creation

So you're probably wondering what happened when David came home
and discovered that his pristine new car had become spotted with pink
stains. He came home from his trip on a Saturday night, and on Sunday
afternoon I said, "David, will you come down to the garage with me?" I
told him the story about the cherry limeade, and I showed him the pink
spots on the carpet in his car. It made him sad, I think, because he knew
that his car would never be like new again. But he wasn't angry with me,
and he told me he didn't want the car to be so important that I had to be
always living in fear of messing it up. He knows that nothing stays new
forever in this world. In fact, over the next couple of years, additional
wear and tear eventually overtook the pink spots.

But something else interesting happened that showed us a picture of
what God is doing in this world, where everything gets old and wears out.

That December we were helping to load Angel Tree gifts into a fellow church member's car—a car that looked amazingly similar to that
car I had driven for twelve years—the one that died in the driveway and
had been hauled off for parts. And as I looked inside, I realized that it
didn't just *look* like my old car—*it was my old car!* The mechanic had
replaced the transmission and sold it to a family at my church.

He had put a new heart into the car! What was old had been made
new on the inside. The car was given a new beginning. Although it had
the same aging body that showed plenty of signs of wear and tear, it was
new on the inside where it really matters.

That's us. We know that, as the years pass, our bodies are showing
the signs of age—supple has turned into sagging. But that is just our

bodies. On the inside, he's making us new. Our hearts have a new ori-
entation, a new direction, a new power, so that we can say with Paul,
"Though our outer self is wasting
away, our inner self is being renewed
day by day" (2 Cor. 4:16).

> *The newness of God in my life will be completed on the day Christ resurrects my body and makes it new.*

When we have been made new on
the inside, it fortifies us to endure the
inevitable oldness and deterioration
that is a reality of living in these bodies of flesh in a world that still longs to
be transformed by this same newness. We begin to think differently as
we saturate ourselves in the written Word and our minds are renewed
(Rom. 12:2). The Word of God does the work of God creating ongoing
newness. As we listen to, chew on, and live out what we read in the Word
of God, the Spirit bears fruit in our character so that our lives become
marked by a new resource to love the unlovable, a fresh spark of joy even
in the midst of sorrow, a pervasive peace even when our circumstances
are chaotic, an unexplainable patience in the face of frustration, words
marked by kindness instead of criticism, a love for what is good instead
of a fascination with what is evil, an unwavering faithfulness when it
would be easier to quit, a compassionate gentleness when it would be
easier to close our eyes to need, and an uncompromising self-control
when it would be easier to give in to temptation.

Do you have the sense that God is remaking you from the inside out?
Do you have a new sense of peace, a new heart for forgiveness, a new
longing for purity, a new hunger for his Word, a new thirst for his Spirit?
Can you look back over recent months and see how God is at work in
you making you new?

Or do you see yourself bound by old habits, weighted down with
old grudges, still stinging from old hurts, confused and deceived by old
ways of thinking?

Would you have to look back many years to identify a time when
you felt God was at work changing you and making you alive to him? If
you are honest, is there a deadness in your heart toward God?

Or would you have to admit that you don't think there has ever been a time in your life that you've sensed God doing a supernatural work in giving you a new heart toward him, a new appetite for him, a new sense of purpose and joy in God himself?

The newness of God can begin in your life right now. Today.

I don't know about you, but I don't want to stay my same old self, trapped in my old sinful tendencies. I don't want to surrender to "that's just the way I am, the way I've always been; I can never change." *I want to be made new.*

I want the newness that only comes by being touched by God, not just at a few points in my past but in a deep and daily ongoing way. I don't want to spend the rest of my life in the newness of when I came alive to Christ in my teens, or the lessons he taught me in my twenties, or how he met me in the hard places in my thirties and forties. I don't want to depend on yesterday's fresh experiences with him. I want there to be an ongoing freshness in my walk with him. And you do too, don't you?

Here is the hope we find as we begin to see Jesus in Genesis 1—that though we've made a mess of things, though we've made ourselves at home in the darkness, though we have filled our lives with so many things and yet find ourselves empty, lifeless, and restless—Jesus can and will illumine us, shape us, fill us, breathe new life into us, and give us rest. We can be made new on the inside through the power of the living Word.

How Genesis Points to What Is Yet to Come: "I Am Making All Things New"

When we read Genesis 1, we see not only a picture of our beginnings, but also a preview of our future. The Bible begins by telling us that "God created the heavens and the earth" (Gen. 1:1). When we come to the end of the Bible we might expect an ending, but what we find is a new beginning. In Revelation, John tells us about his vision of "a new heaven and a new earth, for the first heaven and the first earth had passed away" (21:1).

When John wrote that he saw the new heaven and new earth coming down out of heaven from God, he was not describing a literal descent of a second earth from the sky. He was describing the final culmination of the regenerating work of Christ, that day when this earth will be made new.

In Revelation 21:5, we read, "He who was seated on the throne said, 'Behold, I am making all things new.'" When we read these words, we tend to think of "new" as a replacement for the old. But this does not say that God is making new things; it says that he is making all things new—new in quality, freshness, brightness, and strength. This earth will be completely re-created. It will be recognizable but purged of every trace of sin and the curse.

This new heaven and new earth will be lit by the same light that lit creation even before God "made the two great lights" to rule the day and night (Gen. 1:16). This new creation will have "no need of sun or moon to shine on it, for the glory of God gives it light, and its lamp is the Lamb" (Rev. 21:23). Just as the pre-incarnate Christ lit the world at creation, so will the very presence of the glorified Christ light the new creation.

In this new environment from God, we will enjoy fruitfulness even more abundantly than what Adam and Eve enjoyed in the garden. While the trees bore fruit in the garden (Gen. 1:12), in the new earth, the "tree of life with its twelve kinds of fruit" will yield "its fruit each month" (Rev. 22:2).

The newness that began in the interior of our lives when we became a new creation in Christ will finally be complete. The image of God that was marred by sin will be restored. "The Lord Jesus Christ . . . will transform our lowly body to be like his glorious body, by the power that enables him even to subject all things to himself" (Phil. 3:20–21). Somehow God will use the seed of our earthly bodies to make for us bodies fit for the new heaven and the new earth. Somehow he will take from the matter that has been long buried, or spread on the sea, or in the wind, and fashion it into something glorious. We will have been remade into his image so that "we shall be like him" (1 John 3:2).

Just as our bodies will be remade without the loss of our personal identities, so will the rest of creation be remade in perfection. God's purposes of redemption through Christ have never been limited solely to humanity. His intention has always been to reveal his glory in and through the creation and re-creation of the natural world. This will not be simply a return to Eden. It will be the same creation that God called into being in Genesis 1, yet much more. It will be nothing less than creation glorified.

This is what is ahead for us. "There remains a Sabbath rest for the people of God, for whoever has entered God's rest has also rested from his works as God did from his" (Heb. 4:9–10). This will be the seventh-day rest that every Sabbath since Eden has pointed toward and has implanted in us a longing for—finally like it was in the garden at the beginning, only better, and this time, forever. God's people in God's place, enjoying God himself in their midst for all time.

Creation

GENESIS 1:1–2:3

Getting the Discussion Going

1. It's true that we love *new*, isn't it? What is something you have enjoyed particularly when it was new or because it was new? Of what do you wish you had a "new one" even now?

Getting to the Heart of It

2. Let's open to Genesis 1. In a sense, verses 1 and 2 present a situation that God addresses in the rest of the chapter. What is the situation and what did God do?

3. In the Personal Bible Study, you were asked to list what God did in the days of creation. What stood out to you?

4. Genesis 1 tells us that God made us in his own image. How would you explain to someone what it means to be made in the image of God, and why this is significant?

5. Many of the things we discover about God, the world, and humanity from Genesis 1:1–2:3 go against common beliefs in the culture around us. How would you use Genesis 1 and 2 to challenge the following statements?

~ This world as we know it was formed by chance as new forms of life developed from matter that spontaneously became more complex.

∼ The sun, moon, and stars influence a person's destiny.

∼ God is one with nature.

∼ The human body is inherently evil.

∼ Every thing and every day is equally sacred as well as ordinary.

∼ What makes a person good is how he or she treats the people and the
   world around him or her.

∼ God was lonely, so he created people.

6. Genesis 2:7 tells us that "God formed the man of dust from the
ground and breathed into his nostrils the breath of life, and the man
became a living creature." How should this knowledge impact how we
see ourselves?

7. How does God's breathing into humanity's nostrils the breath of life
picture what God does in someone who comes to life spiritually (regeneration)?

Getting Personal

8. The big question of this week was, "How can I begin again?" In
Genesis 1 we've seen the Father, the Son, and the Spirit in their creative, life-giving work. And we recognize that it is the same Father,
Son, and Spirit who work in us now to give us new life. Some people
can point to a specific date when they know that they were born a
second time—changed by God from a spiritually dead person into a
spiritually alive person. Others, especially some who grew up hearing
about Christ, or those who attend a Bible study over a period of time
and grow gradually in their understanding of the gospel, may have
a hard time nailing down a particular point in time when they were
reborn. But that instantaneous event was there nonetheless when God
through the Holy Spirit, in an unseen, invisible way, called each one
to new spiritual life. It is this work of God that gives us the spiritual
ability to respond to God in faith. Would any of you be willing to tell us
about how God's Word and the Spirit of God brought you to life spiritually and how it changed you?

Getting How It Fits into the Big Picture

9. Throughout this study, we are seeking to grasp how the passage we're studying fits into the bigger story of God's plan of redemption. How does Genesis 1 help us understand not only how history began but also where history is headed?

The Fall

Genesis 2:4–3:24

Personal Bible Study

The Fall

GENESIS 2:4–3:24

1. Read Genesis 2:4–25. Briefly describe what Eden was like and the life that Adam and Eve enjoyed there.

2. Genesis 2 ends by telling us that Adam and Eve were "both naked and were not ashamed" (v. 25). What do you think this means?

3. From other passages in Scripture we know that there is such a being as Satan. He was created perfect but fell away from virtue through pride and he carried many other angelic beings with him in his rebellion against God. He presented himself in the garden at the beginning of history as a serpent to tempt the first man and woman. What light do these verses give us on the identity and actions of this serpent?

∼ Matthew 13:19

∼ John 12:31

∽ Revelation 12:9

⏱ 4. In the chart below, compare the record of what God said to Adam in Genesis 2:9, 16, and 17 with how the Serpent and Eve portray what he said in Genesis 3:1–5. How did they challenge and change God's word?

God	Serpent/Eve	Challenge and Change
"You may surely eat of every tree of the garden, but of the tree of the knowledge of good and evil you shall not eat." (2:16–17)	Serpent: "Did God actually say, 'You shall not eat of any tree in the garden'?" (3:1)	
"You may surely eat of every tree of the garden." (2:16)	Eve: "We may eat of the fruit of the trees in the garden." (3:2)	
"The tree of life was in the midst of the garden, and the tree of the knowledge of good and evil." (2:9)	Eve: "The tree that is in the midst of the garden." (3:3)	
"But of the tree of the knowledge of good and evil you shall not eat." (2:17)	Eve: "You shall not eat . . . neither shall you touch it." (3:3)	
"You shall surely die." (2:17)	Eve: "Lest you die." (3:3)	
"For in the day that you eat of it you shall surely die." (2:17)	Serpent: "You will not surely die." (3:4)	

5. What do we learn from this scene of temptation and sin about how Satan tempts us and about what is needed to stand firm against temptation?

6. Read Genesis 3:6. What were the three appeals to Eve that led her to take and eat?

7. Adam and Eve sought to cover up their sin by making coverings for themselves made of fig leaves, but this was inadequate. What are some modern-day cover-ups and excuses we try to string together to make ourselves okay with God?

8. God entered the garden looking for Adam and Eve, and he asked three questions in verses 9 and 11. What are they, and why do you think he asked them?

9. In Genesis 3:15, God's curse on the Serpent states that an offspring of the woman will "bruise" or "crush" the Serpent's head, while the Serpent will bruise the heel of the promised offspring. What do the following Scriptures reveal about how Satan bruised the "heel" of the offspring of the woman, Jesus Christ?

~ Matthew 16:23

~ John 8:39–44

~ John 13:2

🕐 10. How do the following Scriptures reveal how Christ has and will bruise or crush the "head" of Satan?

～ Colossians 2:13–15

～ Hebrews 2:14–15

～ Revelation 12:11

～ Revelation 20:7–10

11. In Genesis 3:4–24 we begin to see how things changed dramatically after Adam and Eve's sin. In the chart below, see if you can identify some of the things that changed (the first space has been filled in for you as an example).

Before the Fall	After the Fall
Adam and Eve were made in the image of God. (Gen. 1:26)	*The image of God in Adam and Eve became marred by sin.*
Adam and Eve exercised dominion or authority over the animals. (Gen. 1:26)	
Adam and Eve lived under God's blessing. (Gen. 1:28)	
Adam and Eve were given the responsibility and the ability to subdue the earth. (Gen. 1:28)	

Adam was formed from the dust of the ground and given life. (Gen. 2:7)	
The plants in the garden grew easily and in abundance. (Gen. 2:9)	
Adam and Eve lived in the garden. (Gen. 2:15)	
Adam and Eve enjoyed one-flesh intimacy with each other. (Gen. 2:23)	
Adam and Eve were naked and not ashamed. (Gen. 2:25)	

12. We are so used to speaking of "Adam and Eve" that we generally fail to notice that not until Genesis 3:20 is Adam's wife actually called "Eve." Up to this point, she has been called a "female" (1:27), a "helper fit" for Adam (2:18), a "woman" (2:22, 23), and a "wife" (2:24, 25; 3:8). But those are all descriptive terms and not names. Why is it significant that Adam named his wife Eve, and why do you think it falls at this place in the story?

13. Because of the faith of Adam expressed in the naming of Eve, God did for Adam and Eve what they could not do adequately for themselves: he provided a covering of animal skins, perhaps the skin of a

lamb. How does this point to the covering God has provided for us in our sin?

14. God had promised that if they ate of the tree of the knowledge of good and evil, they would surely die. Now an animal has been slain, but they are still alive. What should this have told them about sin and about God?

15. How does the account of Adam and Eve's fall point to Christ? Find the connections in the New Testament passages below, following the example given in the first block of the chart.

The Fall	Christ
"The Lord God formed the man of dust from the ground." (Gen. 2:7)	1 Cor. 15:47–49 *Just as Adam was made of dust and returned to dust when he died, so are we made of dust. But Christ remakes us into his image so that our bodies will be resurrected and glorified.*
"The Lord God . . . breathed into his nostrils the breath of life." (Gen. 2:7)	John 5:21; 1 Cor. 15:45; 1 John 5:12
"But of the tree of the knowledge of good and evil you shall not eat, for in the day that you eat of it you shall surely die." (Gen. 2:17)	Matt. 26:26; John 6:51–52
"A man shall leave his father and his mother and hold fast to his wife, and they shall become one flesh." (Gen. 2:24)	Eph. 1:23; 5:31–32

"She took of its fruit and ate, and she also gave some to her husband who was with her, and he ate." (Gen. 3:6)	Rom. 5:12–21
"They heard the sound of the LORD God walking in the garden in the cool of the day." (Gen. 3:8)	Luke 19:10
"Cursed are you. . . . Cursed is the ground because of you." (Gen. 3:14, 17)	Gal. 3:13–14; Rev. 22:3
"Cursed is the ground because of you; . . . thorns and thistles it shall bring forth for you." (Gen. 3:17, 18)	John 19:2
"I will put enmity between . . . your offspring and her offspring." (Gen. 3:15)	Mark 1:24
"He shall bruise your head, and you shall bruise his heel." (Gen. 3:15)	Heb. 2:14; 1 John 3:8; Rev. 20:7–10
"The LORD God made for Adam and for his wife garments of skins and clothed them." (Gen. 3:21)	Isa. 61:10; Rom. 4:7; Rev. 3:14–18
"He drove out the man, and . . . placed the cherubim and a flaming sword . . . to guard the way to the tree of life." (Gen. 3:24)	John 14:6; Heb. 10:19–22; Rev. 22:2

Teaching Chapter

You Don't Have to Hide

A few years ago I picked up *The Kite Runner* in an airport bookstore as I prepared to board a flight, and as I began to read, I was immediately transported through its pages to the streets of Kabul, Afghanistan.

The novel begins with the words, "I became what I am today at the age of twelve, on a frigid overcast day in the winter of 1975." That was the day Amir crouched behind a crumbling mud wall and stayed silent as his most loyal friend was robbed of innocence and dignity. "That was a long time ago," Amir says, "but it's wrong what they say about the past, about how you can bury it. Because the past claws its way out." For twenty-six years Amir tried to bury his shameful betrayal—forget it, cover it up. And then he got a phone call from an old friend who had known his secret all along.

"*Come,*" Rahim Khan said to him. "There is a way to be good again."

If you have read *The Kite Runner,* then I know you feel the import of those words and what it will mean for Amir to find a way to right his wrong. But even if you haven't read this book, isn't there a place inside you that feels the heartbreak as well as the hope in these words?

There is a way to be good again.

It strikes at the core of our being. Because we too carry regret and shame for who we are and what we've done. We too have unsuccessfully tried to hide away and cover over what has brought us deep shame. We too long for relief from bearing the weight of our past failures and ongoing hypocrisies. We too long for a way to be good again.

Just as Amir looked back at an overcast day in the winter of 1975, the day he kept silent, perhaps there is a day you look back at as the day when shame became a permanent resident in your heart. Perhaps it was that first morning when you woke up in bed with a man who was not your husband. Perhaps it was that afternoon when someone who was supposed to take care of you took advantage of you. Perhaps it was the day you first began to shade the truth, cut corners, or take care of yourself at the expense of someone else. Perhaps it was the night you first went where you said you would never go. And ever since you first took steps to cover up where you were and what you did, you've been hiding—from the people closest to you, from your own conscience, and from God himself.

Or perhaps there is no specific day you can point to. Perhaps your heart has become loaded down with shame a little bit at a time. You are so aware of all the ways you do not measure up. It pains you to take a long look in the mirror, because you see someone who has failed again and again. There are certain people you can't stand to be around because they have said no to what you have said yes to, and their very presence seems to heap shame on you. And even though you may come to church, you would be embarrassed for anyone to know how long it has been since you had any kind of meaningful personal prayer time with God because shame has built up such an insurmountable barrier. You keep hoping that maybe someday you'll figure this out and be free to come out of hiding.

Genesis 3 is for you. For one thing, it explains how we have come to have this bent toward trying to cover up what bring us deep shame. We have all inherited this nature from our parents and from our ultimate parents, Adam and Eve. But we've also been offered the same hope that was promised to Adam and Eve—a way to be good again.

The First Adam: Tested and Tempted in a Garden Paradise

There was a time when everything about the earth and everyone on the earth was good—completely and perfectly good. "God saw everything that he had made, and behold, it was very good" (Gen. 1:31). Adam and Eve fully enjoyed the goodness that was all around them and even within them.

The man and his wife were both naked and were not ashamed. (Gen. 2:25)

Adam and Eve lived in a garden paradise with every need provided for, their lives infused with purpose and enjoying unhindered intimacy with each other and with God. And in the middle of all this abundance were two trees. With one tree came a promise, and with the other came a warning.

> The tree of life was in the midst of the garden, and the tree of the knowledge of good and evil. . . . And the LORD God commanded the man, saying, "You may surely eat of every tree of the garden, but of the tree of the knowledge of good and evil you shall not eat, for in the day that you eat of it you shall surely die." (Gen. 2:9, 16–17)

The tree of life offered more than just unending life. To eat of the tree of life was to enjoy a life that was qualitatively different. It was a life enjoying the rest and provision of God. To eat of the tree of the knowledge of good and evil would not merely enable those who ate to know what good and evil are. To eat of it was to assume the right to decide for oneself what is good and what is evil rather than depend on God to define good and evil.

Through this prohibition, God put Adam to the test. Adam was created with every ability to pass this test of obedience to God. Will he believe God's word and trust God's plan? Or will he doubt and defy God's word and reject God's provision? *Oh, how we wish Adam had passed this test, don't we?*

God put this tree in the middle of the garden to test and train Adam to call good "good" and evil "evil." But into the goodness of the garden of God, a serpent appeared. The Serpent had his own plans for the tree, which were the very opposite of its intended purpose. Satan intended to use the tree to tempt Adam to decide for himself what is good and what is evil.

This Serpent was no ordinary reptile. He was none other than Satan himself. The subtle cunning and the deceit with which Satan approached Eve are like the sinuous, back-and-forth movements of a snake. His ability to look so good and appealing when he was so evil and his purpose was so destructive was like a reptile's ability to camouflage itself in its surroundings. This Serpent intended to strike at God's very heart by destroying that which was most precious to him—the unfettered intimacy he enjoyed with those he created.

It is to the woman that the Serpent spoke, perhaps beginning with a bit of a sarcastic snarl, questioning the clear word God had given to Adam.

> He said to the woman, "Did God actually say, 'You shall not eat of any tree in the garden'?" (Gen. 3:1)

The serpent was planting the idea that God had been unreasonable, that something was wrong with a God who would come up with such a random prohibition. And Eve, who had known nothing but the goodness and bounty of God, began to listen as Satan smuggled in the assumption that God's word was subject to her judgment.

And we still entertain this suggestion, don't we? We do it when we question God's clear instructions and cast them into the categories of unreasonable, out-of-touch, unnecessarily restrictive, and harsh.

Did God actually say I should remain faithful to my marriage vows when we've fallen out of love?

Did God actually say I should give away such a significant portion of my income when it might be misused?

Did God actually say I am supposed to forgive that person who has hurt me again and again?

Satan still comes to us suggesting that what God has commanded is unreasonable and is intended to make us miserable rather than deeply satisfied.

The Serpent not only questioned God's word; he also added to God's word when he suggested that God had said, "You shall not eat of *any* tree in the garden." God had provided a vast garden from which Adam and Eve were free to eat. Only one tree was prohibited. By adding to what God had actually commanded, the Serpent sought to make the prohibition of God seem ridiculously restrictive. And Eve fell for it! Then she made her own addition to what God had actually said.

And the woman said to the serpent, "We may eat of the fruit of the trees in the garden, but God said, 'You shall not eat of the fruit of the tree that is in the midst of the garden, *neither shall you touch it*, lest you die.'" (Gen. 3:2–3)

Eve has begun to think dark thoughts about God and chafe under his command rather than fix her thoughts on what she knows is true about God and rest under his authority.

So the Serpent questioned God's word and added to God's word, and finally he denied God's word:

But the serpent said to the woman, "You will not surely die." (Gen. 3:4)

Eve's receptivity emboldened the Serpent so that he said outright that God had not told her and Adam the truth. Satan suggested not only that God was unreasonable and restrictive but also that he was just plain wrong, and therefore untrustworthy.

> *Christ took my shame upon himself so I don't have to hide.*

When the Serpent said, "You will not surely die," we have the first denial of judgment for sin. But it is certainly not the last. How many people throughout the rest of Scripture and still today continue to laugh off the notion that judgment is coming, suggesting that it is a lie intended to manipulate people into conformity rather than a warning given for protection?

Satan not only suggested God was lying to her; he suggested God was withholding from her.

For God knows that when you eat of it your eyes will be opened, and you will be like God, knowing good and evil. (Gen. 3:5)

The Serpent suggested to Eve that she did not need God to know what is right and what is wrong. She could become her own moral compass.

Have you listened to that lie? Have you allowed the voice of our culture to convince you that only you can define what is right and wrong for you? Have you heard Satan sneer that what God has said is wrong is really not that black-and-white, really not such a big deal? The real question is, are you going to allow God to judge and define what is good and what is evil, or are you going to take the reins of those decisions in your life? This is no small thing. It is this question—and Adam and Eve's response to it—that changed the course of the entire world.

Eve should have said to the Serpent, "Look at this place I am living in! I have an ideal husband, and I am an ideal wife. We walk with the God who made us. He knows us, and we know him. I draw my identity from being made in his image. He has provided everything I need, including giving my life a sense of meaning and purpose. How could I ever think he has withheld anything from me that is good or desirable? Of course he knows what's best! Yet you have the audacity to suggest that I stand in judgment over him?"

Eve should have run screaming through the garden to report this rebellion against God to her protector, Adam. Adam should have protected his wife and defended God by confronting Satan's twisting of God's clear word.

But instead, Eve betrayed her frustration with this one restriction as she entertained the idea that God derived some sort of glee in keeping her down. There was a tingle of potential rebellion rushing through Eve. Adam was not deceived but willfully chose to rebel against God's clear command, assuming there would be no consequences. Eve listened to the Serpent. Adam listened to Eve. And no one listened to God.

Eve stood there looking at the tree and it looked "good for food." A flicker of discontent with the fruit of all the other trees caused sparks to fly. She saw that it was "a delight to the eyes" and the flame ignited as she disparaged the beauty of all that God is and all he had provided. Seeing that "the tree was to be desired to make one wise" (Gen. 3:6), she threw another log onto the fire as this false promise of wisdom burned an image in her mind of becoming the smartest person in the room. If only she had doused the flames of this prideful desire and confronted the deceit of the tempter with the truth of God's word. But she didn't.

> She took of its fruit and ate, and she also gave some to her husband who was with her, and he ate. (Gen. 3:6)

What is described so simply and what sounds so natural was actually cosmic and disastrous. And the consequences for Adam and Eve were immediate. The Serpent had said that their eyes would be opened and they would be like God. And he was half right. Their eyes were opened, but they were not like God. Their eyes were opened so that they saw their own nakedness. Their flaws were now out there—uncovered. And they couldn't bear the exposure. Instead of seeking God and openly confessing their guilt, they attempted to conceal it, sewing fig leaves together to hide from each other. They got behind a tree to hide from God. And they made up excuses in an attempt to hide the truth from even their own eyes.

Adam and Eve were not only filled with shame; they also were captured by fear. They remembered what God had said: "In the day you eat of it you shall surely die." Today was that day. And they discovered that the Serpent's statement, "You will not surely die," was also half true. They didn't die physically, at least not immediately (though now it was clear that one day they would go to earthly graves). But they did die spiritually. They went from having lives marked by blessing, openness, intimacy, and ongoing life, to lives marked by curse, hiding, alienation, and death.

This could be the end of the story. God had every right to bring about the judgment of death right then. But this serves as the beginning of a greater story. Because while we hide in shame and fear, God seeks for us in grace and mercy. While we clearly deserve to die, God comes to us to grant us life.

> And they heard the sound of the LORD God walking in the garden in the cool of the day, and the man and his wife hid themselves from the presence of the LORD God among the trees of the garden. But the LORD God called to the man and said to him, "Where are you?" And he said, "I heard the sound of you in the garden, and I was afraid, because I was naked, and I hid myself." (Gen. 3:8–10)

Here we see one of the first pictures in Scripture of what our God is like personally. He takes the initiative to seek after sinners. "Who told you that you were naked?" God asked Adam. There was only one way that could have happened, and God knew the answer to his question even before he asked it. "Have you eaten of the tree of which I commanded you not to eat?" (Gen. 3:11).

At this point Adam could have come clean and confessed his sin. But instead of making a brokenhearted confession, he offered an excuse. And the blame game began. Adam blamed "the woman whom you gave to be with me" (Gen. 3:12), and Eve blamed the Serpent. And all were called to account under the judgment of God.

God didn't question the Serpent. There was no need for that since there was no possibility of his redemption. He sentenced the Serpent with a curse—not yet utter destruction, but that will come one day. For a season God will use him in a way that will ultimately bring greater glory to himself.

> The LORD God said to the serpent, "Because you have done this, cursed are you above all livestock and above all beasts of the field; on your belly you shall go, and dust you shall eat all the days of your life. I will put enmity between you and the woman, and between your offspring and her offspring; he shall bruise your head, and you shall bruise his heel." (Gen. 3:14–15)

This curse was the converse of the blessing with which God had blessed all of his creation. The joyous dance of creation now became a dirge. Yet in the midst of God's curse we hear a word of grace (the first glimpse of the gospel): an offspring of the woman will engage the Serpent in combat and win.

Beginning with Eve's first offspring—her son Cain—her descendants began to wonder if each new baby might be the offspring who would destroy the Devil, who had led them into so much suffering. But sure enough, each of those children eventually died. The rest of the Old Testament is the story of longing for and God's preparing a people from which the promised offspring would come. And the New Testament is the story of the coming of the promised offspring and his battle with, and ultimate defeat of, the ancient Serpent.

While God cursed Satan personally, and cursed the ground because of Adam's sin, neither Adam nor Eve was cursed personally. They were objects of God's tender mercy. But they would nevertheless experience the effects of the curse.

> To the woman he said, "I will surely multiply your pain in childbearing; in pain you shall bring forth children. Your desire shall be for your husband, and he shall rule over you." (Gen. 3:16)

The aspects of Eve's life that were intended to bring the greatest pleasure in her life will now be invaded by pain. This is not merely the physical pain of labor and delivery but the pain of infertility and miscarriage, birth defects and learning disabilities. This is the pain of birthing a child into a broken world and mothering a child in the midst of this broken world. Her children will be born but will not live forever. They will be born into the reality of sin and death.

She was made to be her husband's companion and helper. But now she will fight against the desire to dictate to him and dominate him. Rather than look to her husband for guidance, she'll seek to manipulate him. And rather than gently guiding and guarding her, he will lord over and exploit her. Rather than the unfettered one-flesh intimacy they once knew, their relationship will be riddled with self-centered strife.

The center of Adam's life also became a struggle.

> And to Adam he said, "Because you have listened to the voice of your wife and have eaten of the tree of which I commanded you, 'You shall not eat of it,' cursed is the ground because of you; in pain you shall eat of it all the days of your life; thorns and thistles it shall bring forth for you; and you shall eat the plants of the field. By the sweat of your face you shall eat bread, till you return to the ground, for out of it you were taken; for you are dust, and to dust you shall return." (Gen. 3:17–19)

While Adam was created to tend and keep the garden, now it is not going to come easily. Work wasn't supposed to be like this. It will now be exasperating toil. The ground is going to resist him. Instead of bearing fruit, it will grow weeds. And ultimately he will be buried in this ground, and his body will turn back into its dust.

We might expect that Adam's response to such a bitter curse would be rage or despair. But even before Adam and Eve heard of their judgment, they heard the promise of their redemption. This curse was laced with grace. And the first thing we see Adam do is express faith in what God has promised.

> The man called his wife's name Eve, because she was the mother of all living. (Gen. 3:20)

His naming her Eve wasn't rugged self-determination to overpower the curse, but solid hope in spite of the curse. Adam caught the promise couched in the curse—that the offspring of the woman will crush the head of the Serpent. By naming his wife Eve, Adam demonstrated that he believed what God had promised. While he was no longer capable of leading his posterity into life, he had put his hope in one to come who will restore what was lost through disobedience.

Christ was alienated from God so that I can draw near.

And this is where we, too, find hope. We grieve over the hurts that the curse causes in our lives—difficulty conceiving, disappointment in marriage, dead-end jobs, disease-ridden bodies. But we do not grieve as those who have no hope.

Here Adam shows all of us who have inherited his nature of sin how to stare the curse of death in the face and celebrate the promise that this curse is not God's final word. God's final word is his Son, Jesus, who said, "I tell you the truth, those who listen to my message and believe in God who sent me have eternal life. They will never be condemned for their sins, but they have already passed from death into life" (John 5:24 NLT). This was Adam's hope, though he could not have articulated it this way. And this is our sure and certain hope while living in a world that is still so deeply impacted by this curse.

God followed this first gospel promise by preaching the first gospel sermon—not with words but in symbol and action. He showed how a sinful creature can become acceptable to his holy creator. It was the initial declaration of the fundamental fact that "without the shedding of blood there is no forgiveness of sins" (Heb. 9:22), an illustration of substitution, the innocent dying in place of the guilty.

And the LORD God made for Adam and for his wife garments of skins and clothed them. (Gen. 3:21)

Adam received grace in the midst of the curse—a covering for his nakedness provided wholly by God.

The Second Adam: Tested and Tempted in a Barren Wilderness

Adam failed the test in the garden. He failed to live up to all that God intended for him. And because he disobeyed, Adam lost for us the perfect environment, the perfect fellowship, that he and Eve enjoyed with the Creator.

But when the fullness of time had come, God sent forth his Son, born of woman. (Gal. 4:4)

This is the one who was to come, the one of whom Adam was only a type (Rom. 5:14). This is the offspring God had promised in the curse. This is the hope of every descendant of Adam who has placed his or her faith in God's promise. This is Jesus.

The New Testament calls Jesus the "last" or "second" Adam (1 Cor. 15:45). Like the first Adam, he too was tested by God and tempted by Satan—not in a garden paradise where all of his needs were met, but in a barren wilderness where he was weak from hunger and deprived of water.

In Matthew we read that the Spirit had just descended on Jesus at his baptism and a voice from heaven said, "This is my beloved Son, with whom I am well pleased" (Matt. 3:17), much like God's "very good," over Adam in the garden of Eden. But then Matthew tells us (4:1) that the Spirit led him into the wilderness for something less pleasant. Here Jesus would be tested.

Now, why did Jesus's obedience need to be tested? He did this for our sake, so that he would know how to sympathize with us when we face temptation while living in the wilderness of this world. But more than that, Jesus's obedience was tested so that it would be the authentic obedience of our fully God, fully human Savior, not the assumed obedience of an out-of-touch deity. His obedience in the face of temptation is the merit that is transferred to us in the great exchange, in which he takes our sin upon himself and gives to us his own glorious righteousness. This is the righteousness of Christ that is credited to us—proven in the trenches of temptation.

Just as Satan entered the garden to tempt Adam and Eve, so Satan entered into the wilderness in a diabolical attempt to subvert God's plan for redemption by tempting Jesus to fall into sin and disobedience, which would disqualify him as the sinless Savior.

> Then Jesus was led up by the Spirit into the wilderness to be tempted by the devil. And after fasting forty days and forty nights, he was hungry. And the tempter came. (Matt. 4:1–3)

Will Jesus question God when tempted? Will he complain? Will he yield? Or will he stand fast?

Satan came to Jesus tempting him to trust in himself to meet his own needs rather than rely on God to provide for him. But Jesus responded to Satan, saying:

> It is written, "Man shall not live by bread alone, but by every word that comes from the mouth of God." (Matt. 4:4, quoting Deut. 8:3)

Unlike Adam and Eve, who suspected God was withholding from them, Jesus knew that God provided everything he needed. And whereas Adam and Eve allowed Satan to question, deny, add to, and twist the word of God, Jesus overcame temptation by the power of God's sure and certain, unchanging, unimpeachable Word.

Next, Satan took Jesus to the pinnacle of the temple where he blatantly misused the words of Psalm 91 in an effort to manipulate Jesus into forcing God's hand into a spectacular display of protecting his Son from death.

> If you are the Son of God, throw yourself down, for it is written, "He will command his angels concerning you," and "On their hands they will bear you up, lest you strike your foot against a stone." (Matt. 4:5–6)

Unlike Adam and Eve who allowed themselves to be manipulated by Satan's twisting of God's word to presume upon God's mercy,

Jesus refuted Satan with God's Word in confidence of God's loving protection.

> Jesus said to him, "Again it is written, 'You shall not put the Lord your God to the test.'" (Matt. 4:7)

But Satan was not finished. He showed Christ all the kingdoms of the world and their glory—exactly what Christ had come to reign over. And he offered it to Jesus if only Jesus would worship him.

Satan was offering an easier way to come into the authority that will be his anyway. He was tempting Jesus to avoid the cross. But he offered authority on earth only, not in heaven (which Satan cannot, of course, offer). This was authority over a world marked by sin and death rather than authority over sin and death. Satan was offering the world, but it's not really a world worth having. Besides, Jesus had not come to set up an earthly kingdom. He was here to redeem the earth for his Father and bring the kingdom of heaven to earth. And to do this, he had to suffer and die. So, once again, Jesus responded to Satan's temptation with the Word of God:

Christ became a curse for me, so that I can enjoy God's blessing.

> Then Jesus said to him, "Be gone, Satan! For it is written, 'You shall worship the Lord your God and him only shall you serve.'" (Matt. 4:10)

Satan slithered into the wilderness to tempt Jesus in an attempt to thwart God's plan and purposes. But Jesus clung tightly to the Word of God and rested in the provision of God. And what Satan intended for evil, God would use for good. God used Satan's evil tempting for the good purpose of strengthening Jesus as he began his earthly ministry.

This is not the last time the second Adam faced testing by God and temptation from Satan. Like Adam was tested and tempted in the garden of Eden, Jesus was also tested and tempted in the garden of Gethsemane. The test, which came from God, was exactly the same as that which God gave to Adam: Will you do as God says? And the temptation, which came from Satan, was exactly the same as Satan used on Adam: "Or will you do as you choose?"

There in the garden of Gethsemane, Satan once again tempted Jesus to avoid the cross. And this temptation was not faced down without a struggle. There in the garden, the most significant spiritual struggle of all time took place. The writer to the Hebrews describes it for us:

> Jesus offered up prayers and supplications, with loud cries and tears, to him who was able to save him from death, and he was heard because of his reverence. Although he was a son, he learned obedience through what he suffered. And being made perfect, he became the source of eternal salvation to all who obey him. (Heb. 5:7–9)

Jesus was put to the test in the garden of Gethsemane as he was tempted by Satan. And Jesus passed the test. He overcame the temptation. He obeyed God, saying, "Not as I will, but as you will" (Matt. 26:39) and became "obedient to the point of death, even death on a cross" (Phil. 2:8).

Adam and Eve faced temptation about a tree in a bright, sunny garden, a paradise with no pressure. But Christ faced temptation about a tree in a dark garden, a garden given the name that meant "oil press," and certainly he felt squeezed like an olive in a press on that dark night, to the point that his sweat was like drops of blood.

If Adam and Eve obeyed God about the tree, they would live. If Jesus obeyed God about the tree, he would die.[1]

Jesus obeyed. And through his obedience he gained for us far more than Adam lost for us through his disobedience.

Adam lost for us the beautiful "naked and not ashamed" of the garden. But at the cross, Christ hung naked and full of shame. It wasn't his own shame. It was your shame and my shame. He "endured the cross, despising the shame" (Heb. 12:2) so that "everyone who believes in him will not be put to shame" (Rom. 10:11).

Adam lost for us the perfect fellowship with God he enjoyed as he shared life with his maker in the garden. But those "who once were alienated and hostile in mind, doing evil deeds" have now been "reconciled in

[1] I am indebted to Timothy J. Keller for this key insight from his sermon "Paradise in Crisis," Redeemer Presbyterian Church, New York, January 11, 2009.

his body of flesh by his death, in order to present [us] holy and blameless and above reproach before him" (Col. 1:21–22). On the cross Jesus cried out, "My God, my God, why have you forsaken me?" (Matt. 27:46). You see, Christ on the cross experienced an infinite alienation from God, the alienation that you and I deserve because of our sin. Christ experienced it in our place so that we can enjoy the fellowship with God that is even better than Adam enjoyed in the garden. This is why we can "draw near to the throne of grace" with confidence (Heb. 4:16).

Adam lost for us the blessing of God that made everything "very good." Because of his rebellion, the blessing became a curse, everything good became infiltrated with evil, what was so beautiful became broken. But once again, Christ has gained for us more than Adam lost for us. "Christ redeemed us from the curse of the law by becoming a curse for us—for it is written 'Cursed is everyone who is hanged on a tree.'" (Gal. 3:13). Because of this we will enjoy far more than the blessings of the perfect garden paradise.

> In him we have redemption through his blood, the forgiveness of our trespasses, according to the riches of his grace, which he lavished upon us, in all wisdom and insight . . . according to his purpose, which he set forth in Christ as a plan for the fullness of time, to unite all things in him, things in heaven and things on earth. (Eph. 1:7–10)

Adam ate the fruit of the tree of the knowledge of good and evil. But could there ever have been a tree that bore more fruit of the knowledge of both good and evil than the tree upon which Christ died? On that tree hung the only person who has ever been perfectly good. And yet he took upon himself all of our evil so that we, along with all of creation, might be restored and cleansed and made good again.

The cross reaches through the centuries, saying to us, "There's a way to be good again." You do not have to spend your life hiding who you really are and what you've done. Whatever it is, Christ died for it. His sacrifice was sufficient for it. So won't you come out of hiding and come clean with him by just confessing it all to him? He doesn't want to condemn you; he wants to cleanse you. No matter what it is, he can make you good again.

In *The Kite Runner*, when Rahid Khan tells Amir that there is a way for him to be good again, it means that he must go back—back to Afghanistan where his shame began. He can make things right if he will rescue the son of the friend he betrayed and bring him home to become his own. And we're satisfied as readers when we come to the last page of the book, because this is exactly what Amir does. His great wrong has been righted by his own courageous heroism and the adoption of this boy as his own son.

So many of us would like this kind of opportunity. We never seem to cease wanting to accomplish our own redemption. We are sons and daughters of Adam and Eve thinking that we can somehow make up for the shameful failures of our past if only we can try a little harder, have a little more time. We so want to be good again—on our own terms, through our own efforts.

When we open up the Bible, it speaks to us, telling us that there is a way to be good again. But it is not up to us to redeem ourselves. From eternity past, God intended that the sin-bringing Adam would point us to the sin-bearing second Adam. We are all children of Adam by birth. It is only by rebirth that we become children of God, as we place our faith in the second Adam. Either we are connected to Adam and destined to die in our shame, or we are connected to Christ and destined to live forever with him, sharing in his glory.

> The sin of this one man, Adam, caused death to rule over many. But even greater is God's wonderful grace and his gift of righteousness, for all who receive it will live in triumph over sin and death through this one man, Jesus Christ. (Rom. 5:17 NLT)

How Genesis Points to What Is Yet to Come: A New Garden with No More Curse

Life for Adam and Eve began in a garden paradise built around the tree of life where God himself walked with them. And for all those who belong to Christ, life will continue into eternity in a restored garden paradise built around the tree of life where God will live with us. Through Christ, God has made a way for us to come back into his garden, where he will be our God and we will be his people. No more hiding. No more alienation. No more pain. No more curse.

The garden of God—the kingdom of God on the earth—is where the Bible and history began, and its restoration is where the whole Bible and all of history is headed. We read about this restored garden in the very last chapter of the Bible:

> Then the angel showed me the river of the water of life, bright as crystal, flowing from the throne of God and of the Lamb through the middle of the street of the city; also, on either side of the river, the tree of life with its twelve kinds of fruit, yielding its fruit each month. The leaves of the tree were for the healing of the nations. No longer will there be anything accursed. (Rev. 22:1–3)

The Serpent will not be able to slither into this garden like he did in Eden. "Nothing unclean will ever enter it" (Rev. 21:27). When this garden becomes our eternal home, Satan will have finally experienced exactly what God promised in Eden so very long ago when he said, "He shall bruise your head, and you shall bruise his heel." Satan bruised the heel of the woman's offspring when Christ was "wounded for our transgressions" (Isa. 53:5). In Christ's resurrection, when he took from the Devil the power of death, and when Christ returns to this earth in power, "the devil who had deceived them [will be] thrown into the lake of fire and sulfur," and "will be tormented day and night forever and ever" (Rev. 20:10).

On that day, the curse will be gone for good. That is our sure hope in the midst of the sorrow we experience living in this broken world in these broken bodies. But for now, we live in an in-between time—in between the Devil being defeated through Christ's resurrection, and the Devil and the curse being destroyed when Christ returns. So for now, the curse is an ongoing reality in our lives. Paul described the frustration we feel living in the here and now: "For the creation was subjected to futility, not willingly, but because of him who subjected it, in hope that the creation itself will be set free from its bondage to corruption and obtain the freedom of the glory of the children of God" (Rom. 8:20–21).

Paul does not say we wait eagerly to be taken away from this world to live forever in some ethereal heaven that is away from this earth, but that we "wait eagerly for . . . the redemption of our bodies" (Rom. 8:23). Certainly we know that to be "away from the body" is to be "at home with the Lord" (2 Cor. 5:8). And if we die before Christ returns, we can be confident that we will be safe in his presence. But our final destination is not somewhere away from here without our redeemed bodies. Christ will return to this earth and will "bring with him those who have fallen asleep" (1 Thess. 4:14). We will return to this earth with Christ and be united with our resurrected, glorified bodies to reign on this renewed earth with Christ. "For as in Adam all die, so also in Christ shall all be made alive. But each in his own order: Christ the firstfruits, then at his coming those who belong to Christ" (1 Cor. 15:22–23).

Christ's resurrection provides a picture of the ultimate future for God's people and all of his creation. Because Adam and Eve's sin brought about a curse not only on themselves but also on the rest of creation, redemption must also involve God's entire creation. The world to come will be startlingly new as the curse of sin and death will be forever gone, but it will also be the very same creation that God called into being in Genesis 1:1. Jesus's return will restore his people to a better paradise than Adam and Eve enjoyed. In renewed bodies we will live forever with God on this renewed earth.

The Fall

GENESIS 2:4–3:24

Getting the Discussion Going

1. Imagine for moment, if you can, what it must have been like to live in the garden of Eden before the serpent slithered in with his temptation. What would have been wonderful about that pre-fall existence Adam and Eve enjoyed?

Getting to the Heart of It

2. God did not explain to Adam *why* eating from the tree of the knowledge of good and evil was prohibited. He simply expected them to trust and obey him. Usually we don't mind obeying as long as it makes sense to us. Why do you think God did not explain the logic behind this prohibition?

3. Notice that God was not in the garden all the time. He came to walk in the garden in the cool of the day, but for the most part, Adam and Eve had to operate on God's word that had been given to them. That is what faith is still about: living according to what God has said. What makes living by faith so challenging?

4. Looking back at the Personal Bible Study you worked on, what was especially interesting or challenging to you?

5. What do we learn about how to successfully withstand temptation when we compare the way Adam and Eve dealt with temptation to the way Christ handled the temptations of the Devil?

6. Though we think of Genesis 3 being primarily about sin and the curse, there are also some wonderful pictures of grace and presentations of the gospel. How do you see the gospel of grace in this part of God's story?

7. Many people feel and express anger with God when the brokenness of this world impacts them in ways that bring pain. How could you use what you've learned in this study of Genesis 3 (perhaps also using the truths in Romans 8 and Revelation 21 and 22) to help someone who is angry with God to put the blame where it belongs and place their hope in Christ?

Getting Personal
8. The big idea of this week was that we do not have to keep hiding from God, from each other, and from ourselves. We can come clean with God. There is a way to be good again. What do you think it takes to really believe this and live in the freedom and joy of this truth?

Getting How It Fits into the Big Picture
9. Throughout this study, we're seeking to grasp how the passage we're studying fits into the bigger story of God's plan for redemption. An argument could be made that none of the rest of the Bible would make sense if it did not include Genesis 3. How would you support that argument? How does Genesis 3 help us to make sense of the rest of the Bible, of the world we live in, and of ourselves?

Week 4

Noah and
the Flood

Genesis 6–9

Noah and the Flood

GENESIS 6–9

1. Skim chapter 5 of Genesis, reading verses 28–32 more carefully. What is the pattern repeated in this account of the descendants of Adam?

2. What does the name Lamech gave to his son, Noah, indicate about his hopes for this child?

3. Read Genesis 6:1–7. There are numerous speculations on what exactly the "sons of God" having children with the "daughters of man" means and who the Nephilim were, and it is difficult to determine definitively from the biblical text. But we do know that the "sons of God" are those who by faith walk with God. So why is it a problem that these "sons of God" are marrying the "daughters of man," who do not by faith walk with God?

4. Remembering that God breathed into man's nostrils the breath of life (Gen. 2:7), what does he mean when he says, "My Spirit shall not abide in man forever" (Gen. 6:3)?

5. What does Genesis 6:5–6 reveal about the heart of man and the heart of God?

6. How does the picture presented in Genesis 6:5–7 differ from or serve as a contrast to that of Genesis 1 and 2? (See especially 1:21–31.) Note the contrast in the second column of the chart below.

"And God saw everything that he had made, and behold, it was very good." (Gen. 1:31)	Gen. 6:5
"Then God said, 'Let us make man in our image, after our like-ness.'" (Gen. 1:26)	Gen. 6:6–7a
"So God created the great sea creatures and every living creature that moves, with which the waters swarm, according to their kinds, and every winged bird according to its kind." (Gen. 1:21)	Gen. 6:7

7. God is so grieved by what he sees in the heart of man that he wants to *un*create what he created. What reason can you think of that he cannot destroy *all* of humanity?

8. In this bleak and seemingly hopeless scene, there is still hope. How would you describe the hope found in Genesis 6:8?

9. In Genesis 6:9, we learn that Noah was "a righteous man, blameless in his generation. Noah walked with God." Which came first: the favor or grace of God, or Noah's righteousness, and why does this matter?

10. In contrast to Noah, who was righteous, Genesis 6:11 says that all people and the whole earth were corrupt and that God had determined to destroy them. God gave Noah instructions to build an ark that would hold Noah and his family and two of every living thing. What does this signal about God's intentions in the flood and after the flood, and what does God state about his intentions in regard to Noah?

11. Read Genesis 6:11–8:19. What are two or three details from these verses about the flood and Noah's experience that stand out to you as significant. Why?

12. Recognizing that the day is coming when the world and all that are in it will once again fall under God's judgment, what can we learn from this story about (1) the nature of that judgment; (2) who and what will be destroyed by it; (3) who will be preserved in it; and (4) what we can expect after it?

13. Using the chart below, compare and contrast God's blessing and instructions to Noah with those God gave to Adam at creation.

"God blessed them." (Gen. 1:28)	Gen. 9:1
"Be fruitful and multiply and fill the earth and subdue it." (Gen. 1:28)	Gen. 9:1
"Behold, I have given you every plant yielding seed that is on the face of all the earth, and every tree with seed in its fruit. You shall have them for food." (Gen. 1:29)	Gen. 9:3

14. Read Genesis 9:8–17. How would you summarize the covenant promise God made to Noah, and why do you think he made it?

15. Read the following verses in which God's "bow" is described:

> If a man does not repent, God will whet his sword;
> he has bent and readied his bow;
> he has prepared for him his deadly weapons,
> making his arrows fiery shafts. (Ps. 7:12–13)

> He has bent his bow like an enemy,
> with his right hand set like a foe . . .
> he has poured out his fury like fire. (Lam. 2:4)

> Then the LORD will appear over them,
> and his arrow will go forth like lightning. (Zech. 9:14)

How might these verses offer insight into the imagery God used when he said to Noah, "I have set my bow in the cloud" as a sign of his covenant promise not to destroy the earth and all flesh again?

16. When Adam sinned, his shameful nakedness had to be covered in a provision from God, and Noah's shameful nakedness must also ul-

timately be covered by a provision from God. Go back to Genesis 6:8. What has God provided to cover Noah's shameful nakedness?

17. How does Noah point to Christ? Look up the verses in the second column of the chart below and write a statement that relates to the statement about Noah in the first column.

Noah	Christ
Noah's name means "rest." (Gen. 5:28–29)	Isa. 11:10; Matt. 11:28 *Jesus is our rest. He is the one who provides rest for our souls.*
"Noah found favor in the eyes of the LORD." (Gen. 6:8)	Matt. 3:17
"Noah was a righteous man." (Gen. 6:9)	Luke 23:47
Noah was "blameless in his generation." (Gen. 6:9)	Luke 1:35
Noah "walked with God." (Gen. 6:9)	Luke 2:52; 4:4; 6:12
Noah was given work to do by God—to build an ark that will provide protection from judgment. (Gen. 6:14–21)	John 17:4
Noah's work resulted in the "saving of his household" and "every living thing." (Gen. 8:17; Heb. 11:7)	Rom. 8:21; Heb. 3:6

Noah did "all that God commanded him." (Gen. 6:22; 7:5)	John 15:10; Phil. 2:8
Noah brought his whole family and every living creature out of the ark with him. (Gen. 8:18–19)	Isa. 11:6–7; John 18:9

18. How does the ark point to Christ? Look up the verses in the second column of the chart below to write a statement about Christ that relates to the statement about the ark in the first column.

Ark	Christ
The ark was a divine provision of grace. (Gen. 6:13–14)	John 3:16; Rev. 13:8
The ark was a refuge from divine judgment. (Gen. 6:17–18)	Acts 4:12; Rom. 5:9–10
God invited Noah and his family to come into the ark. (Gen. 7:1)	Matt. 11:28; Acts 16:31
The ark was a place of absolute security. (Gen. 6:14; 7:16; 8:18–19)	John 10:28; 18:9; Col. 3:3; 1 Pet. 1:5
The ark bore the judgment of God in the form of the flood. (Gen. 7:17–18)	John 12:32–33; 1 Pet. 2:24
All of those outside the ark perished. (Gen. 7:21–23)	Acts 13:40–41

Teaching Chapter

What Will Have the Last Word in Your Life?

As I sit here sipping my hot tea this morning, it is clear that the transformation is complete. I have become my mother.

I went for many years without the morning hot tea and afternoon iced tea ritual my mother has always enjoyed. But it must be in the genes.

My husband sees my mom in me in the way I set my fingers along the car door window when riding in the passenger seat in the car. I don't remember ever observing this in my mother and deciding I wanted to do it, yet when I see my fingers on the car door, I realize this is exactly what my mother does.

It shouldn't surprise me. All I need do is look in the mirror to see that I am a reflection of where I came from.

We are all born with traits and tendencies inherited from our mothers and fathers—some good and some bad. These things are in our hardwiring so that they just come naturally. But does where we come from and the environment we live in have the last word in who we are and who we will become? Do we have to succumb to the genetics we inherited, the culture we live in, or the choices we've made?

A long season of Natalie Grant's life was shaped by a voice from without and within that threatened to have the last word in her life. She first heard it waiting in line with her college boyfriend at the grocery store. "You always ask me if you look pretty," he said. Then, pointing to the picture of a woman on the cover of a magazine, he said, "This is what I think is beautiful."

Looking at the rail-thin model on the cover, with her perfect skin and flawless hair, Natalie knew that she could never look like that. But she could try, she thought.

After leaving the store, she and her boyfriend went out to lunch at a restaurant nearby. It was the first of innumerable times over the coming years when Natalie would lock the door of a bathroom stall, kneel down on the dirty floor, shove her finger down her throat, and expel what she had just eaten. And it felt good. She felt free of the food, in control of her life, and hopeful that by this she could gain the acceptance and approval she craved from the person whose word had so much power in her life.

Eventually Natalie dropped down to 96 pounds. Her collarbone stuck out, and she thought she was beautiful. Other people thought she was beautiful too, and told her so. But then her teeth began to turn yellow from the constant purging. Her hair began to fall out, and the boyfriend drifted away. What she initially thought had given her freedom and control had actually turned her into a slave.

But a boyfriend's unrealistic expectations and bulimia's false promises did not have the last word in Natalie's life. The day came when Natalie heard the word that had much more power than the word she had listened to from her boyfriend, from our beauty-crazed culture, and from her own self-loathing: "I've never heard God speak audibly," Natalie said, "but the Holy Spirit speaks to us on the inside, and one day, huddled down with my head over the toilet, I heard him saying, 'My grace is enough. My grace is enough' as that Scripture began to move from my head to my heart. I remember looking at that toilet and saying, 'I am kneeling to the wrong God. I'm kneeling to this god of myself because this is what I do to make myself feel better and to feel accepted, and to look a certain way. I'm kneeling to the wrong god, and this will destroy me.'"[1]

Freedom came when the voice of God spoke grace into her life so powerfully that it drowned out all lesser voices. God's grace became the defining word in her life instead of bulimia.

---

[1] Adapted from "Natalie Grant: Her Heart Revealed" (http://www.cbn.com) and "From Hunger to Healing," Focus on the Family radio program (September 2, 2009).

As we look at Genesis 6, we see that Noah had many voices in and around him seeking to define him. There were the voices in the culture inviting him to join in debauched living, voices suggesting he not take this ark building so seriously, voices ridiculing his lonely stand against the world, and angry rants at how his obedience to God heaped condemnation on everybody else.

Perhaps even more unavoidable was the voice inside Noah—his own voice—questioning his own ability to hear God clearly, lamenting the effect his choices were having on the rest of his family, wincing at the knowledge of his own shortcomings, wondering if one hundred years of building a boat on dry ground would only leave him looking like a fool.

But most unavoidable was the voice of God giving instructions and making promises.

So what or who will have the last word in Noah's life? Will the words of ridicule heaped upon him by his neighbors have the last word? Will his fears and failures have the last word?

This is a question we want answered because we have the same question about our own lives. Will my religious upbringing or my current doubts and questions have the last word? Will my sexual experimentation or my marital faithfulness have the last word? Will my initial spiritual fervor or my current apathy toward God have the last word? Ultimately, will my own thoughts and feelings, successes and failures, have the last word in my life?

Or will someone else, something else, get the last—the lasting and definitive—word in my life now and in my eternal future?

Noah: A Sinner Saved by Grace

Noah's life began shaped by a grand expectation. For generations, whenever a son was born, moms and dads hoped that he would be the one to be the offspring that God had promised (Gen. 3:15). They hoped he would be the one who would break the curse that had brought so much frustration and difficulty to life while working the land, as well as death when the work was done.

So when Lamech fathered a son, he "called his name Noah, saying,

'Out of the ground that the LORD has cursed this one shall bring us relief from our work and from the painful toil of our hands'" (Gen. 5:29). Perhaps Noah, whose very name meant "comfort and rest," would be the one! But 595 years after Noah was born, it happened to Lamech too—he died. Evidently Noah was not the Promised One.

Noah was born into a world that had devolved significantly from the beauty and purity of the garden that Adam and Eve were forced to leave. By the time Noah was born, the population had grown significantly in number. But as they grew in number, they also increased in wickedness.

> The LORD saw that the wickedness of man was great in the earth, and that every intention of the thoughts of his heart was only evil continually. (Gen. 6:5)

Humanity had become thoroughly and pervasively evil—*every* intention, *only* evil, *continually.* No goodness, no kindness, no joy—just never-ending selfishness and never-enough indulgence.

This is the world Noah was born into and the nature he was born with. Noah was a natural-born sinner like everyone around him. The same selfishness came naturally to him, and the same debauchery tempted him. But Noah was not like everyone around him. Noah's life was not guided by what came naturally to him based on his environment and inherited tendencies. How do we know?

> Noah found favor in the eyes of the LORD. (Gen. 6:8)

Noah found favor, or grace, with the Lord. Or perhaps it would be better to say that grace found Noah.[2] And when grace found Noah, grace determined to have the last word in Noah's life. His surroundings and his sinful nature and his evil ancestry certainly spoke into his life and had their impact, but they simply did not have the final say about who Noah would be or what would happen to him.

Most of my life, I assumed that Noah found favor in God's eyes *because of* his righteousness—that God looked at humanity and found the one person who sought to please him and therefore granted him

---

[2] Alec Moyter, *Look to the Rock: An Old Testament Background to Our Understanding of Christ* (Grand Rapids, MI: Kregel, 1996), 43.

favor and provided salvation in the ark. But that is not the case at all. The grace came before the goodness.

It was the grace of God poured out on Noah, based not on Noah's goodness but on God's choice, that made Noah righteous. Noah did not earn this favor from God. It was a gift, pure and simple and undeserved. In fact, God's favor is never something that can be earned or purchased. It is always a

> *My sinful nature will not have the last word in my life—God's favor will save me from myself.*

gift. The grace that found Noah changed Noah. In fact, it shaped everything about his life and identity.

> Noah was a righteous man, blameless in his generation. Noah walked with God. (Gen. 6:9)

When we are told that Noah was a "righteous" and "blameless" man, it does not mean that Noah never sinned. Like all other sinners who find acceptance with God, Noah received this righteousness by faith. Though he was surrounded by moral evil and perversion, the grace at work in his life implanted in him the desire to keep himself pure and uncontaminated. Like his great-grandfather Enoch before him, Noah "walked with God," meaning that Noah was a man who oriented his life away from the world and toward God. He saw himself and his sin in the light of God's holiness and God's grace, which made him want to stay close to God and walk with him throughout his life.

While Noah found and knew the grace of God, he did not see and understand it as we can, because grace has come to us in the flesh and blood of Jesus Christ. "We have seen his glory, glory as of the only Son from the Father, full of grace and truth" (John 1:14). And though Noah may not have seen and understood the grace that found him, it still had the power to change him from who he was according to the nature passed along to him by his mother and father. As he responded to and was covered by this grace, he was accepted by God because of this grace.

To know the favor of God is not to be loved as you are by nature but to be loved for who you are in Christ. It is not that you have never done wrong or naturally do right, but that God's grace gives you eyes to see your own sinfulness and a heart of repentance. God's grace in your life transforms you into a person who loves the world around you less even as you have an increasing affection for God. Most significantly, grace gives you faith to believe in the Promised One.

Noah: A Sinner Protected by Grace

While Noah had found favor in the eyes of the Lord, God looked at the rest of humanity and saw only corruption and violence. So God decided to treat humans exactly as they deserved to be treated. God determined to destroy them. But not all of them. God had every intention to fulfill his promise to send the offspring who would crush the head of Satan and break the curse on all creation. He had not forsaken his plan for the whole earth to be filled with the glory of God. He intended to preserve one righteous man and his family. With this man, Noah, God would start over.

God's wrath would fall in the form of raindrops that would wipe out every living thing. Noah would not escape the judgment that was about to fall, but he would be protected in it. He was to build an ark in which he would find protection. The storm of God's judgment would rain down its full fury on the ark, but Noah, safely inside with his family, would be preserved.

God's instructions must have made little sense to Noah. To invest one hundred years in building a huge wooden boat on dry ground when he had likely never even seen rain falling from the sky, let alone flood-waters, required a radical reliance on the word of God. The writer to the Hebrews tells us that "*by faith* Noah, being warned by God concerning events as yet unseen, in reverent fear constructed an ark for the saving of his household. By this he condemned the world and became an heir of the righteousness that comes by faith" (11:7). In other words, Noah believed what God told him about something that he had never seen and in fact had no categories for. Noah took God at his word. And sure enough, what God had warned about and prepared Noah for finally happened.

> Then the Lord said to Noah, "Go into the ark, you and all your house-hold, for I have seen that you are righteous before me in this generation." (Gen. 7:1)

The righteousness that had come to Noah by faith worked its way in and through his life and was lived out not only through his radical *belief* in God's word but through his radical *obedience* to God's word. Four times the narrative expounds on the nature of his obedience. In Genesis 6:22 we read, "Noah did this; he did *all* that God commanded him." After receiving God's instructions for going into the ark and taking his family and all the pairs of animals with him, we're told, "Noah did *all* that the LORD had commanded him" (Gen. 7:5). Two more times in this chapter we read that Noah did as God had commanded him.

What a picture of grace at work in the life of a sinner whose natural bent is to go his own way, trust in himself, and seek to gain the approval of others. Noah set himself against all of that so he could single-heartedly give himself to obeying God.

Then the day came that Noah had invested a century of sweat preparing for. He and his wife along with his sons and their wives, and two of every animal went into the ark. "And the LORD shut him in" (Gen. 7:16). The single heavy, pitched-covered door of the ark was locked tight by an act of God. Noah did not shut himself in. The world outside did not shut him in. Because it was the Lord who shut him in, he knew they would be safe. Water would not leak through the door and sink the boat. Desperate, drowning people would not break open the door and thereby overwhelm the boat.

There they were, shut inside the boat that all the people of his day must have thought would be Noah's oversized coffin. And then the rain began to fall. Water not only fell from the sky, but it also gushed from beneath the ground so that all of creation became a watery chaos.

This is not the cute little story of children's storybooks and cheery nursery decor. Just go to Babies-R-Us and see what you find. I looked. In addition to all the Noah's ark–themed toys and bedding, you'll find a Noah's ark Fun Rug, Noah's ark stepstool, potty chair, and toy chest. On each item you'll find a cheery, white-haired Noah and his wife surrounded by animals of every kind, ready to board a big wooden boat.

But this is a sanitized picture of the whole sad story. The real panorama is not one we want to plaster and paint around a child's room, even though it is true. Noah's ark floated in the midst of a grim and gruesome scene. While Noah and his family nestled safe inside the boat with all of the animals, the wider view reveals the rest of humanity—all of those who refused Noah's warnings and rejected Noah's God, all of those who, instead of being safe inside the ark, were swept away in a tidal wave. The bigger picture around the ark was that of families on rooftops, struggling and failing to keep their heads above the water, and a sea of floating corpses. Not exactly what we want to wallpaper around the baby's bed.

This story of unbridled wickedness and condemnation, of death and destruction, serves as a warning to all those who refuse God's offer of grace. It prefigures what will happen to all who refuse to enter into the safety and protection provided in Christ. The day is coming when all those who have rejected Christ will be destroyed, although next time it won't be by flood but by fire (2 Pet. 3:7).

Many people today, as in Noah's day, refuse to believe that a time of judgment is really coming. And let's face it. It's unpleasant. It sounds old-fashioned. We'd rather not talk about it or just be vague about it. The story of Noah and the ark shouts to all those who persist in living apart from God about what is to come. It invites all to accept God's offer of protection and safety found only by being united to Christ.

In the ark we see in shadow form the salvation provided through Jesus Christ:

- Just as building the ark seemed foolish to all those who would perish in the storm, so "the word of the cross is folly to those who are perishing, but to us who are being saved it is the power of God" (1 Cor. 1:18).
- Just as the ark was provided by God so that those who believed God's word would not perish in the flood, "God so loved the world, that he gave his only Son, that whoever believes in him should not perish but have eternal life" (John 3:16).
- Just as the ark was the only refuge for those who wanted to survive the storm, so "there is salvation in no one else" but Jesus (Acts 4:12).

~ Just as the ark provided absolute security for those who hid themselves inside, so is there absolute security for those whose lives are "hidden with Christ in God" (Col. 3:3).

~ Just as all those outside the ark perished because they refused to believe the truth and be saved, so will all those outside of Christ perish "because they refused to love the truth and so be saved" (2 Thess. 2:10).

There is an ark of safety—the person of Christ—and the door is open to you. Have you entered in? Have you responded to the grace that has come to you in Jesus? Or are you lingering on the outside somewhere— distracted by the world, disgruntled by what you will have to leave behind, delayed by doubts or questions?

Won't you enter in? Won't you hide yourself in Christ where there is safety and rest?

Noah had to have been happy that all of his family was inside the ark with him, safe and dry. They carried with them God's promise that while everything that lived on the earth would die, all who were safely in the ark would live. Rather than experience God's wrath, they would receive his covenant promise. Rather than die in the flood, they would emerge from the waters of death into resurrection life.

But as happy as they were to be safely together, and as noisy as all the animals and the sounds of the rushing waters must have been, surely it did not drown out the screams of those who refused to listen to the warnings Noah had given about the judgment to come. Because Noah was a righteous man who walked with God, Noah's heart must have broken as he heard the desperate cries of those who were not safely inside the ark.

And though you may find yourself safe from the storm of judgment in the ark of safety provided in Christ, if someone you love has so far refused to believe that judgment is coming and has scoffed at the suggestion of the need to enter into the safety of Christ, your heart is broken, too. Rest inside the boat does not come easily unless all those you love deeply are safe inside with you.

This cannot be skipped over lightly, but neither can it be settled simplistically. It can only be saturated in prayer. It can only be sought through diligence on our knees. The heart that is heavy with the knowledge that someone we love is outside the ark is a heart that aches with the burden of Christ himself, who said with tears, "O Jerusalem, Jerusalem, the city that kills the prophets and stones those who are sent to it! How often would I have gathered your children together as a hen gathers her brood under her wings, and you would not!" (Matt. 23:37).

Like Noah, we live a blameless life joyfully obeying God's commands. Like Noah, we put our faith in a loving Father whose Son said, "It is not the will of my Father who is in heaven that one of these little ones should perish" (Matt. 18:14). And ultimately, we pray that it will not be our loved one's rebellion and resistance that will have the last word in his or her life, but God's grace and mercy.

> *God's wrath will not have the last word in my life—God's protection will keep me safe.*

Noah: A Sinner Preserved by Grace

While Noah and the ark is a story of judgment and death, it is also a story of grace and new life, a story of a promise kept to send a flood, and a promise made to never destroy the earth again through a flood. This is the story of how a world of evil was cleansed and given a fresh start.

When Noah finally emerged from the ark with his family and the animals, he was like a new Adam, the father of a new humanity. The world had been washed clean so that it was like a new Eden. Except this was not the pre-fall paradise. The curse was not gone. Sin was still a reality that had to be dealt with. And so before he began a new life in this new world, Noah built an altar to make a burnt offering to God. This was an offering of gratitude for salvation. But it was more than that. We know that because, as it burned, it was "a pleasing aroma" to the Lord (Gen. 8:21). This is the language used throughout the Old Testament for an atoning sacrifice offered in faith that pointed to the once-for-all, all-sufficient sacrifice to come. Though Noah could not see Christ or speak of Christ, the sacrifice he offered on the altar pointed to Christ. This is precisely what made it pleasing to God.

God then made a promise that took into account his expectation that Noah and his descendants would sin:

> I will never again curse the ground because of man, for the intention of man's heart is evil from his youth. Neither will I ever again strike down every living creature as I have done. While the earth remains, seedtime and harvest, cold and heat, summer and winter, day and night, shall not cease. (Gen. 8:21–22)

Then we read that "God blessed Noah and his sons" (Gen. 9:1). Clearly, the story has moved from judgment to blessing. This is the first time we read of God blessing anything or anyone since he blessed Adam and Eve in the garden before they sinned (Gen. 1:28). This new beginning in many ways resembled the first beginning recorded in Genesis 1 and 2, particularly in the command to be fruitful and multiply. But there was a key difference. It now rested upon a covenant of grace based on shed blood. Though humanity had forfeited the blessing of God given to Adam and Eve in the garden and abdicated their position as ruler over creation, by his grace, God gave his blessing once again.

God also instituted some new protections, since sin still reigned in the world. To protect them from the animal kingdom, people could now eat animals, which would cause animals to fear them. To protect them from other people, people could put to death someone who murdered another person. And to protect them from another flood, God made a covenant promise that despite their sin, he would never again send a flood that would destroy the whole earth. In a sense, we could say that, in this promise, God was really protecting them from God.

He called it "my covenant" (Gen. 9:9, 11) because it did not require any assent, action, or ratification from Noah—not even acknowledgment. This was God's self-motivated promise of mercy that would last throughout the remainder of human history. God bound himself with the promise that he will never again send a flood that will kill all living creatures and destroy the earth. Then God put forth a sign of his covenant.

> I have set my bow in the cloud, and it shall be a sign of the covenant between me and the earth. When I bring clouds over the earth and the bow is seen in the clouds, I will remember my covenant that is between me and

you and every living creature of all flesh. And the waters shall never again become a flood to destroy all flesh. (Gen. 9:13–15)

What is interesting about this sign of a bow in the clouds is who the sign is for:

When the bow is in the clouds, *I* will see it and remember the everlasting covenant between God and every living creature of all flesh that is on the earth. (Gen. 9:16)

This sign is not so much for man but for God. This bow in the clouds will remind God of his own promise. But it also had to be a comforting sign to Noah and his family. Though their feet were again on the solid ground of earth, the sound of rushing torrents had surely left its echo in their ears. The next time they saw clouds gathering and darkness coming, their fears would surely flourish as they wondered, "Is God's judgment about to rain down again? Is he coming again to wipe out the world?" Then they would look up and see the bow.

The bow illustrated exactly why God could make this promise of mercy. Throughout the Old Testament, the word "bow" refers to a weapon of war or a dispenser of wrath. So the bow that God placed in the sky was not merely a curve of light shining through the rain. This sign represented an archer's bow, a weapon. The psalmist described God's bow, saying, "If a person does not repent, God will sharpen his sword; he will bend and string his bow. He will prepare his deadly weapons and shoot his flaming arrows" (Ps. 7:12–13 NLT).

But this bow is not hung in the sky and strung tight with arrows at the ready, pointing toward the earth. It is loose and hanging at the warrior's side, pointing into the heavens. The bow in the clouds is a sign that God is no longer at war with those who have found grace. By setting his bow in the heavens, God was saying that even though humanity is sinful, he will not come again in war against the earth.

God can hang up his bow for only one reason. It is not because Noah and his descendants will no longer sin, and it's not because he will now overlook sin. He can hang up his bow because its arrows have been spent on someone else. God chose to aim the arrows of his wrath and judgment toward an innocent Christ rather than toward guilty sinners.[3]

Whenever we begin to think that the grace extended to us, the grace that gets the last word in our life, is free, the bow in the clouds reminds us that the grace we enjoy has come to us at great cost.

Like the rainbow that appeared in the sky, in Christ, "the grace of God has appeared, bringing salvation for all people" (Titus 2:11). And just as the rainbow serves as an "everlasting" sign to show his intentions of grace toward his people, we have been raised up with Christ "so that in the coming ages he might show the immeasurable riches of his grace in kindness toward us in Christ Jesus" (Eph. 2:7).

I suppose it would be nice if this were the happy ending of Noah's story. If it ended here, he and his little family could walk off into the sunset of a cleansed creation, with the backdrop of the burning sacrifice on the altar to signify their faith and obedience and a bow in the clouds to signify God's eternal promise to them.

Had some human admirer chronicled the history of Noah, the last part of his story would likely be omitted. But the fact that it is recorded and that no effort is made to cover up or excuse Noah's sin is evidence that the characters of the Bible are painted in the colors of truth and reality by inspiration of the Holy Spirit.

Noah's story is the story of a man who walked with God, believed God, waited for God, and depended on God. But sadly, it is also the story of a man who, in the final chapter of his life, dishonored and failed God. Noah is just like us. He not only needed God's saving grace; he needed God's sustaining grace.

Genesis 9:20 tells us that "Noah began to be a man of the soil, and he planted a vineyard." It takes years for a vineyard to produce grapes, so it must have been some time after the flood when Noah used the grapes from the vineyard to make wine. Because he was a seasoned man of the soil, he knew exactly what would happen when, as Moses

---

[3]Numerous pastors and theologians present God's bow as picturing a warrior's bow, including Michael D. Williams, *Far as the Curse Is Found* (Philipsburg, NJ: P&R, 2005), 96–98; Timothy J. Keller, "Lord of the Earth" sermon, December 10, 2000, Redeemer Presbyterian Church, New York; and Charles Haddon Spurgeon, "The Eternal Truth of God," sermon, Metropolitan Tabernacle, London, 1865. But other theologians disallow this, citing inadequate support for the idea in the text, including the editors of the *ESV Study Bible*, and O. Palmer Robertson, *The Christ of the Covenants* (Phillipsburg, NJ: P&R, 1980), 125.

tells us, "he drank of the wine and became drunk and lay uncovered in his tent" (v. 21).

Obviously the flood had not purged the world of wickedness. If God had wanted to do that, he would have had to eradicate the entire human race. But this God would not do because he had promised that the off-spring of Eve would one day crush the head of Satan.

What seems to be a sad ending to Noah's story is redeemed only because of what we remember from the beginning of his story: "Noah found favor in the eyes of the LORD" (Gen. 6:8). This favor had not come to Noah because of his good behavior, and he could not lose it through his bad behavior.

The good news of the end of Noah's story is the good news at the end of our stories. If God's grace has found us and is clearly at work in us, we do not have to fear that sins in our past or sins in our future will disqualify us from enjoying the benefits of God's gracious covenant. God has bound himself to us, and nothing can come between us.

> *My future failures will not have the last word in my life—God's promise will secure my hope.*

Your genetic predispositions, your sinful tendencies, the moral failures of your past, the culture you live in, the path you have taken so far in your life—none of these are destined to have the last word in your life. God's grace toward you in Christ has the last, the lasting, and the determining word in your life, as it did when it found Noah:

~ Grace invites you to walk with God and away from the world.

~ Grace empowers you to obey over the long haul.

~ Grace keeps you from having to endure the wrath of God you deserve.

~ Grace promises you that the storms in your life are not punishment for your failures but preparation for your fruitfulness.

~ Grace covers your sin so completely that it cannot be canceled out by your bad behavior. It is there, on the other side of your repentance, to woo you back and welcome you home.

⁓ Grace binds you to Christ so that neither death nor life, nor angels nor rulers, nor things present nor things to come, nor powers, nor height nor depth, nor anything else in all creation, will be able to separate you from the love of God in Christ Jesus our Lord (Rom. 8:38–39).

How Genesis Points to What Is Yet to Come: "As Were the Days of Noah"

The disciples asked Jesus the question, "What will be the sign of your coming and of the close of the age?" (Matt. 24:3). Jesus answered their question by referring them back to the story of Noah: "As were the days of Noah, so will be the coming of the Son of Man" (Matt. 24:37). So we have to ask, in what way(s) will it be like it was in Noah's day? Jesus said that in the days before the flood, people were absorbed in their daily activities, ignoring Noah's warnings about the judgment to come, enjoying life. They could not imagine a devastating flood and therefore would not believe they were in any danger.

> They were unaware until the flood came and swept them all away, so will be the coming of the Son of Man. (Matt. 24:39)

Jesus was saying that is the way it will be at his second coming. Many people will be busy going about life, having persisted in denying that God will pour out his judgment on sin, and like the people in Noah's day, they will be "swept away." Then Jesus added to this picture two scenarios in which one person is taken and the other left:

> Two men will be in the field; one will be taken and one left. Two women will be grinding at the mill; one will be taken and one left. (Matt. 24:40–41)

Many have read this passage and imposed on it a particular view of the end times to suggest that believers will be taken to be with Christ somewhere other than on this earth, while unbelievers are left behind.

But is that a correct assumption based on Jesus's statement that it will be like it was in Noah's day? Who were the ones taken in the day of Noah, and who were left? Genesis 7:23 says that "only Noah was left, and those who were with him in the ark." Was it not those who refused to respond to the "gospel" preached to them by Noah who were taken when they were swept away in the flood? And was it not Noah and his family who were left?

Surely Jesus was saying that those who have rejected God's offer of protection in Christ will be swept away or taken, while those who have hidden themselves in him will be left to rule and reign with him in the cleansed creation of the new earth. And if this is so, we do not sing, "The Son has come, and you've been left behind," as a dirge but as a dance.

The apostle Peter also wrote about the day of the Lord, when Christ will return, and he also drew on Noah's story to help his readers understand what that day will be like. He described a coming day of judgment when the ungodly will be destroyed—not by flood but by fire. On that day, the cursed creation will not be swept away by water but melted away by flames:

> In the last days scoffers will come, mocking the truth and following their own desires. They will say, "What happened to the promise that Jesus is coming again? From before the times of our ancestors, everything has remained the same since the world was first created." They deliberately forget that God made the heavens by the word of his command, and he brought the earth out from the water and surrounded it with water. Then he used the water to destroy the ancient world with a mighty flood. And by the same word, the present heavens and earth have been stored up for fire. They are being kept for the day of judgment, when ungodly people will be destroyed. . . . On that day, he will set the heavens on fire, and the elements will melt away in the flames. But we are looking forward to the new heavens and new earth he has promised, a world filled with God's righteousness. (2 Pet. 3:3–7, 12–13 NLT)

On that day, all who have hidden themselves in the ark of God—the person of Jesus Christ—will be protected from the flames, just as Noah and his family were protected from the flood. Our Savior, Jesus Christ, will deliver us safely to the new heaven and new earth he has promised. But this time we will not begin again as sinners living in a cursed environment, like Noah and his family did. Sin and its effects on us and our environment will be gone for good. There will be no more curse. Grace will have had the last word. "'Tis grace hath brought me safe thus far, and grace will lead me home."[4]

---

[4]John Newton, "Amazing Grace," 1779.

Noah and the Flood

GENESIS 6–9

Getting the Discussion Going

1. If you had been a news photographer during the time of Noah as he prepared for and built the ark and as he gathered the animals and prepared to enter the boat and after the rain started falling, what interesting scenes might you have captured? Are there any animals you wish had missed the ship?

Getting to the Heart of It

2. In the Teaching Chapter, we saw that Noah was a sinner saved by grace, protected by grace, and preserved by grace. Let's work our way through these three. First, when we read that "Noah found favor in the eyes of the Lord," or that "Noah found grace in the eyes of the Lord," what does that mean?

3. Has it always been your understanding that God initiated and provided Noah's righteousness, or like Nancy described as her own past understanding, have you thought that Noah was the only righteous one and, because of that, he found favor with God? What difference does it make?

4. As we see Noah and his family and the animals protected inside the ark, we discover an Old Testament picture of the saving work of Jesus Christ. All who "hide" in Christ will be protected from judgment. As you made the connections between the ark and how it pictures Christ

in the Personal Bible Study section, which aspects were most meaningful to you?

5. As Nancy described, we tend to turn this into a cute children's story,
and even as adults we are pained to face up to the stark reality of the
divine judgment and gruesome death in this story. Why do you think
we are so uncomfortable with it, and why is it important that we not
conveniently delete it from the story?

6. Though Noah was a righteous man in that he embraced God's covenant from the heart, he was still a sinner. What were the signs of that
when he emerged from the ark and began to build a new life on dry
land?

7. How was Noah *preserved* by grace, and what verses in the Bible come
to mind to assure you that you are preserved by grace?

Getting Personal

8. The big question of this week was, "What will have the last word in
your life?" Though Noah inherited a sin nature and was surrounded by
wicked sinners, sin did not have the last word in his life. Would you be
willing to share how you dealt with this question personally this week?
Is there anything other than the grace provided to you in Jesus Christ
that threatens to have the last word in your life?

Getting How It Fits into the Big Picture

9. Throughout this study, we're trying to grasp how some of these familiar stories fit into the bigger story of God's plan for redemption. How
do you see the continuing threads of the promised offspring and the
restoration of all things in Genesis 6–9?

The Tower of Babel

Genesis 10:1–12:3

Personal Bible Study

The Tower of Babel

GENESIS 10:1–12:3

1. Genesis 10 provides us with a "table of nations"—an overview of the descendants of Noah's three sons. This includes where they lived and the nations that descended from each of them. Skim the chapter noting the repeated word or idea found in Genesis 10:5, 18, and 32.

2. Genesis 11:1–9 actually tells us about something that happened in the middle of all the generations listed in Genesis 10. Think of it this way: chapter 11 gives us the details about what happened in Peleg's lifetime (Gen. 10:25). While this may seem insignificant now, we'll come back to Peleg after we learn more about what happened at Babel during his lifetime to discover why he is significant.

3. To understand the story of the Tower of Babel in Genesis 11, we have to remember the instruction God gave to Noah and his sons in Genesis 9:1: "Be fruitful and multiply and fill the earth." What do you think this meant, and why do you think this instruction was given by God?

🕐 4. Read Genesis 11:1–2. Immediately we see the problem in relation to God's clear instruction. What is it?

5. Repeatedly in verses 3–4 the people say, "Come, let us . . . ," inviting all the people of Babel to work together on a great project. What do you think is the problem with their plans? Note your answers in the chart below.

The People's Plan	The Problem
"Come, let us make bricks, and burn them thoroughly." (Gen. 11:3)	
"Come, let us build ourselves a city." (Gen. 11:4)	
"Come, let us build ourselves . . . a tower with its top in the heavens." (Gen. 11:4)	
"Come . . . let us make a name for ourselves." (Gen. 11:4)	
" . . . lest we be dispersed over the face of the whole earth." (Gen. 11:4)	

6. According to Genesis 11:6, why did God frustrate the people's attempt to accomplish this great feat?

🕐 7. How was God's action of dispersing people all over the face of the earth and giving them many different languages both a judgment and a preservation?

8. Read Genesis 12:1–3. How do these three verses offer tremendous hope in light of the grim situation of humanity in Genesis 10–11?

9. Using the chart below, compare Genesis 11:1–9 with Acts 2:1–11, looking for contrasts between what happened in Babel and what happened at Pentecost.

Babel	Pentecost
The people used their own initiative to gather together to make plans apart from God, in defiance of God.	*The disciples gathered together to pray and wait for God to take the initiative to give them the power they needed to accomplish the commission Jesus had given them.*
Human beings sought to climb their way up to God.	
Communication was restricted, as people could no longer understand each other to plot rebellion.	
God came to judge and disperse the people into many nations.	
God intervened so that people with one language and culture were no longer able to understand each other.	
People sought to make a name for themselves through their own achievement.	
The rebelling Babel resulted in the disintegration of the human family into different races and nationalities.	
From Babel the people were dispersed over the face of all the earth.	

A Name for Myself

What would it be like to have made such an impact on the world that you need only one name for people to know exactly who you are? Think Elvis, Cher, Hitler, Lincoln, Einstein, Michelangelo, Oprah. Certainly they are people who have literally made a name for themselves. And this is the dream of many, many people.

> Fame! I'm gonna live forever. I'm gonna learn how to fly—high!
> Fame! I'm gonna live forever. Baby, remember my name.[1]

Jake Halpern is a journalist who wanted to understand more about our culture's love for fame. In his book *Fame Junkies: The Hidden Truths Behind America's Favorite Addiction*, Halpern writes about visiting a convention for child-star wannabes. Walking through the hotel lobby he felt a tug at his elbow. He writes:

> "Excuse me, sir," said a young man of about twenty in a thick-as-molasses Kentucky drawl. "Would it be okay if I gave you my headshot?" Without thinking I nodded, and he produced a large glossy photo with his name spelled out in block letters. "I'd like to be a celebrity," Brent said as we began talking. "To be honest with you, I'd like the whole deal. I see these celebrities on TV who don't like their picture getting taken, and I can't understand it. I want it all. I want the money, I want the women, I want the publicity, I want the people hounding me around trying to take my picture. I know that sounds really bad—it makes me sound conceited—but I guess in a sense I am."[2]

---

[1] From the song "Fame," in the musical of the same name. Lyrics, Jacques Levy; music, Steve Margoshes.
[2] Jake Halpern, *Fame Junkies: The Hidden Truths Behind America's Favorite Addiction* (New York: Houghton Mifflin Harcourt, 2006), 30.

But Halpern discovered that it is not just children who want to make a name for themselves. He later visited Hollywood's premier retirement home, Woodland Hills. And there he met a man named Hal Riddle, an eighty-five-year-old former character actor. Riddle strove throughout his career to become a movie star, but the only parts he got were small supporting roles on television shows such as *Charlie's Angels*, *Little House on the Prairie*, and *The Mary Tyler Moore Show*. Nothing ever turned him into a household name. Yet even at eighty-five, Riddle clung to the hope that fame was still within his grasp. "Fame is really an addiction," he said. "And when it takes you as a child, and when you build on it your whole life, even if you look around and all you see is ruins, you can't leave the ruins."[3]

But the most interesting thing I found about the book *Fame Junkies* is actually not in the book. It is in a news story I read about the book in which the author admits that the taste of fame he experienced as he traveled the country on the book tour to promote the book made him hungry for fame himself. "We live in rural New Mexico, and my wife's a doctor who does work with the Navajo. I came home from the whirlwind to a house where tumbleweed literally blows across the street, and I felt a sense of—almost—withdrawal," he says. "It passed, but the irony was not lost on me."

We roll our eyes at the parents who would set their children on the quest for fame. We feel so embarrassed for those pathetic people who are willing to be humiliated by the judges in an *American Idol* audition just to get a few minutes of television time, but we too have a taste for fame, don't we?

We want to achieve something. And more than that, we want to be noticed for what we've accomplished. We long to emerge from the shadows of being ordinary and unnoticed to enjoy the spotlight, at least for a few fleeting minutes—to simply be somebody—to be taken note of, to appear impressive, to be the envy of somebody else who also longs to be somebody.

We have come by this appetite for attention quite naturally. In fact, it is as old as Genesis 11 and the story of the people who built the tower of Babel. But first, a little background.

---

[3] Ibid., 190–91.

God's Intention

Adam was put on this earth to glorify and enjoy God. Then the Serpent told Eve that if she and Adam ate of the tree, "you will be like God," and Adam and Eve fell for it. Their own glory became more desirable than God's glory. But even as they faced banishment from the garden and the curse of God, they also received the grace of God—a promise that an offspring of the woman will one day restore the garden paradise of God. So Adam and Eve and all of their descendants began to wait in hope for God to fulfill his promise.

After the flood, God gave Noah and his sons the same instructions he had given to Adam and Eve: "Be fruitful and multiply and fill the earth" (Gen. 9:1). God's intention was still for the earth to be filled with people who would worship him. The tenth chapter of Genesis shows us that Noah's sons got married and had children and that their children had children. When we read through the list of the nations that descended from Noah's sons, Japheth, Ham and Shem, we see that obviously they were fruitful as instructed. But there was a problem.

Babel's Ambition

God had said to "fill the earth." They were supposed to spread out so that God's whole earth would be inhabited by people who called on the name of the Lord. But they weren't spreading. They "found a plain . . . and settled there" (Gen. 11:2). They decided to stay put in Shinar. They were clustering together, finding security in numbers. They wanted to build a city "lest we be dispersed over the face of the whole earth" (Gen. 11:4).

So what is the problem with sticking together? It doesn't really sound like that big of a deal, does it?

Building a city was an expression of their contentment with this world, of their unwillingness to wait for the city that God will bring. They did not want to venture forth, trusting God to guide, preserve, and keep them. The wanted a permanent city. To settle and stay together was seditious defiance of God's clear instruction to fill the earth.

Why would they do this? Because they longed for the security that comes from being surrounded by other people who look like them and talk like them and think like them (just as we do). In a great city they would be less vulnerable living in this world that is under a curse. They would also be more productive. They imagined all that they could accomplish and all that they could become if they just worked together. They were not just after security; they also wanted significance. They really had no concern about spreading the glory of God to every corner of this earth. They really just wanted a piece of glory for themselves. And if God wouldn't give it to them, they would just go up to heaven and get it from him. They intended to build a tower that would reach up into the heavens and in this way "make a name" for themselves.

Rather than obeying God and trusting him for their security and significance, they took matters into their own hands and determined that they would create their own security and significance—on their terms and in their timing.

How would they do this? Their strategy is revealed in several sound bites from the scene of the rebellion:

> They said to one another, "Come, let us make bricks, and burn them thoroughly." And they had brick for stone, and bitumen for mortar. Then they said, "Come, let us build ourselves a city and a tower with its top in the heavens, and let us make a name for ourselves, lest we be dispersed over the face of the whole earth." (Gen. 11:3–4)

Did you see the strategy in there—the thrice-repeated call, "Come, let us . . . " This is a group project and they are inviting everyone to join in. These people are not gathering together to pray and spur each other on to trust in God. They are gathering together to organize rebellion. "Come, let us make bricks"; "Come, let us build a city and a tower"; "Come, let us make a name for ourselves." None of them want to stand alone in obedience to God. They want to find others to reinforce their desire to do things their own way and conveniently ignore the command of God as well as the promise of God.

There were no stones for building on the plains of Shinar, so they used their ingenuity and the latest technology to manufacture bricks. With dusty bricks and crumbly asphalt they thought they could build a city that would keep them safe. They thought they were geniuses. They fully expected to go down in the history books for such innovation and invention.

They would storm the gates of God and invite themselves in. And this would be an impressive feat. In this way they would make a name for themselves that would live on even after they died. But this whole plan to thwart the plan of God and storm the gates of God was absurd, and God responded with appropriate scorn.

God's Observation

Don't miss the mocking tone in verse 5:

> And the LORD came down to see the city and the tower, which the children of man had built.

By calling them "the children of man," it is as if God was saying, "Like father, like son." These kids are doing what their father Adam did. They are rebelling. By saying that the Lord "came down," Moses, the author, was simply making fun of their grand plan. They thought their tower would reach into heaven, but it is so, so far from heaven that God has to "come down" to see it.

This city of man is not my home. Christ is preparing a home for me where I will be safe and secure.

Have you ever stood at the bottom of the Sears Tower or the Empire State Building? It is so impressive, standing at the bottom and looking up, isn't it? But have you ever seen the Sears Tower or the Empire State Building while looking out the window of an airplane high above Chicago or New York City? They look like they are built of Legos. Can you imagine how this tower of Babel must have looked to the Almighty God of the universe, who sits high and lifted up, enthroned in the highest heavens?

God saw the ridiculousness of their plans, and he also saw the danger in their plans:

> And the LORD said, "Behold, they are one people, and they have all one language, and this is only the beginning of what they will do. And nothing that they propose to do will now be impossible for them." (Gen. 11:6)

God knows what humans are capable of. He knows we are very ingenious and industrious. He made us that way. And he knows that if he allows humanity to stick together and work together, they will accomplish a great deal. It's not that God feared that they would come so far that they would pose any threat to him. It is that they would pose a threat to themselves. As they increased in technology and accomplishment and affluence, it would become harder and harder for them to see their need for God. They would sense no need for salvation through the promised offspring. Their self-sufficiency would harden their hearts toward God.

God's Intervention

So in mercy, God intervened.

> "Come, let us go down and there confuse their language, so that they may not understand one another's speech." So the LORD dispersed them from there over the face of all the earth, and they left off building the city. (Gen. 11:7–8)

The people had been saying, "Come, let us . . . " to each other. And now the triune God said in counsel with himself, "Come, let us go down."

They were one people with one language, but God was about to divide them into many peoples who speak many different languages. This would make it harder for them to communicate with each other in order to make their God-belittling global plans. The Lord limited their progress in order to limit the damage.

Babel's Confusion

> Therefore its name was called Babel, because there the LORD confused the language of all the earth. (Gen. 11:9)

Moses wrote Genesis initially for the children of Israel who were awaiting entrance into the Promised Land, and when he wrote that the place was called Babel, and that Babel means "confusion," he was insulting the great city of Babylon that the children of Israel knew all too well. Of course, when the people of Babylon gave that name to their city, they weren't naming it "confusion." To them, in their language, Babylon meant "the gate of God." They saw their city as a place where men might ascend up into heaven and take their place next to the gods. But, ironically, the name ended up sounding very much like the Hebrew word for confusion. In a sense, the people of Babel did make a name for themselves, but it wasn't at all the way they intended.

So who were these people who worked so hard to make a name for themselves? If we look back in Genesis 10, the leader of this mighty kingdom, Nimrod, is named (vv. 8–10), but his children, if he had any, are not. There is only one person from the time of the tower of Babel who is named along with his posterity. We find his name in Genesis 10:25:

> To Eber were born two sons: the name of the one was Peleg, for in his days the earth was divided.

Eber is the name from which we get the term "Hebrew." Peleg, whose name must mean "divided," got his name from God's response to the incredible sin committed by the people of his day. Peleg was given what the Babylonians wanted and couldn't provide for themselves—a name that went down in history as significant. One of Peleg's descendants would be Terah. And Terah would have three sons—Abraham, Nahor, and Haran. And, of course, one of Abraham's descendants would be the Promised One, Jesus.

Abraham's Alienation

By the time Terah was born, it was becoming more and more difficult to wait for the Promised One. Evidently Terah grew weary of waiting and made his home in Ur of the Chaldeans, which is in modern-day southern Iraq. Ur, a large and powerful city, was the center of the cult of the moon god.

We'd like to give Terah the benefit of the doubt and believe that even though he made his home in Ur, certainly he didn't succumb to worshiping the moon god. But we can't do that. Joshua removed all doubt, writing that "Long ago, your fathers lived beyond the Euphrates, Terah, the father of Abraham and of Nahor; and they served other gods" (Josh. 24:2). So Terah and his sons were certainly not in a position to be or to produce the godly offspring. They were pagan idol worshipers deserving the wrath of God.

Obviously Abraham, Terah's son, was a pagan among pagans. He was not looking for Yahweh or for his promise to become reality. He did nothing to deserve to be the one through whom the Promised One would come. And even if he was worthy of it, the reality is that his wife, Sarah, was barren (Gen. 11:30). Frankly, it was quite impossible that Abraham could be the father of a whole new humanity. And that makes

> *I don't have to build a tower to find my way to God. God has come down in the person of Jesus Christ.*

him perfect to show us exactly how God accomplishes his saving work. Because we don't deserve it. Apart from him we would not look for it. Yet God comes to us and calls us out of the lives we are living far away from him. Like his command to Abraham, God commands us to leave behind what we have found in the world that gives us a sense of security and significance—our plans for our family, our expected inheritance, the convenience of living near family, our familiar culture and established home.

God's Provision

Just as God came into the garden of Eden and found Adam hiding, and just as God spoke to Noah in the midst of his evil generation, God came to Ur and spoke to Abraham right there in the shadow of the family idols.

> Now the LORD said to Abram, "Go from your country and your kindred and your father's house to the land that I will show you." (Gen. 12:1)

What God was about to do with and through Abraham had nothing to do with what Abraham could contribute or accomplish. It had everything to do with who God is and what he would do through Abraham. God intended to freely give Abraham what the men of Babel sought to get for themselves, apart from God. Whereas the people of Babel in the previous chapter had repeatedly said, "Let us make . . . ," here we hear God say repeatedly, "I will make."

I will make of you a great nation, and *I will bless* you and make your name great, so that you will be a blessing. *I will bless* those who bless you, and him who dishonors you I will curse, and in you all the families of the earth shall be blessed. (Gen. 12:2–3)

God promised to make Abraham into not just a great city but a great nation. God was going to give him a great name. God was going to be his security, and God was going to give his life significance. He had done nothing to deserve this. And he was not told to do something to earn this. God's promise of blessing was a sheer gift of grace.

Abraham will be made into a mighty nation entirely by the power of God. It will be different from all the failed efforts and faded accomplishments of those who came before him. Cain built a city, but it was destroyed in the flood with all his descendants. The Babylonians built a city, but it was left half-finished as a monument to their arrogance when God scattered them. Ur of the Chaldeans was a mighty city that is now only an archaeological site. These are cities built by men, and they do not endure.

There is a clear distinction here, and as we look at it, we realize that there is also a clear choice, a choice we have to make, just like the people of Babel and Abraham had to make. And so I have to stop here and ask you, which is it going to be in your life? Is your life going to be all about what *you* will do, what *you* will accomplish, what *you* can build, or what *you* can make of yourself?

Or is your life going to be all about what *God* has done, what *God* will do, and what God will give to you and make of you?

Do you want your life to be about building a monument to yourself and your ingenuity and abilities and accomplishments?

Or do you want your life to be about God seeking you out when you weren't even looking for him, calling you to leave everything behind to follow him? Do you long for your life to be about God blessing you, protecting you, and filling your life with significance, with himself?

God came to Abraham and called to him while living in the land of Ur. But obeying God would cost Abraham everything he held dear. He was to leave his country and his people—everything familiar and dear to him. And we hear the same gospel call, don't we? "If anyone would come after me, let him deny himself and take up his cross and follow me" (Matt. 16:24). Or as Martin Luther wrote, "Let goods and kindred go, this mortal life also."[4]

And what did Abraham do? Look at verse 4: "So Abram went." Did he have to think it over for a while? I don't know. There's no evidence of it. He left with all his possessions, taking everything, because he had no intention of going back.

Abraham set out for the land of Canaan, and when he got there, "the LORD appeared to Abram" (Gen. 12:7). Now, God had not appeared on the earth since he came to judge the Serpent, the woman, and the man in the garden of Eden. He had spoken with Cain, with Noah, and earlier with Abraham. He had judged Cain and the flood generation and Babel, not as one who appeared, but rather as one who sits in heaven. And now, suddenly, he appeared to Abraham.

This time he appeared not to curse but to bless. And Abraham's response was to build an altar to the Lord. This was not a tower built out of a heart of rebellion so that he could demand an audience with God. This was an altar built with a heart of worship and wonder so that he could confess his dependence on God and remember this place where he had met with the God who made such precious promises to him.

When we met Abraham in the Scriptures, he lived in a city. But God immediately told him to leave that city and his family and go to the place he would show him. Yet when Abraham went, he didn't find a city to make his home in, and he didn't build a city. In fact, Hebrews says that Abraham lived in the land of promise "as in a foreign land, living in tents with Isaac and Jacob, heirs with him of the same promise" and that he was "looking forward to the city that has foundations, whose designer and builder is God" (Heb. 11:9–10).

Abraham's son Isaac also lived without a city. If it was a city here on earth that he wanted, he could have gone back to the city Abraham had left. But he and his descendants didn't. Why? Because "they desire a better country, that is, a heavenly one." And what will their willingness to wait get for them? "Therefore God is not ashamed to be called their God, for he has prepared for them a city" (Heb. 11:16).

---

[4]From Martin Luther, "A Mighty Fortress," 1527–1529.

Isaac's son Jacob also lived as a stranger on earth. One night, as he lay his head down on a stone to sleep, he had a dream. It wasn't a tower to heaven that he saw but a ladder that reached into heaven on which angels were going up and coming down. Jacob heard God speaking to him from heaven, assuring him of his promises. And Jacob called the place Bethel, saying, "This is none other than the house of God, and this is the gate of heaven" (Gen. 28:17).

The Babylonians thought the name of their city meant "gate of god"—a place where they, in their greatness, would commune with the gods. But in his dream Jacob saw the true gate into the city of God. Jacob did not need to build a city; God is providing a city he will live in forever. Jacob did not need to build a tower; God will provide a ladder and come down. Jacob did not need to make a name for himself. God will give him a new name—Israel (Gen. 32:28). He can wait for God to accomplish all that he has promised.

In time God did set up an earthly city, Jerusalem, the holy hill of God where he dwelt in his temple. But Jerusalem was only a copy, a foreshadowing of the heavenly city God has prepared for those who love him. Earthly Jerusalem was not a place of security. The people there eventually rebelled, so God sent another city to conquer them. The name of that city was Babylon. King Nebuchadnezzar of Babylon showed forth the character of the whole city when he boasted, "Is not this great Babylon, which I have built by my mighty power as a royal residence and for the glory of my majesty?" (Dan. 4:30). Do you hear the same spirit here that we saw in those who built the tower there so long before?

Babylon is the spiritual city of sin. It represents those who trust in themselves and make their home here, apart from God. This present life is all they want or need. Babylon is the enduring God-hating, self-loving, arrogant, self-confident city of man.

Eventually, the people of God who were taken to Babylon returned from exile to their homeland to rebuild their temple and their city. But the temple and the city were never as glorious as they had been. And by the time of Christ, the Roman Empire, a new Babylon, reigned over the people of God.

Throughout his ministry, even those closest to Jesus hoped that he was the Messiah who would finally make Jerusalem the great city of the world, safe and secure. Even after Christ's resurrection his disciples said to him, "Lord, will you at this time restore the kingdom to Israel?" (Acts 1:6). But Jesus had a different kind of kingdom building in mind, a better city. And once again he wanted his people to disperse—but this time it was not a judgment but an assignment.

Babel's Redemption

Just before he ascended into heaven Jesus told his disciples:

> But you will receive power when the Holy Spirit has come upon you, and you will be my witness in Jerusalem and in all Judea and Samaria, and to the end of the earth. (Acts 1:8)

When that power came, they finally understood that Jesus had not come to set up a temporary, earthly city. He had come to conquer death, atone for sin, and thus provide an eternal, heavenly dwelling place for all who will trust in him instead of themselves.

> When the day of Pentecost arrived, they were all together in one place. And suddenly there came from heaven a sound like a mighty rushing wind, and it filled the entire house where they were sitting. And divided tongues as of fire appeared to them and rested on each one of them. And they were all filled with the Holy Spirit and began to speak in other tongues as the Spirit gave them utterance. Now there were dwelling in Jerusalem Jews, devout men from every nation under heaven. And at this sound the multitude came together, and they were bewildered, because each one was hearing them speak in his own language. And they were amazed and astonished, saying, "Are not all these who are speaking Galileans? And how is it that we hear, each of us in his own native language?" (Acts 2:1–8)

People from "every nation under heaven" were there in Jerusalem. Representatives of those who were scattered in the day of Babel were re-gathered for this feast. They were divided by one thing—language. But suddenly God came, and the apostles began to speak so that everyone heard the gospel in his own language.

God came down in mercy to reverse the judgment of Babel. Those who heard the gospel in their own language there in Jerusalem went back to their own people to share the unifying message of Christ. Today, the gospel continues to go out as we obey Jesus's final instructions: "Go therefore and make disciples of all nations, baptizing them in the name of the Father and of the Son and of the Holy Spirit, teaching them to observe all that I have commanded you. And behold, I am with you always, to the end of the age" (Matt. 28:19–20). (Can you see here how God redeems even our sinful disobedience to use it to accomplish his God-glorifying purposes?)

Our Decision

We have a city. And our home is not built with bricks and asphalt that is doomed to break down but with the gold of the kingdom of God. Christ himself is preparing this place for us, and even now he is the anchor of our souls so that we will not be swept up in the world's frenzied attempts to make this world a permanent home and to find our security and significance here.

I have one trophy, my own little monument to myself. I'll have you know that I won first place in the Olathe, Kansas, optimist club oratorical contest when I was in the ninth grade. I will be glad to let you come to my garage and hunt with me for the box that holds the tiny tower to my achievement on which my name is engraved.

> *I don't have to make a name for myself.
> I will glory only in the name of Christ.*

Perhaps you have a trophy or two yourself. Maybe there is a display of state championship trophies at some high school on which your name is engraved. Maybe there is an office building that bears the name of your company, a library built on a campus somewhere that bears the name of your family's foundation, a mailbox in front of one of the nicest houses in town with your name on it. Perhaps there is an honor roll that lists your child's name, a World's Greatest Mom plate on your shelf, a World's Greatest Boss mug on your desk, or a diploma from a prestigious university on your wall.

These are all very nice. There's nothing wrong with them. But can you see that the monuments we build to our own achievement and the ways we try to make and maintain a name for ourselves in this world always eventually get packed away, covered over? Monuments to our own achievements simply don't last in this world.

The day will come when your name and your mark on this world, which is passing away, will be reduced to your name engraved on a grave marker. If your life is about making a name for yourself and building monuments to yourself in the here and now, this is what it will come to, and all it will amount to.

But, my friends, if you are willing to put all of your hopes in the promises of God—if you are willing to come away from the security and significance that this world offers—if you will hear and respond in obedience to the call of God, he will give you the security of an enduring city whose architect and builder is God. He will give you the significance of a name written in his book of life. Nothing is more significant or more secure than that.

Here is what Jesus promises to those who overcome the attraction of the Babylons of this world, those who overcome the temptation of this world to trust in themselves, to make something of themselves:

> To the one who conquers I will give some of the hidden manna, and I will give him a white stone, with a new name written on the stone that no one knows except the one who receives it. (Rev. 2:17)

Oh, my friends, this is the name we want—not a name we can make for ourselves, but the name Christ will give to us known only to him! *O God, give us the wisdom and grace not to settle for making a name for ourselves! Jesus, fill us with a holy longing for the name you will give us that is known only to you!*

This leaves each of us with a choice to make: Am I going to keep trying to make a name for myself, or am I willing to wait on God, trust God, for the name that he will give to me? Is my life going to be about making a name for myself, or is it going to be about lifting up and proclaiming the only name that is truly worthy of honor and glory—the name of Jesus Christ?

God has highly exalted him and bestowed on him the name that is above every name, so that at the name of Jesus every knee should bow, in heaven and on earth and under the earth, and every tongue confess that Jesus Christ is Lord, to the glory of God the Father. (Phil. 2:9–11)

Is my life going to be about building towers to my own achievement? Or am I willing to glory in the only tower of true greatness—the cross of Christ?

Can I be honest and tell you where this hits home with me? Could I risk being real with you about where I feel the rub in my little world as I read this story and consider this question?

The most influential voices in publishing today (including many in Christian publishing) say that to be an author in this climate, you have to be willing to promote yourself—"build your brand." You have to use all the tools of social network marketing; you need to twitter to build your audience and speak to build your platform. And I get that. It makes perfect sense to me.

But I keep asking myself, *Do I really want to build a career or a ministry for myself, with my own ingenuity and charisma and creativity?* I've worked in publishing for over twenty-five years. I've been a publicist for many leading Christian authors. I know how to bake the bricks of personal promotion that are used to build a following. Is that what I am going to do?

Or am I willing to wait on God? Am I willing to listen for his voice and follow where he leads me, which is always away from anything and everything in this world in which I am tempted to find my security and significance apart from Christ alone? Am I willing to be faithful and fruitful in the work he has given to me regardless of whether anyone ever knows my name? Am I willing to forsake building a monument to myself so that I can give myself fully to being used by him to build his kingdom in my generation? Am I willing to put my hope in the Promised One—in Christ alone—to be my sole source of security and significance?

That's the question for me. What's the question for you? Where do you face the daily temptation to secure your own future or make a name for yourself? What will it look like for you to trust God to bless, to build, and to provide the security and significance you long for?

Here is the gospel in this account of the tower of Babel: God has not left us here to work our way up to him or to make something of ourselves apart from him. That may be the American dream, but it isn't the promise of the gospel. The truth of the gospel, and the mercy of God, is that he has come down to us. *He* will build a city for us. *He* will give us a name that will endure.

How Genesis Points to What Is Yet to Come: Praise from Every Tribe and Language and Nation

When God put an end to the prideful rebellion of those who built the tower of Babel, it was a foreshadowing of the day to come when Christ will finally put an end to the world-loving ways of those opposed to God and his people represented throughout the pages of Scripture by the city of Babylon. Here, early in the Scriptures, we see that salvation history is going to be a "tale of two cities"—the city of man, which is epitomized by Babel and throughout the rest of Scriptures by her offspring, Babylon, and the city of God, which is identified with Jerusalem throughout the Scriptures.

Babylon is the spiritual city of sin, and she has a good ride throughout the Scriptures. She is even used by God to discipline his chosen people, taking them into captivity. And as long as this earth and its systems endure, the God-hating, self-loving city of Babylon will endure. In Revelation, Babylon is portrayed as "the great prostitute" (Rev. 17:1). She has used her gaudy allures to seduce "the kings of the earth" (Rev. 17:2). She is "drunk with the blood of the saints, the blood of the martyrs of Jesus" (Rev. 17:6). The "saints" are our brothers and sisters in Christ that she has taken such great joy in torturing because the name of Christ is so much more precious to them than their own name and their own security.

But Babylon will not endure forever. Human power and human evil will run its course. Christ will come again, and he will put an end to the evil influence of Babylon and to Babylon's persecution of God's people.

John was given a glimpse of this future, when Babylon the Great will come to her appointed end:

> Fallen, fallen is Babylon the great! . . . she will be burned up with fire; for mighty is the Lord God who has judged her. (Rev. 18:2, 8)

While Babylon, the city of man, the harlot bride of the beast, is destined for certain destruction, the New Jerusalem, the beautiful bride of Christ, is being prepared to celebrate the marriage supper of Christ the Lamb and to live forever with him in the city of God. When that day comes, we will finally see the full redemption of what happened to the people who built the tower of Babel. We saw a partial redemption on the day of Pentecost. But the dispersion and confusion of Babel will be fully redeemed at this great gathering when all the people of God will stand together before God's throne.

> I looked, and behold, a great multitude that no one could num-
> ber, from every nation, from all tribes and peoples and lan-
> guages, standing before the throne and before the Lamb, clothed
> in white robes, with palm branches in their hands, and crying
> out with a loud voice, "Salvation belongs to our God who sits on
> the throne, and to the Lamb!" (Rev. 7:9–10)

The love of God will reach into every nation and tribe and people and language group. Every race, every cultural heritage, every language will be there before God in heaven. The praise that Jesus will receive from all the languages will be more beautiful because of its diversity than it would have been if there were only one language and one people singing. God will replace all our failed attempts at a perfect world with his own holy city, New Jerusalem. The ideal human culture we long for will not rise up from our genius or even from our generous compassion; it will come down from God's grace, ready for us to enter in. The city of God, safe and secure.

> And he carried me away in the Spirit to a great, high mountain,
> and showed me the holy city Jerusalem coming down out of
> heaven from God, having the glory of God, its radiance like a
> most rare jewel, like a jasper, clear as crystal. It had a great, high

wall. . . . The kings of the earth will bring their glory into it, and its gates will never be shut by day—and there will be no night there. (Rev. 21:10–12, 24–25)

We'll have the significance we have longed for as the bride of Christ, and we'll have the security we've longed for in the city of God. "A mighty fortress is our God. His kingdom is forever."[5]

---

[5]Ibid.

Discussion Guide

The Tower of Babel

GENESIS 10:1–12:3

Getting the Discussion Going

1. As you read the story of the tower of Babel this week, could you almost picture in your mind a movie version of this scene? Try to if you can. What are the people like? How is this group project progressing? What is God's tone of voice? What are the scenes like as families are split and dispersed and people can no longer understand each other?

Getting to the Heart of It

2. What are your thoughts about this picture of people sticking together to build a city in defiance of God and building a tower to get to God on their own terms? What is this about?

3. Looking back at the work you did in the Personal Bible Study, what was especially interesting or challenging to you?

4. There is some humor in this story (whether or not we recognize it) in the way God responded to the tower-building project. There is also judgment and mercy. How do you see humor as well as judgment and mercy here?

5. Some people have said that the story of the tower of Babel is in the Bible as an explanation of why there are different people groups and languages in the world. Do you think that is why Moses told this story? If not, why do you think Moses included this part of primeval history for

his original readers, the children of Israel who were preparing to enter the Promised Land?

6. There's nothing inherently wrong in our desires for security and significance, is there? The question is where we will look to have those needs met. How do you think we can distinguish between legitimate and illegitimate ways of having those needs met?

Getting Personal

7. The big question of this week was, "How will you meet your needs for security and significance?" As you look back over your life so far, do you see evidence of trying to secure your own future or make a name for yourself? Would you be willing to share that with the group?

Getting How It Fits into the Big Picture

8. Throughout this study, we're trying to grasp how some of these familiar stories fit into the bigger story of God's plan for redemption. What part does Genesis 10–11 play in understanding God's story of salvation through the Promised One?

Week 6

Abraham

Genesis 12–15

Personal Bible Study

Abraham

GENESIS 12–15

1. Read Genesis 12:1–9. Hebrews 11:8 says, "By faith Abraham obeyed when he was called to go out to a place that he was to receive as an inheritance. And he went out, not knowing where he was going." Try to imagine what it must have been like for Abraham, at age seventy-five, to hear the call of God while living in Ur, to leave the life he had known behind and set out, not even knowing what his final destination would be. Why do you think he did it?

2. Abraham traveled the Promised Land from end to end, symbolically taking possession of it for his descendants, lingering at Bethel, Hebron, and later, Mount Moriah to build altars, even though the Canaanites were still in the land. In Genesis 12:7–8 we read that "the Lord appeared to Abram" and along with building an altar, Abraham "called upon the name of the Lord," indicating that he and his large entourage publicly proclaimed Yahweh's name in the middle of all the pagan Canaanites. How do Abraham's altar building and calling on the Lord's name reflect a work of grace going on in Abraham's life?

⏱ 3. Throughout these chapters, the Lord repeatedly speaks to Abraham, giving instructions and making promises and then expanding and clarifying those promises. What does God promise and then how does he expand or clarify it in the following verses?

	God's promises to Abraham in Genesis 12, 13, 15, 17
Nation	Gen. 12:2a
	Gen. 17:5
Blessing	Gen. 12:2b
	Gen. 12:3a
	Gen. 12:3b
Land	Gen. 12:7
	Gen. 13:15
	Gen. 17:8
Offspring	Gen. 13:16
	Gen. 15:4
	Gen. 15:5

⏱ 4. All of God's promises to Abraham were fulfilled in physical ways to Abraham and his descendants by birth. But they are also being fulfilled in spiritual ways to Abraham's descendants by faith. And they will be fulfilled in eternal ways when Christ returns and his kingdom is consummated in the new heaven and the new earth. Let's look back to see how God's promises were fulfilled in the Old Testament, how they are being fulfilled in believers today, and what we have to look forward to in these promises being fulfilled into eternity.

Below is a series of verses in biblical order. Write the reference for each passage in the chart that follows, indicating whether the passage reflects a fulfillment of God's promises to Abraham and his descendants physically, spiritually, or eternally. Some fulfillments may have more than one reference, and some references may seem to fit in more than one category. You may even have a box that is left empty. Do not stress over having the "right" answers, but allow this exercise to expand your understanding of how God has fulfilled and will fulfill the promises he made to Abraham.

Sarah conceived and bore Abraham a son in his old age. (Gen. 21:2)

The LORD has greatly blessed my master, and he has become great. He has given him flocks and herds, silver and gold, male servants and female servants, camels and donkeys. And Sarah my master's wife bore a son to my master when she was old, and to him he has given all that he has. (Gen. 24:35–36)

Thus the LORD gave to Israel all the land that he swore to give to their fathers. (Josh. 21:43)

Who is like your people Israel, the one nation on earth whom God went to redeem to be his people, making for yourself a name for great and awesome things? (1 Chron. 17:21)

You have made me king over a people as numerous as the dust of the earth. (2 Chron. 1:9)

You multiplied their children as the stars of heaven. (Neh. 9:23)

Abraham was the father of Isaac. . . . The father of Joseph the husband of Mary, of whom Jesus was born, who is called Christ. (Matt. 1:2, 16)

For the promise to Abraham and his offspring that he would be heir of the world did not come through the law but through the righteousness of faith. (Rom. 4:13)

And the Scripture, foreseeing that God would justify the Gentiles by faith, preached the gospel beforehand to Abraham, saying, "In you shall all the nations be blessed." So then, those who are of faith are blessed along with Abraham, the man of faith. For all who rely on works of the law are under a curse. (Gal. 3:8–10)

The promises were made to Abraham and to his offspring. It does not say, "And to offsprings," referring to many, but referring to one, "And to your offspring," who is Christ. (Gal. 3:16)

If you are Christ's, then you are Abraham's offspring, heirs according to promise. (Gal. 3:29)

Blessed be the God and Father of our Lord Jesus Christ, who has blessed us in Christ with every spiritual blessing in the heavenly places. (Eph. 1:3)

They desire a better country, that is, a heavenly one. . . . He has prepared for them a city. (Heb. 11:16)

But you are a chosen race, a royal priesthood, a holy nation, a people for his own possession. (1 Pet. 2:9)

And I heard every creature in heaven and on earth and under the earth and in the sea, and all that is in them, saying, "To him who sits on the throne and to the Lamb be blessing and honor and glory and might forever and ever!" (Rev. 5:13)

A great multitude that no one could number, from every nation, from all tribes and peoples and languages, standing before the throne . . . (Rev. 7:9)

All nations will come and worship you, for your righteous acts have been revealed. (Rev. 15:4)

God remembered Babylon the great, to make her drain the cup of the wine of the fury of his wrath. (Rev. 16:19)

	Physical Fulfillment to Abraham and his Descendants by Birth	Spiritual Fulfillment through Christ to Abraham's Descendants by Faith	Eternal Fulfillment to Come in the Consummation
Nation			
Blessing			
Land			
Offspring			

5. Though Abraham made a great start in the life of faith, he stumbled significantly (Gen. 12:10–20). How does his going to Egypt and his deceit there reflect a lack of faith, and what were the consequences?

6. Read Genesis 13. Despite the fact that Abraham descended to self-serving deception in Egypt, he was still a man of faith. Like us, he was a mix of self-centered reliance and trust in God. How are his

actions in chapter 13 a contrast to his lack of faith and deception in chapter 12?

7. Read Genesis 14. Lot chose to make his home near Sodom, and when he and his family were carted away by a cadre of kings who ravaged Sodom, Abraham could easily have responded in apathy, seeing it as Lot's getting what he deserved based on the choice he made. But instead, the herdsman Abraham became General Abraham, taking 318 men and defeating those who had taken Lot and bringing back all the possessions taken from Sodom along with Lot and Lot's family. Earlier Abraham was tested by want in the famine and failed, and here he was tested by success. What do verses 17–24 reveal about how Abraham responded to this test?

8. When we begin reading Genesis 15, we see that it begins with "After these things," so we know that what is about to happen is related to what has just happened in Genesis 14. Abraham had just rejected what anyone around him would have said was a very good deal. The king of Sodom offered to divide with Abraham everything recovered from the defeated kingdoms , which would have made Abraham incredibly rich. The agreement would have also created an alliance that would have provided Abraham with some protection, should those kings want to take revenge. How does this shed light on what God promised and why in Genesis 15:1?

9. God was revealing himself to Abraham here in a new way and inviting Abraham to trust him in a new way. Putting your own name in place of Abraham's name, what would it mean to you personally to hear God say to you in your own situation and circumstance, "Fear not, _____, I am your shield; your reward shall be very great" (Gen. 15:1)?

⏱ 10. Genesis 15:6 is quoted in three New Testament passages (Rom. 4:3; Gal. 3:6; and James 2:23). What does Paul's discussion of this verse in Romans 4 add to our understanding of the relationship between believing God and righteousness?

〰 Romans 4:4–5

〰 Romans 4:10

〰 Romans 4:20–22

〰 Romans 4:23–24

⏱ 11. Read Genesis 15:7–21. Today, if you are in court and swear to "tell the truth, the whole truth, and nothing but the truth," you confirm your oath by placing your hand on a Bible. In the office of a notary public, you may be asked to confirm an oath by raising your hand. In Abraham's day, an oath was confirmed by a ceremony in which animals were cut into two parts along the backbone and placed in two rows facing each other across a space marked off between them. The two parties to the oath walked together into the space between the parts and spoke their promises there, thereby pledging that if they did not fulfill their oath, they would be cut in two like the animals. When God "cut a covenant" with Abraham, why was it only God, manifested in the form of a smoking firepot and blazing torch, and not Abraham also, who passed through the pieces?

12. In Genesis 15:12–16, God explains how, when, and why the land would be given to Abraham's descendants. This divine preview of history with its precise predictions and explicit dating taught Abraham that God is sovereign in history. According to the following verses, for

what purposes did God postpone the time when Abraham's descendants would take possession of the land?

~ Genesis 15:13 fulfilled in Exodus 1:11

~ Genesis 15:14 fulfilled in Exodus 12:12 and 12:36

~ Genesis 15:15 fulfilled in Genesis 25:8

~ Genesis 15:16 fulfilled in Numbers 21:24–25

Teaching Chapter

The Day You've Waited For

I spent my elementary school years living in the town of Leavenworth, Kansas, which was adjacent to Fort Leavenworth, a military base. Families would move to town and spend a year and then move on. Just about the time I got to be good friends with someone, she would move away.

When I was in the third grade, a military officer from Norway spent a year at Fort Leavenworth, and I became best friends with Bente Skipenes, his daughter. I have a photograph we took in my front yard together when that sad day came that she moved back to Norway, and I can picture myself sitting in the chair looking out the window after she left, so very sad. That was when my dad made me a promise. He said, "When you are sixteen, I will send you to Norway to see Bente." And that was a promise I held on to. Bente and I wrote letters over the years that followed, and I looked forward to the day when I would turn sixteen and my dad would send me to Norway to see her.

But when I turned sixteen, my dad's business was facing some setbacks, and as much as he wanted to send me, it was not a good time for the trip. Bente and I continued to keep in touch, but I put my dreams about the day when I would go to see her on the back burner, pretty much out of sight.

Fast forward to July 2002. I was signing copies of my book *Holding on to Hope* on the first day of its release, and a couple from Norway was first in line to get a copy. They told me they wanted to publish the book in Norwegian and asked if I might be willing to come to Norway to do some promotion for it.

"You don't understand," I told them with a huge lump in my throat. "I've wanted to go to Norway my whole life."

Months later I sat on the flight from Oslo to Bardufoss, where my friend Bente and her husband, Trygve, were coming to pick us up. As I looked out the window, I said to David, "I'm about to do something I have wanted to do my whole life." This was a day for which I had longed for thirty-four years.

Then a dose of reality hit me. *What am I doing? I haven't seen this friend for thirty-four years, and I am about to spend three days in her home! What if we have nothing in common? What if we can't communicate? What if David hates it and blames me for bringing him here?* Even though it was a day I had longed for, I realized that the next three days might end up being the longest three days of my life!

Has there been a day out in the future that you have longed for? Do you remember counting down the days until your wedding? Do you remember counting down the weeks until the birth of your child? And did that turn into longing for the day when your child would start kindergarten so you would finally get some time alone? Perhaps you have longed for the day when your business is in the black, or the day when you make your last mortgage payment, or the day you retire.

Has someone made a promise to you that you long to see fulfilled? The promise of a financial settlement or inheritance? The promise made by a family member to deal with an addiction? A boss's promise to give you that promotion and raise when business picks up? Is there a day out there you are looking for and longing for? Do you have any kind of assurance that it is really coming? And if it does come, do you think it will live up to your longing?

Abraham, the man described as the father of faith and the friend of God, had his heart set on a day out in the future, based on promises made to him by God himself. We don't find this stated exactly this way in Genesis. We do find it in the words of Jesus, recorded in John 8. The people of Jesus's day took great pride in their pedigree of being descendants of Abraham, and they asked Jesus, "Are you greater than our father Abraham?" Jesus answered, "Your father Abraham rejoiced that he would see my day. He saw it and was glad" (John 8:53, 56).

This was a stunning statement—perplexing to those Jesus spoke to that day and pregnant with meaning for us today. What was Jesus saying here? In what way did Abraham "see" the day of Jesus? And why did it make him glad? These are the questions we want to ask and answer as we look together at Genesis 12–15.

A Longing for the Day All of God's Promises Will Be Fulfilled

The longing for a day to come was put into Abraham's heart on the day that God came to him while he was living in the land of Ur. God gave him a command as well as a series of promises:

> Now the LORD said to Abram, "Go from your country and your kindred and your father's house to the land that I will show you. And I will make of you a great nation, and I will bless you and make your name great, so that you will be a blessing. I will bless those who bless you, and him who dishonors you I will curse, and in you all the families of the earth shall be blessed." (Gen. 12:1–3)

Later, when Abraham reached Canaan, God confirmed to Abraham that the land he had promised to show him was the land he was now standing on:

> To your offspring I will give this land. (Gen. 12:7)

So, in addition to the general promise of blessing, God now added a tangible, earthly pledge of what he would do—*the land I've brought you to is going to belong to your children and your children's children.* But there was one big problem. Abraham did not have any children. His wife was barren. He was seventy-five years old at this point.

In Genesis 13, we read that God came to Abraham again to expand upon and clarify his earlier promise:

> Lift up your eyes and look from the place where you are, northward and southward and eastward and westward, for all the land that you see I will give to you and to your offspring forever. (Gen. 13:14–15)

Earlier God had promised to give Abraham the land he was standing on, but he didn't say how far it would extend or how long he would have it. Now God told Abraham that the land as far as his eye could see would belong to his family *forever*. And then God added:

> I will make your offspring as the dust of the earth, so that if one can count the dust of the earth, your offspring also can be counted. (Gen. 13:16)

Just as God expanded the territory, God also expanded the promise of the descendants who will fill it. Earlier Abraham was promised *a* descendant who would inherit the land. Here Abraham was promised *numerous* descendants—as uncountable as "the dust of the earth." Abraham, who didn't have a single child, was told that one day he wouldn't be able to count the number of his children.

But years later, Abraham still had no child of his own who would inherit the great promises of God, which raised a natural question:

> "O Lord GOD, what will you give me, for I continue childless, and the heir of my house is Eliezer of Damascus?" And Abram said, "Behold, you have given me no offspring, and a member of my household will be my heir." (Gen. 15:2–3)

Abraham was not being rebellious or disrespectful. This was no shaking his fist in the face of God, accusing him of not being good or failing in his promise. He was genuinely thinking that perhaps his highest-ranking servant would be the one who would inherit the promises God had made to him.

> *My calm confidence is that every promise of God is fulfilled to me in Christ.*

Abraham recognized that he was powerless at this point. He had nothing he could use to nudge God's promise toward becoming reality. But it is to this place of recognizing the utter impossibility of the situation in human terms that God has purposefully brought him. Of course Abraham cannot do it. God will do it all.

> And behold, the word of the LORD came to him: "This man shall not be your heir; your very own son shall be your heir." (Gen. 15:4)

In grace, God stooped down to explain his promise to Abraham in terms Abraham could understand. *You are not going to have an offspring through adoption. You are going to father a child in your old age.* Later, after Abraham had taken things into his own hands and had a child with Sarah's servant, Hagar, God came to Abraham again making his promise even clearer, saying about Sarah, "I will give you a son by her" (Gen. 17:16).

In addition to repeating and clarifying his promise regarding offspring, God also expanded on it:

> And [God] brought [Abraham] outside and said, "Look toward heaven, and number the stars, if you are able to number them." Then he said to him, "So shall your offspring be." (Gen. 15:5)

Anytime Abraham began to wonder if God was going to fulfill his promise, he could wait until dark, look up at the sky, and have his confidence rekindled.

As we take stock of the promises God made to Abraham, we can see why Abraham had such longing implanted in his heart.

- ∽ God promised to give Abraham a son (Gen. 15:4) by his wife Sarah (Gen. 17:16), and through that son, many descendants, and that, in fact, the number of his descendants will be so numerous that they will be beyond counting (Gen. 13:16; 15:5).
- ∽ God promised to make Abraham into a great nation (Gen. 12:2), and that, in fact, Abraham will be the father of many nations (Gen. 17:4).
- ∽ God promised to make Abraham's name great so that he will be a blessing (Gen. 12:2), and that, in fact, *all* the families of the earth will be blessed or cursed through him, based on their response to his offspring (Gen. 12:3).
- ∽ God promised to give the land of Canaan to Abraham's offspring (Gen. 12:7; 13:14–15; 15:18–21), and that, in fact, the land he will give to them will belong to them forever (Gen. 17:8).

Regarding God's promises to Abraham, the writer of Hebrews in the New Testament offers what appears, at first, to be the good news followed by the bad news. The good news:

> Therefore from one man, and him as good as dead, were born descendants as many as the stars of heaven and as many as the innumerable grains of sand by the seashore. (Heb. 11:12)

Then the bad news:

> These all died in faith, not having received the things promised." (Heb. 11:13)

Wait a minute. Abraham had descendants, but they, like Abraham, died without having received what God had promised to them? No possession of the land? It's true. According to Hebrews, Abraham made his home in the Promised Land of Canaan "as in a foreign land, living in tents with Isaac and Jacob, heirs with him of the same promise" (Heb. 11:9). In fact, the only land Abraham ever owned in Canaan was a cave in which he buried his wife, Sarah. And even though the children of Israel took possession of the land under the leadership of Joshua, it was constantly under siege and repeatedly invaded and overtaken by their enemies. How can this be?

This is exactly why Abraham rejoiced to see Jesus's day. Abraham understood that while he and his descendants enjoyed tastes and glimpses of all that God promised to him over the years of his lifetime, the land and the descendants and the blessings were given as tangible, material pointers toward a greater fulfillment to come. Abraham understood that everything God promised to him would ultimately be fulfilled through the promised offspring. Abraham understood in part what Paul stated clearly about Christ: "All the promises of God find their Yes in him" (2 Cor. 1:20).

- Jesus is the offspring promised to Abraham that the birth of Isaac pointed toward. All those who belong to Christ are "Abraham's offspring, heirs according to promise" (Gal. 3:29).
- Jesus is the head of a great nation made up of "disciples of all nations" (Matt. 28:19) because he died "to gather into one the children of God who are scattered abroad" (John 11:52).
- Jesus is "King of the nations" (Rev. 15:3), the one through whom all the families of the earth are eternally blessed or eternally cursed based on their response to him.

⌖ Jesus is the one who has gone to prepare a place for us (John 14:2), a "homeland," a "better country, that is, a heavenly one" (Heb. 11:14, 16).

Jesus is the ultimate offspring of Abraham. Jesus is the one through whom all the families of the earth will be blessed. Those who find life in him will be as numerous as the stars in the sky. It is Abraham's connection to Christ that will make his name great, and Christ's Spirit in Abraham that will make Abraham fruitful.

Can we think together for a minute about the implications of this? I have to warn you that the truth that Jesus has fulfilled all of the promises made to Abraham may disrupt or offend your politics or what you may have heard from Bible-prophecy teachers about what must take place in this world before Christ returns. To rightly understand the hope we have in Christ now and in the future, we have to understand the implications of Christ's fulfilling all of the promises made to Abraham. God's promise to bless those who bless him and curse those who curse him has been fulfilled in Christ. Blessing and cursing come not to those who bless or curse a particular people group or national entity but to those who bless or curse Christ, the promised offspring of Abraham.

Likewise, it is no longer the land of Palestine that has been given by God to physical descendants of Abraham—be they descendants of Ishmael or Isaac. God's promise of a land where his people can dwell with him in safety forever is fulfilled ultimately in the city that Abraham was looking for, the "city that has foundations, whose designer and builder is God" (Heb. 11:10). Clearly the land Abraham looked forward to and longed for most was not a piece of Middle Eastern real estate but the place Jesus has gone to prepare for us. Certainly no descendant of Abraham by faith will enter this heavenly land and think that God has not lived up to all of his promises to his people.

This not only has implications for our politics and end-times perspectives; it has much more personal import to those of us who have staked our futures on the promises of God. It tells us something very significant about the nature of God's promises—both how and when we can expect them to be fulfilled.

We see in Abraham's experience that God kept his promises. But they certainly didn't come about in the timing or the way that Abraham and his offspring expected. While Israel enjoyed the very real blessings of land and nation and descendants, these tangible, earthly fulfillments were given to point and prepare them for their ultimate fulfillment through Christ. All of the promises to Abraham and his descendants are in no way abolished or replaced, but are fulfilled in a different and superior way.[1]

It is easy to pluck a promise out of the Bible and "claim it" with little thought to who the promise was originally made to or the conditions for receiving the promise. We make the assumption that we have every right to claim the promise for the here and now in physical, tangible terms. We discount the value of the promise being fulfilled in spiritual and eternal terms. Our assumption ignores the nature of God's promises—that every blessing God intends to give us comes through Christ. "Blessed be the God and Father of our Lord Jesus Christ, who has blessed us in Christ with every spiritual blessing" (Eph. 1:3).

This is what God intended from the day he promised to bless Abraham and make him a blessing—that we would enjoy all of his blessings through Christ.

A Longing for the Day the Righteousness Credited to Him Will Be Revealed

Abraham could have looked at the promises made to him and discounted them or been indifferent to them, or he could have simply seen them as too good to be true and disregarded them. But that is not what he did. Instead, he went against intuition and logic, against what he saw and felt. He believed God. And because he believed God, a miraculous and mysterious transaction took place. The narrator of Abraham's story tells us:

> [Abraham] believed the LORD, and [the Lord] counted it to him as righteousness. (Gen. 15:6)

Abraham believed that God could and would do exactly what he said he would do. This belief was no mere assent to the possibility. The

---

[1] I was helped greatly in understanding God's promises to Abraham by Bob Deffinbaugh,"The Promised Blessings and Their Fulfillment in God's Perfect Plan" (http://www.bible.org), and also by Chris Wright, "A Christian Approach to Old Testament Prophecy Concerning Israel," in *Jerusalem Past and Present in the Purposes of God*, ed. P. W. L. Walker (Cambridge, UK: Tyndale, 1992), 1–19.

promise of God was no longer something outside of him, but a part of him. God's promise pierced Abraham's heart and became his. Later Paul wrote about what happened, saying:

> In hope he believed against hope, that he should become the father of many nations, as he had been told, "So shall your offspring be." He did not weaken in faith when he considered his own body, which was as good as dead (since he was about a hundred years old), or when he considered the barrenness of Sarah's womb. No distrust made him waver concerning the promise of God, but he grew strong in his faith as he gave glory to God, *fully convinced* that God was able to do what he had promised. That is why his faith was "counted to him as righteousness." (Rom. 4:18–22)

All these promises of blessing that he did not deserve, that he repeatedly put into jeopardy, that he had no power to bring about—Abraham saw that they were all grace, and Abraham embraced grace.

Before this time, Abraham had heard from God and even obeyed God. Certainly he demonstrated his belief in God's promise to him when he left Ur. So why at this particular point in time was Abraham's belief counted to him as righteousness?

The text says that Abraham "believed the LORD." What was it specifically that Abraham believed that brought this about? Was it his belief in owning the land, in having a great name, or in being a blessing that was counted as righteousness? In Galatians 3, we discover a specific answer to our question:

> Now the promises were made to Abraham and to his offspring. It does not say, "And to offsprings," referring to many, but referring to one, "And to your offspring," who is Christ. (Gal. 3:16)

Abraham believed God, not just in general but in respect to the promise of a child from his body who would bless the world and be its Savior. This is what Abraham believed that was credited to him as righteousness.[2] Abraham embraced the grace to come in Jesus Christ. He didn't know the offspring's name or when he would come, but he looked

---

[2] In his sermon "The Covenant with Abraham," at Park Cities Presbyterian Church, Dallas, TX, October 6, 2004, Sinclair Ferguson states, "Abraham believed God not just in general, but with respect to the promise of the coming Savior. He trusted this coming Savior, and God counted it to him as righteousness."

forward in faith, understanding the offspring promised to Adam and Eve would be one of his own descendants.

Now, we have to be clear that his believing what God said about the promised offspring was not some sort of good work that became righteousness. Genesis says that Abraham believed the Lord and it was "*counted* to him as righteousness." This term, "counted" or "credited" or "reckoned," is an accounting or bookkeeping term. Genesis 15:6 tells us that a deposit was made to Abraham's spiritual account in the sight of God. This was not wages that Abraham earned, and neither was it something that magically appeared out of nowhere; this was real righteousness. But it was not Abraham's righteousness. Abraham believed God, and that faith became the channel through which Abraham received the perfect righteousness of another.

And this is another reason why Abraham rejoiced to see Jesus's day. Abraham longed for the day the righteousness that was credited to him would be revealed. And when Christ came, living a life of sinless obedience and loving devotion to God, true and perfect righteousness was revealed. Paul put it this way:

> For in [the gospel] the righteousness of God is revealed from faith for faith, as it is written, "The righteous shall live by faith." (Rom. 1:17)

Abraham couldn't see the source of this righteousness clearly. Faith for Abraham required that he trust God for how and from where or from whom this very real righteousness would come. From our vantage point we can see the source of this righteousness more clearly. But, like Abraham, we must believe that the righteousness of Christ is sufficient, that it is weighty enough, and that God is good enough to give it to us, who have no real righteousness of our own.

There is only one way we can receive this wonderful gift of righteousness deposited by the grace of God to our personal account. It is by placing our faith fully in Abraham's offspring—Jesus Christ. Faith that saves is not simply faith that believes in God or even tries hard to obey God's commands. The righteousness of Christ is not credited to those who are seeking after being spiritual or sincere about their religious beliefs. Saving faith is putting all our hopes in what God has promised—

specifically the promise of his Son, Jesus Christ, and in his life, death, and resurrection.

Abraham looked forward in faith to God fulfilling the promise of sending the Righteous One, the one who provided the righteousness credited to him. This is why Jesus could say that Abraham rejoiced to see his day.

A Longing for the Day the Covenant's Curse Will Be Removed

While Abraham believed God in regard to what God promised him, he still struggled with doubts. Does it help you to know that? Does it help you to know that you can embrace the grace that God has given to you in the person of Christ and yet still struggle with doubts about it, still have questions about how his promises will all come about? When God reaffirmed his promise to give Abraham possession of the land, Abraham said:

> O Lord GOD, how am I to know that I shall possess it? (Gen. 15:8)

Likely Abraham's doubts were not limited to his questions about how and when God would or could come through on his promises. More likely Abraham's doubts were fed by what he knew about himself—his history of idol worship, his cowardly failure to protect Sarah from the Pharaoh in Egypt, which put the promised offspring in jeopardy, his willingness to have a child with Hagar in faithless desperation to have a child of his own. Surely what caused Abraham to doubt God's heretofore unfulfilled promises was more about his own failings and frailty than about his doubts about God's power and provision. God was covenanting to be Abraham's God, but Abraham must have doubted whether he could be God's man.

Isn't it our own history and humiliating failures that cause us to doubt whether we can really expect to experience all that God has promised to us through Christ? Even though we know that it is Christ's righteousness and not our own that matters, don't we still fear that because of who we are, and what we've done, or what we've failed to do, or what we're afraid we might do in the future, we cannot be sure that we will ever really possess what God has promised to us through Christ?

God did not rebuke Abraham for his question but provided for Abraham, and for us, a gruesome and yet ultimately beautiful picture that assuaged Abraham's doubts. Let it assuage your doubts too, though you'll have to get past the weirdness of it to see the wonder in it. When Abraham asked how he could know that God would fulfill his promises, God told him:

> Bring me a heifer three years old, a female goat three years old, a ram three years old, a turtledove, and a young pigeon. (Gen. 15:9)

Then we read:

> He brought him all these, cut them in half, and laid each half over against the other. But he did not cut the birds in half. And when birds of prey came down on the carcasses, Abram drove them away. (Gen. 15:10–11)

Notice that God did not give Abraham instructions on what to do with the animals. Abraham seemed to have instinctively known what to do. That's because this was a common custom in Abraham's homeland. The way in which two parties solemnized a promise or covenant was by killing an animal and dividing it in two so that the two covenanting parties could walk between the sundered body of the animal. The ceremony dramatized a self-imposed curse should either of them break their pledge. In essence, as they walked between the carcasses they were saying, "May this be done to me—may I be cut in two—if I do not live up to my part of the covenant."

So Abraham slaughtered and arranged the animals, and we read that, "a deep sleep fell on Abram" (Gen. 15:12). This was not just nodding off from all the hard work of collecting and cutting up these animals. This was a deep sleep brought upon Abraham by God, reminiscent of the sleep imposed on Adam when God formed Eve from his rib.

But if Abraham is in a deep sleep, how will he walk through the sundered animals to solemnize his part in the covenant? In fact, he will *not* take this walk of commitment. God knew that Abraham could not walk blameless before him, as he had commanded (Gen. 17:1). Abraham could not fulfill his part of the covenant. So Abraham was not invited or allowed to walk between the pieces of the animals. But something or someone certainly walked the bloody path:

> When the sun had gone down and it was dark, behold, a smoking fire pot and a flaming torch passed between these pieces. (Gen. 15:17)

What was this "smoking fire pot" and "flaming torch"? Moses would see something similar in the burning bush (Ex. 3:2). The Israelites would see something similar at Sinai when they stood at the foot of the mountain that burned with fire and was wrapped in smoke (Ex. 19:18). The Israelites would see it again when they followed the pillar of cloud by day and the cloud of fire by night (Ex. 13:21). Abraham realized that this was a visible manifestation of God traversing the bloody path. God alone was making the promise and submitting himself to the curse of the covenant. God assumed the full responsibility for seeing that every promise of the covenant would be realized, and he alone submitted himself to the curse for Abraham's inability to live up to the covenant.

Abraham had no idea what the cost would be for God to fulfill this oath of grace. But this is why Abraham rejoiced to see Jesus's day. That was the day when God, in the person of Jesus Christ, walked the bloody path, marked not with the blood of halved animals but with his own blood. Paul wrote, "When he was hung on the cross, he took upon himself the curse for our wrongdoing" (Gal. 3:13 NLT). By bearing the full consequences of the covenantal pledge to death, Christ delivered us from the curse of our inability to live up to the covenant so that we might become heirs of its blessings.

What does this strange ceremony have to do with you and me today? The writer of Hebrews helps us understand:

> For when God made a promise to Abraham, since he had no one greater by whom to swear, he swore by himself, saying, "Surely I will bless you and multiply you." (Heb. 6:13–14)

God made a promise to Abraham, but to accommodate Abraham's doubt about whether God would come through on his promises, God went even further to make this covenantal oath:

> So when God desired to show more convincingly to the heirs of the prom-
> ise the unchangeable character of his purpose, he guaranteed it with an
> oath, so that by two unchangeable things, in which it is impossible for
> God to lie, we who have fled for refuge might have strong encouragement
> to hold fast to the hope set before us. We have this as a sure and steadfast
> anchor of the soul. (Heb. 6:17–19)

This is one of those passages that answers our *why* questions clearly with a "so that . . . " *Why* did God submit himself to this strange ceremony to make an oath? *So that* we can courageously take hold of the fulfillment of the promises God made to Abraham in the person of Jesus Christ. He is the hope set before us. He is the sure and steadfast anchor of our souls.

My great comfort is knowing that one day the curse of sin will be gone for good.

Do you sometimes feel adrift in this life, wondering who and what you can trust, what is true, what is real, what is reliable? God walked this bloody path to say to you, *You can trust me. You can rely on me. Flee to me as your refuge. Take hold of me as your anchor.*

At the cross, the curse sanction of the covenant made with Abraham was exhausted on Christ. This is why Abraham rejoiced to see Jesus's day! Finally, the curse that had to fall in God's perfect justice fell on Christ so that mercy flows to Abraham and all of his descendants by faith. Abraham rejoiced as he embraced the grace he saw only in shadows on that dark night.

So are you wondering how my visit to my friend in Norway turned out? I stepped off the plane and into the arms of my friend, and it seemed there had never been thirty-four years and millions of miles between us. And our husbands could not have had much more in common—my husband is a gadget guy and a publisher of choral music for the church. Her husband is the IT guy for the local school where he is also the instrumental teacher, and he sings in a choral group that travels all over Europe. That night, as we pulled the comforter over us, sleeping in their daughter's bed, David said, "If they lived in Nashville, we would be friends." Since then, they've been here in Nashville, and we've been back to Norway, along with Matt, on what ended up being the most perfect family vacation of all time.

The day I longed for surpassed my expectations. But it came and went. It was good, but it wasn't perfect. And it certainly wasn't forever. Any day we long for in the here and now, though it might be good, will not last. And sadly, so many days we look for and long for leave us disappointed. They come and go, and so often they don't live up to our expectations.

That is why we must set our sights and hopes on the day Abraham longed for. Because while he saw the day of Jesus's incarnation and was glad, I think there is another day he saw by faith that caused him to rejoice even more—that day when all of his descendants will enter "the city that has foundations, whose designer and builder is God" (Heb. 11:10).

Abraham longed to see the day of Christ, not only when Christ was born to earth the first time but when he will return to earth the second time to usher in the complete and final fulfillment of all that God promised. On that day, Jesus will throw open the doors to the land that Abraham had his sights set on all along.

God is in the process of bringing about fulfillment of all his promises. And he is so good to give us tastes and glimpses of what is to come. These tastes and glimpses are meant to nurture our longing for the day Abraham longed for, the day when faith becomes sight. This will be the answer to all of our deepest longings; this day will deliver our greatest joy. This will be the day when Christ comes again.

On that day, all the true descendants of Abraham will experience a blessing that is far beyond the temporal blessings of this life. As co-heirs with Christ, standing on a redeemed and renewed earth, every part of it—beyond what our eyes can see—will belong to us, not just for a few years but forever. There will be people from every generation there—from Abraham's day, those who looked forward to the coming of the Promised One, and from our day, those who look back at the coming of the Promised One and look forward to his coming again—and the number will be as numerous as the dust of the ground or the stars in the sky.

Finally, we will experience in full the best promise God gave to Abraham:

> I will establish my covenant between me and you and your offspring after you throughout their generations for an everlasting covenant, *to be God to you* and to your offspring after you. (Gen. 17:7)

This is a promise we can take hold of now, a promise to flee to, a promise that is a weighty anchor for our souls, a promise that will be fulfilled when we stand in the new Jerusalem and hear "a loud voice from the throne saying, 'Behold, the dwelling place of God is with man. He will dwell with them, and they will be his people, and God himself will be with them as their God'" (Rev. 21:3).

This, my friends, will be a day worth longing for, a day worth waiting for, a day that will not disappoint.

How Genesis Points to What Is Yet to Come: "My Day"

We often hear people say, "In my day . . . " followed by what they did or didn't do when they were younger as opposed to the way things are done now. And of course when they say "my day," they don't mean a particular twenty-four-hour period in their history. They are referring to a period of time when they were at their best, when they were at the center of things, when they were having their greatest impact.

When Jesus said that Abraham rejoiced to see "my day," he was saying that Abraham, by faith, took pleasure in seeing the time when Jesus would have his greatest impact, when he would be at the center of things, when he would do his greatest work. And, of course, that would be the day Jesus accomplished the work he had covenanted with the Father and the Spirit to do before time began. This was the day when the Son of God offered himself as a substitutionary sacrifice for the sin of mankind.

But we also know there is another day coming—the Day of the Lord—and certainly Abraham must have rejoiced to see this day. The day Christ died on the cross is the day that secured Abraham's hopes of this greater day—the day when everything Christ purchased, everything he made possible through his death and resurrection will become the reality that Abraham and his descendants by faith will live in fully and forever.

In the Old Testament prophecies about the Day of the Lord, we find the near and the distant future brought together in a single vision of things to come. The Old Testament prophets saw the temporal days of the Lord—his days of judgment in their own lifetimes or shortly thereafter—as precursors of and the pattern for one final *dies irae*, the day of the divine wrath. When the Day of the Lord is discussed in the New Testament, it exclusively refers to the second coming of Christ. We read of "the day of the Lord's return" (1 Thess. 5:2 NLT), "the day when our Lord Jesus Christ returns" (1 Cor. 1:8 NLT), "the day when Christ Jesus returns" (Phil. 1:6 NLT), and "the day of Christ's return" (Phil. 2:16 NLT). All these phrases refer to the same day and to the same event: the time of Christ's final and decisive visitation of this world in judgment and salvation. Paul provides insight into the agony and the glory of that day:

> He will come with his mighty angels, in flaming fire, bringing judgment on those who don't know God and on those who refuse to obey the Good News of our Lord Jesus. They will be punished with eternal destruction, forever separated from the Lord and from his glorious power. When he comes on that day, he will receive glory from his holy people—praise from all who believe. (2 Thess. 1:7–10 NLT)

The day of the Lord, then, will be the day of God's wrath and judgment against his enemies, but it will also be the day of salvation for his people. The reason Abraham can rejoice about this day is that on this day, like none other, God will be his shield and his very great reward through Christ. Christ will shield Abraham and his offspring from the wrath of God that is going to fall. Finally Abraham and his offspring will receive the very great reward God promised to Abraham.

> Therefore do not throw away your confidence, which has a great reward. For you have need of endurance, so that when you have

done the will of God you may receive what is promised. For, "Yet a little while, and the coming one will come and will not delay; but my righteous one shall live by faith, and if he shrinks back, my soul has no pleasure in him." But we are not of those who shrink back and are destroyed, but of those who have faith and preserve their souls. (Heb. 10:35–39)

Abraham

GENESIS 12–15

Getting the Discussion Going

1. Probably most of you fit into one of two camps: either you still live near the family you grew up with or at some point you moved away and started a new life and family of your own, like Abraham did. What do you see as the upsides and downsides of each?

Getting to the Heart of It

2. Perhaps you have grown up seeing Abraham as a "hero" of faith. How does what we've read about Abraham so far in Genesis 12–15 build an argument for or against that idea?

3. What question from the Personal Bible Study was especially interesting or meaningful or maybe challenging to you?

4. Evidently Abraham understood what so many people throughout history, and so many of us today, simply have not understood clearly about the nature of God's promises. We become so focused on God's fulfilling his promises in the here and now, in physical ways we can see and feel and enjoy in this life. In the process we diminish and discount the spiritual and eternal nature of God's promises. Often the spiritual and eternal nature of God's promises seem to us to be somehow less-than, even a copout on God's really delivering on his promises. How has tracing the various ways God has fulfilled, is fulfilling, and will fulfill his promises

to Abraham helped you in understanding and perhaps accepting how
God has fulfilled, is fulfilling, and will fulfill his promises to you?

5. How is Genesis 15:1–6 a model for us in dealing with fear and
doubt?

6. We saw that Abraham was not declared righteous until his believing
God's promise related specifically to the promised offspring, the one
who would bring salvation. What significance does this have for us
in regard to faith? How is this different from merely having spiritual
beliefs or a belief that there is a God or that Jesus was a great moral
teacher?

7. What difference does it make that Abraham's believing God was not
a good work through which he earned the righteousness that was credited to him, but rather his believing God was the channel through which
the righteousness of Christ was credited to him?

8. The heart of these chapters of Genesis is the grace of God coming to a
pagan idol worshiper and making promises to a man who, in response,
embraced the grace given to him. How do you see that in these chapters,
and how does it challenge you or move you?

9. Many people in our world today see God as a harsh judge, an arbitrary
power, an uncaring deity. What does the covenant oath ceremony, as
unusual as it is, reveal to us about the person of God?

Getting Personal
10. The big question of this week was, "Is there a day you are longing
for?" We were challenged to nurture our longing for the day when Christ
will return and all the promises made to Abraham and his descendants
will be fulfilled for eternity. Is that a day you long for? Why or why not?
How can we nurture that longing?

Getting How It Fits into the Big Picture

11. Throughout this study, we're trying to grasp how some of these familiar stories fit into the bigger story of God's plan for redemption. The Bible doesn't begin with Abraham's story in Genesis 12; Abraham's story is part of God's story of redemption after the fall of Genesis 3. How does it fit into the bigger story? How does understanding the bigger story help us to put God's promises to Old Testament descendants of Abraham in proper perspective?

Abraham and Isaac

Genesis 16–24

Personal Bible Study

Abraham and Isaac

GENESIS 16–24

🕐 1. Read Genesis 16 and summarize in a couple of sentences what takes place.

2. Egypt plays a prominent part in Abraham's story. In Genesis 12 there was a famine, and Abraham's solution was to go to Egypt, where he succumbed to fear that led to great sin in telling Pharaoh that Sarah was his sister. In Genesis 13 the land chosen by Lot is described as being "well watered everywhere like the garden of the LORD, like the land of Egypt" (v. 10). Now, in Genesis 16, we meet Hagar, an Egyptian who, not surprisingly, was fruitful while Sarah was barren. Why would this repeated theme of the dangers of the allures of Egypt be significant to the original readers, the Israelites, for whom Moses wrote Genesis, as they prepared to enter the Promised Land?

🕐 3. The covenant is stated in its most basic form in Genesis 17:7–8. What is it?

4. As part of this covenant, God changed the name Abram to Abraham and Sarai to Sarah. What is implied by God's changing their names?

The Connection between Circumcision and Baptism

As a sign of his submission to the covenant, Abraham was commanded to be circumcised, reflecting the reality that this relationship with God would penetrate even the most personal areas of his life, leaving a permanent mark of belonging to God. In commanding Abraham not only to be circumcised himself but also to circumcise all the males in his household, God revealed himself as a covenant God who deals faithfully with us as families, not just as individuals. The circumcision of eight-day-old infants in the Old Testament testified that they were not free to choose their own gods but were part of the covenant people belonging to the one true God. Obviously circumcision had no saving power; Abraham was declared righteous long before he took this sign upon himself. Circumcision was a sign of belonging to God's covenant people and the need to submit to the one true God, or face the consequences of being "cut off" from him. Ishmael was circumcised (Gen. 17:26), but he never embraced the promises of God and showed no evidence of a living faith. So, even though he was circumcised, he was not ultimately part of God's covenant people.

Many faithful churches see a connection between the Old Testament covenant sign of circumcision and the New Testament covenant sign of baptism, and therefore, just as infants were circumcised as a sign of God's promise to save, these churches baptize infants as a sign of God's promise to save. Infants are baptized as an act of faith in the promises of God. By baptizing their child, parents acknowledge that God can and will save their child, if that child will look to Christ in repentance and faith. Baptism testifies to the truth that without repentance and faith, the child will face the consequences of being "cut off" from God for eternity. In this view, the primary function of baptism is not to symbolize our response to the promise of the gospel, but to signify and seal the gospel to which we are called to respond in lifelong faith and repentance.

Likewise, many faithful churches do not connect Old Testament circumcision and New Testament baptism in the same way, pointing out that infants are nowhere explicitly mentioned in the New Testament as being baptized. These churches hold to believer's baptism in which those who come to faith in Christ are baptized as a sign of new life in Christ, identifying with his death and resurrection, and marking one as belonging wholly to Christ. Those who hold to believer's baptism would say that the parallel between circumcision and baptism in the new covenant is not between physical circumcision and infant baptism but between spiritual circumcision of the heart and believer's baptism, which signifies regeneration, faith, and union with Christ. In this view, baptism functions first and foremost not as a statement or sign of the *promise* of salvation but as a statement or sign of *the fulfillment of that promise* in the life of one who has personally trusted Christ. By immersion, believer's baptism pictures one's union with Christ's death and resurrection in cleansing of sin and newness of life.

One thing those who practice believer's baptism and those who practice infant baptism agree on is that baptism is the sign and seal of the new covenant, inaugurated by Christ's death and resurrection. It is a symbol of regeneration, cleansing, and repentance in Christ (Acts 2:38; 22:16; Eph. 5:26; Col. 2:12; Titus 3:5–7; Heb. 10:22).

Regardless of which position your church takes, it may be helpful for you to deepen your understanding of the biblical basis for baptism and correct any misunderstandings you have about what it means in your church as well as what it means in churches who do it differently from your own. Most importantly, if you belong to Jesus Christ but have never been baptized, it is important to obey God by taking this sign of belonging to him upon yourself.

5. On the day of Pentecost, which is the birthday of the New Testament church, Peter encouraged the people to "repent and be baptized." Compare Acts 2:38–39 with Genesis 17:7. What similarities

and what differences do you see? Write down your discoveries in the chart below.

Similarities	Differences

6. Paul connects circumcision to baptism in Colossians 2:11–14. How do they relate according to these verses?

7. Read Genesis 18:1–15. Abraham's guests were the Lord (Yahweh) and two angels. But Abraham had no idea of this, at least not at first. How does what Abraham's visitors say in verses 9–10 make obvious to Abraham that his visitors were not ordinary men?

8. Earlier Abraham laughed when God said he would have a son, and God did not rebuke him (Gen. 17:17–22). But when Sarah laughed to herself, God rebuked her (Gen. 18:12–13). What was different about the spirit behind their laughter?

9. Read Genesis 21:1–14 along with Galatians 4:21–31. Paul writes to those in the Galatians church, "Now you, brothers, like Isaac, are children of promise" (Gal. 4:28). What does it mean to be a child of promise?

🕰️ 10. Read Genesis 22:1–19. List a few adjectives you would use to describe Abraham's obedience in this testing by God.

11. Moses, the narrator, tells us upfront that Abraham is being tested, but Abraham didn't know that. When God tests us, his purpose is always for our good (as opposed to Satan's purposes in tempting us, which are meant to harm). How do you think Abraham's faith was strengthened by this test?

🕰️ 12. How do Abraham and Isaac point to God the Father and Jesus the Son? Note your answers in the chart below.

Abraham and Isaac	God the Father, Jesus the Son
"Your very own son shall be your heir." (Gen. 15:4) "I will give you a son by her." (Gen. 17:16)	Gen. 3:15; Luke 1:72–73 *Just as Isaac was promised by God repeatedly, long before he was born, so Jesus was promised by God repeatedly through the prophets, long before his birth.*
"You shall call his name Isaac." (Gen. 17:19)	Matt. 1:21
"Sarai was barren." (Gen. 11:30) "The way of women had ceased to be with Sarah." (Gen. 18:11)	Luke 1:34
"The LORD said to Abraham, 'Why did Sarah laugh and say, "Shall I indeed bear a child, now that I am old?" Is anything too hard for the LORD?'" (Gen. 18:13–14)	Luke 1:34

"Sarah conceived and bore Abraham a son in his old age at the time of which God had spoken to him." (Gen. 21:2)	Gal. 4:4
"He said, 'Take your son, your only son Isaac, whom you love, and . . . offer him there as a burnt offering.'" (Gen. 22:2)	Matt. 17:5; John 3:16
"So Abraham rose early in the morning, saddled his donkey, and took two of his young men with him. . . . And he cut the wood for the burnt offering." (Gen. 22:3)	Acts 2:23
"And Abraham took the wood of the burnt offering and laid it on Isaac his son." (Gen. 22:6)	John 19:17
"Abram gave all he had to Isaac." (Gen. 25:5)	John 3:35

13. While there are a number of ways that Abraham offering up Isaac as a sacrifice points to God offering his Son, Jesus, as a sacrifice, there are key contrasts. Note in the chart below those you find from the passages given.

"But the angel of the LORD called to him from heaven and said, 'Abraham, Abraham! . . . Do not lay your hand on the boy.'" (Gen. 22:11–12)	Matt. 26:53; Rom. 8:32

Teaching Chapter

How Will I Know I Am Loved?

Did you ever have anyone say to you in your search for Miss or Mr. Right, "When you find her or him, *you'll know*"?

I don't know about you, but I found that whole "you'll just know" thing very frustrating—like a secret society I was not cool enough to join. But I also have to admit that when David left the night of our first date, I had a deep sense of, "I found him." I knew.

I'm not sure that David was so sure so quickly, but it soon became obvious to me that David loved me. He told me he loved me. And his eyes and his actions confirmed it. Then the day came that he gave me a tangible sign of his loving commitment to me. He put a ring on my finger and said, "I give you this ring in token and pledge of our constant and abiding love."

He gave me something else when we got married that was not nearly as valuable as the ring, yet to me, it was precious. The day we came back from our honeymoon and I went into work for the first time, there was a gift waiting for me on my desk. It was a new desk sign with my new name, Nancy Guthrie. No longer was I Nancy Jinks. My whole identity had changed and was now linked to him, and he wanted the world (or at least anyone who walked into my office) to know that things had changed, that now I belonged to him.

The ring on my finger, the sign on my desk, the blending of my life into his were tangible signs of his love for me—love that was not squishy and sentimental or merely a feeling, but a decision, an action, a commitment. But that was twenty-four years ago. Today it is not a ring on my finger or a sign on my desk that tells me David loves me. The signs are perhaps more subtle but no less significant.

I know David loves me because he has kept the promises he made to me the day we were married. He promised to take me as his wife, to have and to hold me for better or for worse, for richer, for poorer, in sickness and in health, to love and to cherish me until we die. And he has done that. He *is doing* that.

I know David loves me in his patience with me and his acceptance of me. I do things like lock my keys in the car and leave my purse at the gas station and let pots boil over on the stove. And instead of being annoyed with me, David says that because my pretty little head is so full of so many significant things, I just have no space for these mundane matters. That's grace.

I know he loves me because I can't get to the dishwasher before he has emptied it—not because he enjoys this tedious duty but because it is a simple way he can serve me and sacrifice for me. He sacrificed his late-night ways to begin turning out the lights by ten when he married me. He is continually laying down his life for me.

Marriage was always meant to point us to the intimate, committed relationship God wants us to enjoy with him. So it is not surprising that the things that show me David loves me point to some of the things that show me that God loves me. What David does wonderfully yet imperfectly, God does perfectly.

But I also know that many of us go along accepting easily that we are loved by God, until something happens—something that seems to be completely at odds with love the way we've defined it. We think:

"If God loves me, he would not have made me this way."

"If God loves me, he would never let this happen to me."

"If God loves me, he would never ask this of me."

We've determined what God's love should look like in our lives. And rather than allow him to define love, we have decided that we are the reliable judges of what true love should look like, and if God does not express love for us on those terms, we find it hard to believe he truly loves us.

So let's look at Abraham, this one man God picked out from all of the people on earth to set his love on in a unique way. What did his love for Abraham look like? How did Abraham know that he was loved by God? Did he "just know" by intuition? Or was there something more tangible, more solid that he could look at that filled him with confidence that the God who made him and called him was fully committed to bless him? In looking at how Abraham knew he was loved by God, we'll discover how we too can know that we are loved by God.

I Know You Love Me Because You've Marked Me as Belonging to You

Abraham could never forget the dark night when he saw the flaming torch and smoking firepot traversing between the sundered animal parts. That night God confirmed his oath to him that his very own son would be his heir. But then thirteen long years passed, which served to intensify the impossibility of Abraham and Sarah ever having a child between them. Following an established practice of his day, Abraham had taken Sarah's maid, Hagar, as a wife and had a son with her, which created serious tensions in the tent. For these thirteen years Abraham cherished a hope he dared not share with his wife—that Ishmael would inherit the covenant and the promises of God because, frankly, he and Sarah had become hopelessly old.

As we come to Genesis 17, we find that God is about to speak to Abraham again to give him a far more personal sign of his commitment than the covenant oath ceremony. This sign will go beyond pointing to the righteousness that was credited *to* him and the curse that will be borne *for* him—this will be a sign of the change to be wrought *in* him.

Up to this point God had required little of Abraham other than to leave Ur and believe in his promise. But now God came to Abraham and told him how he wanted him to live:

> When Abram was ninety-nine years old the LORD appeared to Abram and said to him, "I am God Almighty; walk before me, and be blameless, that I may make my covenant between me and you, and may multiply you greatly." (Gen. 17:1–2)

To walk before God is to live in such way that every step is made in reference to God. To be blameless is not to be sinless but to offer to God wholehearted devotion and unqualified surrender. Abraham must walk before his God, not in perfection but in purity. This obedience will not be the *basis* of God's covenant with him but the natural *outflow* of it. No one who lives by faith continues to live their own way. Grace goes to work in the interior of our lives so that our allegiances are directed by God and our perspectives are shaped by God.

God reiterated and even expanded on his promises to Abraham— that he will make him fruitful and the father of many nations, and that kings will come from him. But more than promises of what he will *do* for Abraham, God pledged what he will *be* to Abraham:

> I will establish my covenant between me and you and your offspring after you throughout their generations for an everlasting covenant, to be God to you and to your offspring after you. (Gen. 17:7)

"I will be God to you," God promised. "I will belong to you. I will not just be the God of all creation. I will be God to *you*." This is personal. And he's about to get even more personal as he tells Abraham what his part will be in expressing faith in what God has pledged to him.

> And God said to Abraham. . . . "This is my covenant, which you shall keep, between me and you and your offspring after you: Every male among you shall be circumcised. You shall be circumcised in the flesh of your foreskins, and it shall be a sign of the covenant between me and you. . . . So shall my covenant be in your flesh an everlasting covenant. Any uncircumcised male who is not circumcised in the flesh of his foreskin shall be cut off from his people; he has broken my covenant." (Gen. 17:9–14)

Certainly Abraham must have wondered why such a personal and painful sign was being required to signify this covenant. Why not something soothing and restful like the sign of sabbath God gave at creation? Why not something painless and pretty like the rainbow that was the sign God gave to Noah? To undergo circumcision, for Abraham, meant that he was binding himself to God in this covenant. It was physical evidence that he looked forward to the covenant blessings, even as he submitted to its stipulations.

Circumcision was no mere badge of national membership in the Jewish nation but a physical sign of a loving, cleansing, purifying, identifying, defining relationship between God and his people. It was also a sign of promised judgment for those who rejected God's covenant. What more graphic reminder of having yourself and your descendants cut off could there be than the "cutting off" of part of the organ of progeneration?

God told Abraham that this was an "everlasting covenant" given to his offspring "throughout their generations." So, we have to ask, if we are offspring of Abraham, why aren't we still circumcising our little boys eight days after they are born? Because the circumcision Abraham was commanded to carry out pointed to a cleansing to come that would not only mark the body but also change the heart. This ritual purification became an experienced reality when Christ provided the cleansing that circumcision pointed to.

Not only did Christ fulfill the cleansing aspect of this sign, but also he experienced in our place the judgmental aspect of this sign. He was cut off from God for us, fulfilling the penalty of the covenant, putting an end to circumcision as the mark of one belonging to God. Rather than being marked as belonging to God by circumcision, we are marked as belonging to God in a new way— through baptism.

> *I know I am loved because I've been sealed by the Holy Spirit.*

After his resurrection Jesus sent his disciples out—not to circumcise but to baptize: "Go therefore and make disciples of all nations, baptizing them in the name of the Father and of the Son and of the Holy Spirit" (Matt. 28:19). Baptism is now the sign of covenant membership and the mark of true descendants of Abraham by faith:

> For as many of you as were baptized into Christ have put on Christ. There is neither Jew nor Greek, there is neither slave nor free, there is no male and female, for you are all one in Christ Jesus. And if you are Christ's, then you are Abraham's offspring, heirs according to promise. (Gal. 3:27–29)

For most of my life I've seen the baptism I received as an eight-year-old little girl as an act of obedience in which I declared my resolve to follow Jesus. But now I see that baptism is not primarily about my commitment, or my intentions, or my declaration to the world around me. It is about God's commitment and his intentions, and his declaration of his saving power and promise to the world. Just as the Sabbath is a sign of divine rest, and the rainbow is a sign of divine, not human, resolve, and the oath ceremony of halved animals was a sacrament of God's unilateral commitment to the covenant, baptism is God's announcement of his intention to be our God and make us his own.

How do I know David loves me? I look at my ring and it reminds me that he chose me, that he committed to be a husband to me, that I am marked as belonging to him.

How can you know that God loves you? You look back at your baptism, and remember that "in him also you were circumcised with a circumcision made without hands, by putting off the body of the flesh, by the circumcision of Christ, having been buried with him in baptism, in which you were also raised with him through faith in the powerful working of God, who raised him from the dead" (Col. 2:11–12).

Through baptism God marks us as belonging to him. We know he loves us.

I Know You Love Me Because You've Kept Your Promises to Me

The second way we know that God loves us is that he keeps his promises to us. God made some incredible promises to Abraham—promises reflected even in the names he gave to Abraham and Sarah.

When parents named a child in an ancient culture, they were expressing their *hopes* for what the child would do or become. But when God names someone, he states what the person *will* do and *will* become. Abraham's initial name, Abram, meant "exalted father," and referred not to Abram himself, but to God as exalted Father. But in Genesis 17, God came to Abram and changed his name from Abram to Abraham. The new name pointed to Abraham himself as "father of a multitude." So every time people called him "Abraham" it was as if they were calling out to him, "Hey, you, father of a multitude." When people called him "Abraham," perhaps it was an encouraging reminder of God's promise.

But certainly at times it must have seemed to mock the obvious reality that he had no child at all.

God also changed Abraham's wife's name:

> God said to Abraham, "As for Sarai your wife, you shall not call her name Sarai, but Sarah shall be her name. I will bless her, and moreover, I will give you a son by her. I will bless her, and she shall become nations; kings of peoples shall come from her." (Gen. 17:15–16)

Both Sarai and Sarah mean "princess." But while her birth name, Sarai, looked back at her noble descent as the daughter of a king, Sarah, her covenantal name, looked ahead to her noble descendants. This princess will become the mother of a future King. While her father may have named her "princess," he had no power to make her one. But God, in renaming her "princess," will fulfill the promise of this name.[1]

Imagine this holy moment. God is speaking, making these incredible promises, giving them these new names. And what did Abraham do?

> Abraham fell on his face and laughed and said to himself, "Shall a child be born to a man who is a hundred years old? Shall Sarah, who is ninety years old, bear a child?" (Gen. 17:17)

It was just laughable, utterly impossible. Abraham and Sarah had spent plenty of years waiting and longing for God to give them children. They had dealt with the disappointment month after month when Sarah's period would come again. Then the day came when her periods completely stopped. And continuing to hope for a child, even one child, let alone descendants as numerous as the stars in the sky, seemed ridiculous and beyond reason.

Then Abraham spoke up, seeking to give God an out for what seemed an impossible promise:

> Abraham said to God, "Oh that Ishmael might live before you!" (Gen. 17:18)

"Don't knock yourself out trying to do the impossible," Abraham was

---

[1] Bruce Waltke, *Genesis: A Commentary* (Grand Rapids, MI: Zondervan, 2001), 262.

saying. "I've produced an heir already! Choose him to inherit the promises!" But this was the very reason Ishmael was an unsuitable heir. He
represented an effort of the flesh, and Abraham was not going to receive
the inheritance God promised through his own efforts but through a
work of God so that all of the glory would go to God.

> God said, "No, but Sarah your wife shall bear you a son, and you shall call
> his name Isaac. I will establish my covenant with him as an everlasting
> covenant for his offspring after him. (Gen. 17:19)

Ishmael will be made into a great nation, but he will not be the one
through whom God will establish his covenant. It will be Isaac who
will continue the line that will produce the promised offspring. He
will be the one who will inherit everything that has been promised to
Abraham and his descendants—the nation, the land, the descendants,
the blessing.

Later, just as Abraham had laughed at the absurdity of God's promise of a son through Sarah, Sarah also laughed when she overheard the
Lord repeat the promise:

> The Lord said, "I will surely return to you about this time next year, and
> Sarah your wife shall have a son." And Sarah was listening at the tent door
> behind him. Now Abraham and Sarah were old, advanced in years. The
> way of women had ceased to be with Sarah. So Sarah laughed to herself,
> saying, "After I am worn out, and my lord is old, shall I have pleasure?"
> (Gen. 18:10–12)

Evidently she didn't laugh aloud, but to herself. Maybe she rolled her
eyes at the impossibility. She knew her own body—it was worn out and
dried up. The idea that she could ever become plump and productive
was laughable. God heard the laughter of unbelief inside of Sarah and
called her on it.

> Is anything too hard for the Lord? At the appointed time I will return to
> you, about this time next year, and Sarah shall have a son. (Gen. 18:14)

Sarah had been focused on whether it was too hard for her and
Abraham, and there was no question but that it was. But the Lord turned

her to the real question: "Can I do it?" he asked. And of course he could. He is God Almighty. God will have the last laugh in this matter.

> The LORD visited Sarah as he had said, and the LORD did to Sarah as he had promised. And Sarah conceived and bore Abraham a son in his old age at the time of which God had spoken to him. (Gen. 21:1–2)

Notice that it says *the Lord* visited Sarah and *the Lord* did to Sarah, and she conceived. There is no mention of Abraham in this process. Surely this child had Abraham's DNA, yet this child was conceived by a miraculous work of God.

> Abraham called the name of his son who was born to him, whom Sarah bore him, Isaac. And Abraham circumcised his son Isaac when he was eight days old, as God had commanded him. Abraham was a hundred years old when his son Isaac was born to him. And Sarah said, "God has made laughter for me; everyone who hears will laugh over me." And she said, "Who would have said to Abraham that Sarah would nurse children? Yet I have borne him a son in his old age." (Gen. 21:3–7)

"He will laugh" is an unusual name for a son, but it is the name God commanded Abraham to give to his son. Isaac was named after Abraham and Sarah's laughter of disbelief. But the very act of naming him Isaac in obedience to God's command made him the child of faith. And while Sarah had laughed in disbelief when she heard him promised to her, now she is laughing as she thinks about a woman in her nineties breastfeeding a baby and chasing after a toddler. It is hilariously wonderful, and no house has ever been so full of joy as when this baby was born.

When we read this story, we must recognize that it is not simply about Abraham and Sarah and the miraculous birth of Isaac that God has accomplished. This promised child was always meant to point us toward another promised child. Seeing God's power at work in Sarah prepared God's people to trust that another woman who cannot possibly conceive because she has never even been with a man will in fact conceive by the power of God. Sarah's questions about how this could happen point us to another mother who cannot understand how she will conceive. Just as God assured Sarah by asking, "Is anything too hard for God?" the angel will say to the virgin Mary, "For nothing will be impossible with God" (Luke 1:37).

If Abraham ever wondered in the years to come about whether God was truly committed to him, he need only look in the laughing eyes of his son and see that God was faithful in his promises. Abraham received the promises of God not because he and Sarah worked up enough faith on their own to believe God's promises and hold on to them. It was grace given to them in spite of their doubt and disbelief. God was faithful to Abraham not because of Abraham's faithfulness but in spite of Abraham's faithlessness. God kept all of his promises to Abraham, who did not keep his promises to God.

This is good news for people like you and me who have made so many promises to God that we have not kept. We've promised to build our lives on the foundation of his Word, and we go a whole week not even realizing we left our Bible at church last Sunday. We've promised to raise our children in the teaching and admonition of the Lord, and while we nag about schoolwork, we rarely speak over them the promised blessings of God. We've promised that we will walk in a manner worthy of our calling, yet we so often walk in lock step with the world around us. The good news of the gospel is that even though we fail in keeping our promises to God, he will keep his promises to us.

How do we know God loves us? Because he has done no less a miracle in our lives than he did in Abraham's and Sarah's lives. We were dead—not just sickly—but dead in sin. The same El Shaddai that accomplished what was impossible in the birth of Isaac and the birth of Jesus, has done what is no more possible in human terms in us. "But God, being rich in mercy, because of the great love with which he loved us, even when we were dead in our trespasses, made us alive together with Christ" (Eph. 2:4–5).

He has kept his promise to make us alive together with Christ. We know he loves us.

I Know You Love Me Because You Sacrificed Your Life for Me

Imagine the joy in Abraham and Sarah's household when Isaac was born. This one whose name means laughter brought so much joy and laughter to their tent. Perhaps the only person who didn't find joy in Isaac's birth was Ishmael. Sarah couldn't stand his mocking of Isaac and demanded that Hagar and her son be sent away. Of course Abraham was reluctant, but by sending Hagar and Ishmael away he tightened his grip on God's word that Isaac would be heir of the promises. And precisely because Isaac was the child that God had promised would be the first of unnumbered descendants, what God asked Abraham to do next made no sense.

> After these things God tested Abraham and said to him, "Abraham!" And he said, "Here am I." He said, "Take your son, your only son Isaac, whom you love, and go to the land of Moriah, and offer him there as a burnt offering on one of the mountains of which I shall tell you." (Gen. 22:1–2)

God instructed Abraham to take his precious son up on a mountain and slaughter him as a burnt offering, a sacrifice for sin. His corpse was to be consumed utterly with fire so that the smoke would rise up to God.

The conflict for Abraham was not that a sacrifice was required of him. He was well aware of his own sin and the debt he owed. The conflict was that Isaac was the son of the promise. To put him to death would be to put the promise of a Savior in jeopardy. So while we struggle to make sense of this command in terms of how this seems to conflict with our understanding of a loving God and our experience as parents who love our children, Abraham was conflicted in

I know I am loved because Christ has brought me from death to life.

that way, but also in a far deeper way. Along with the agony of the very idea of putting to death the son who had brought so much joy to his life, he struggled to harmonize this command of God to sacrifice Isaac with the promise of God, who had said, "I will establish my covenant with Isaac" (Gen. 17:21).

On this day the laughter must have come to an abrupt end in Abraham's life. His heart must have been broken. But interestingly, the text doesn't tell us anything about what Abraham felt. It does tell us what he did:

So Abraham rose early in the morning, saddled his donkey, and took two
of his young men with him, and his son Isaac. And he cut the wood for
the burnt offering and arose and went to the place of which God had told
him. (Gen. 22:3)

Abraham did not drag his feet or argue with God. *Early in the morning* he obeyed. As we observe him, we recognize that his faith is the real deal. Genuine faith is always lived out through obedience. Authentic faith is proven, purified, and strengthened when put to the test.

Cutting the wood for the sacrifice at over one hundred years of age, Abraham was thinking it through. *How can God be true to his promise if Isaac is dead? What is God going to do to remain a God who keeps his promises?* Abraham's pondering must have continued on the three-day journey to Moriah. And by the time he got to the place where he parted with his servants, he must have become convinced that the outcome of his sacrifice would not be the end of Isaac.

On the third day Abraham lifted up his eyes and saw the place from afar.
Then Abraham said to his young men, "Stay here with the donkey; I and
the boy will go over there and worship and come again to you." And
Abraham took the wood of the burnt offering and laid it on Isaac his son.
And he took in his hand the fire and the knife. So they went both of them
together. (Gen. 22:4–6)

The writer of Hebrews tells us more precisely what Abraham's words, "I and the boy . . . will come again to you" indicate about his conclusion after thinking it through:

He considered that God was able even to raise him from the dead, from
which, figuratively speaking, he did receive him back. (Heb. 11:19)

Abraham had no idea how it would happen. But he knew the life that had been given to the dead parts of his own body, and he knew that God had promised it would be through Isaac that his offspring would become numerous as the stars in the sky. And putting two and two together he reasoned that the same God who had brought Adam to life from the dust of the ground could bring Isaac back to life from the ashes of his body. Abraham fully intended to sacrifice Isaac as God had commanded, but after three days of thinking it through, his calm conclusion was that God would raise Isaac from the dead.

His confidence in his conclusion, however, must have been tested when Isaac finally broke the silence of the climb:

> And Isaac said to his father Abraham, "My father!" And he said, "Here am I, my son." He said, "Behold, the fire and the wood, but where is the lamb for a burnt offering?" (Gen. 22:7)

Isaac did not yet know that *he* was the lamb that would be slain, and so he asked the question that will be asked again and again throughout the coming centuries: *"Where is the lamb?" When will he come? When will he show up and save us? Where is the lamb who will die for our sins once for all?*

Isaac's question was finally answered when John the Baptist saw Jesus walking toward him and said, "Behold, the Lamb of God, who takes away the sin of the world!" (John 1:29). John recognized that Jesus is the lamb that Isaac and all of the Israelites who descended from him had been looking for—the lamb who would die in their place.

In Abraham's answer to Isaac's innocent question, we hear deliberate vagueness but also an element of hope:

> Abraham said, "God will provide for himself the lamb for a burnt offering, my son." So they went both of them together. (Gen. 22:8)

While we certainly see Abraham's determined obedience in this story, in these words it becomes clear to us that it was not Abraham's iron will to obey God that empowered his every step heading up the mountain. Abraham was not giving himself a pep talk on the climb, saying to himself, "I can do this!" His confidence was not in what he willed himself to do, but in God who would provide.

Abraham and Isaac arrived at the place, built the altar, and arranged the wood. There was nothing left to do but bind Isaac and place him on the pile of wood and plunge the knife into his tender flesh. Clearly a boy who could carry all that wood could easily escape from a man who was at least 110 years old. But Isaac submitted willingly. Certainly he would want this cup of suffering to pass from him. But, like the greater Son whom Isaac clearly points to, he wanted not what he willed but what his father willed. Only when the knife was lifted high did God restrain Abraham.

> But the angel of the LORD called to him from heaven and said, "Abraham, Abraham!" And he said, "Here am I." He said, "Do not lay your hand on the boy or do anything to him, for *now I know* that you fear God, seeing you have not withheld your son, your only son, from me." (Gen. 22:11–12)

This test took Abraham's faith from anticipated obedience to actual obedience, from a disposition to surrender all to a demonstration of total surrender. In the past, while Abraham had demonstrated faith, his faith had also failed. While he passed the test of trust when he left Ur not knowing where he was going, he hesitated a while in Haran and took along his nephew rather than leaving his family behind. He passed the test of wealth by turning down the plunder of battle offered to him by the king of Sodom and by giving a tenth of his wealth to the king of Salem. He passed the test of commitment by circumcising himself and every man in his family. But he failed the test of waiting when he took Hagar as his wife and had a child with her. He failed the test of fear when he told Pharaoh that Sarah was his sister. Now Abraham had passed the supreme test. By raising his hand with every intention of carrying out God's instructions, he demonstrated that now he feared God more than he feared losing what God had given to him.

> And Abraham lifted up his eyes and looked, and behold, behind him was a ram, caught in a thicket by his horns. And Abraham went and took the ram and offered it up as a burnt offering instead of his son. So Abraham called the name of that place, "The LORD will provide"; as it is said to this day, "On the mount of the LORD it shall be provided." (Gen. 22:13–14)

Notice that the mountain did not become a monument to Abraham's obedience but to God's provision. What Abraham was willing to do was a dramatic demonstration of his loving obedience to God, yet this story is not recorded for us primarily to inspire us toward sacrificial acts of obedience to God. It is here to paint in vivid colors the sacrifice *of* God—what God was willing to sacrifice to demonstrate his love for us.

The point of this story is not to convince or convict you that you must be willing to sacrifice for God what is most precious to you. It is that God was willing to sacrifice for you what was most precious to him.

In Abraham's day, God provided a ram as a substitute to sacrifice in place of Abraham's son. But what Abraham really learned from his experience, and what we must see in his experience, is that at the proper time, God would provide a human sacrifice, his own Son, to die as our substitute. This has to be another reason that "Abraham rejoiced" to see Jesus's day. When Abraham saw the day of Christ, the test that made no sense at the time finally made sense.

> *I know I am loved because God demonstrated it at the cross.*

When the day came that God the Father offered up his own beloved Son as a sacrifice, surely Abraham could have stood at the foot of the cross and echoed the words he had heard God say to him on the mountain: "Now I know you love me, seeing that you have not withheld your son, your only son, from me."[2]

When the Israelites read Moses's account of Abraham's test, it burned into their hearts a picture of the unthinkable—that a father would offer his only beloved son as a sacrifice.

Yet it was the will of the LORD to crush him; he has put him to grief. (Isa. 53:10)

For God so loved the world, that he gave his only Son. (John 3:16)

For many, this story of God calling Abraham to offer his son as a sacrifice seems pointless, indiscernible, and cruel. Yet God did not ask Abraham to do anything that he himself would not do. In fact, the command to Abraham was always intended to foreshadow what God would

---

[2] I am indebted to Timothy J. Keller for this profound insight, adapted from his sermon "Real Faith and the Only Son," in the sermon series *The Gospel According to Abraham*, Redeemer Presbyterian Church, June 17, 2001.

do centuries later on the cross of Calvary. The true Father would one day walk his beloved only Son up that same hill on which the Son would be sacrificed. But this time the Father's hand was not stayed.

My friends, do you want to know how you can know that you are loved by God? It is not by looking at your circumstances. You must come to this mountain and look up at this cross. You must see that God "did not spare his own Son but gave him up" for you (Rom. 8:32). Only then can you say, "Now I know. Now I know that I am truly loved, because you have marked me as your own, you have kept your promises to me, you have sacrificed your only Son for me."

> God shows his love for us in that while we were still sinners, Christ died for us. (Rom. 5:8)

The ring David gave me as a sign of his commitment to me has been to the repair shop a few times and is due for another repair. But the sign God has given of his eternal covenant is permanent. I am forever marked as belonging to him by my baptism and by his Spirit, who lives inside me.

The promises David made to me have a time limit. He pledged to be my faithful husband "till death us do part," and that day will no doubt come. But God's promises to me are not for this life only. In fact they are not primarily for this life, but for an eternity to come. All of God's promises will come to their most glorious fulfillment in the new heaven and the new earth, where he will be our bridegroom and we will be his pure bride.

And while David continues to lay down his life for me in big and small ways, he has not made the ultimate sacrifice of offering his life for mine. It is the "Lamb who looks as if he has been slain" whose sacrifice provides my greatest joy and security. His sacrifice will be my focus throughout all eternity, reminding me of my Father's love.

I know he loves me, not through intuition, or because I experience his love on my terms, but because I have by faith stood at the foot of the cross and seen the sacrifice of his beloved Son, which enables me to say, "Now I know you love me."

How Genesis Points to What Is Yet to Come: The Father Seeks a Bride for His Son

If Isaac, the son of promise, was going to be the father of descendants as numerous as the stars in the sky, he would need a wife—and not just any wife. God had told Abraham that the Canaanites would eventually be driven out of the land, so he could not take a wife from among people who were under the curse of God. She also had to be willing to leave her family and relocate to Isaac's home because Isaac could not leave the Promised Land.

Trusting in the providence of God's covenant faithfulness, Abraham sent his servant away to the far country he came from to secure a bride for Isaac. Confident that God had already selected a bride for Isaac, the servant waited by a well to discover God's choice.

> Rebekah, who was born to Bethuel the son of Milcah, the wife of Nahor, Abraham's brother, came out with her water jar on her shoulder. The young woman was very attractive in appearance, a maiden whom no man had known. (Gen. 24:15–16)

Once the servant identified the chosen bride, a great price was paid for her release, and when asked if she would go with Abraham's servant, Rebekah said, "I will go" (v. 58). She then left her family to undertake a long pilgrimage to come to her bridegroom to live with him in a land she would share with him as an inheritance. Rebekah was willing to forsake all for Isaac and agreed to go with Abraham's servant to become the bride of a man she had never seen.

Just as Isaac pictures the Son of God for us, perhaps we also can see in Rebekah the bride the Father seeks for his Son. As the servant of Abraham sought out Rebekah and wooed her to be the bride of Isaac, so has the Holy Spirit wooed us to find our future in the promises of God by becoming the bride of Christ, his church.

The marriage of Isaac and Rebekah did not begin with the love of the couple but with the choice of the father to secure a bride for his beloved son. So did our betrothal to our Bridegroom begin with the sovereign choice of God the Father to take a bride for his beloved Son. Once we were chosen, a great price was paid for our redemption. Just as Rebekah was

made an heir with Isaac of all that God had promised to Abraham, so are
we co-heirs with Christ of all he will inherit. Like Rebekah, we are called
to leave everything behind in order to persevere to our wedding day that
is to be celebrated in a far-off country.

In her ancestry, her beauty, and her purity, Rebekah was a picture of
the bride of Christ. Yet we know that we are not from the right family—we
were born children of the world. Our beauty has been marred and scarred
by sin. We are not pure virgins; we have given ourselves to many other
lovers, spiritually speaking. So how can people like you and me become
the beautiful bride of Christ?

Our bridegroom will make us beautiful. He will make us pure. By his
grace, he will give us his own beauty and purity so that we can be wedded
to him, so we can be "as a bride adorned for her husband" (Rev. 21:2).
Revelation 19 describes the wedding celebration of that day to come when
we, as Christ's bride, come to the marriage dressed in our groom's gift of
grace:

Hallelujah!

For the Lord our God
        the Almighty reigns.
Let us rejoice and exult
        and give him the glory,
for the marriage of the Lamb has come,
        and his Bride has made herself ready;
it was granted her to clothe herself
        with fine linen, bright and pure. (Rev. 19:6–8)

The narrative of Isaac and Rebekah is a beautiful love story. Even
though Rebekah had never seen her bridegroom, she loved him. And ours
too is a beautiful love story. "Though you have not seen him, you love him.
Though you do not now see him, you believe in him and rejoice with joy
that is inexpressible and filled with glory, obtaining the outcome of your
faith, the salvation of your souls" (1 Pet. 1:8–9).

Discussion Guide
Abraham and Isaac

GENESIS 16–24

Getting the Discussion Going

1. What are some of the most meaningful ways your spouse (or a family member or friend, if you are not married) instills confidence that you are loved?

Getting to the Heart of It

2. Abraham is known as the father of faith. But we've also seen last week and this week that he is a real person whose faith sometimes failed. In what ways did Abraham exhibit faith and in what ways did he fail to trust God?

3. How does the sign of circumcision speak of both blessing and cursing? And how does Christ fulfill both the blessing and the cursing of this covenant sign?

4. How would you explain the connection between circumcision in the Old Testament and baptism in the New Testament?

5. When the Lord appeared to Abraham by the oaks of Mamre, he shared a meal with Abraham. What does this suggest about the kind of covenant relationship God wants to have with his people?

6. Laughter is a big part of these chapters—Abraham's laughter, Sarah's laughter on two different occasions, and Ishmael's laughter, as well as

the name given to Isaac, which means "he laughs." What is the difference between some of these instances of laughter? Why do you think this idea of laughter is repeated in this story?

7. Some people are offended that God would test Abraham by telling him to sacrifice his son, even though God never intended for Abraham to kill Isaac. Why do you think God chose to test Abraham in this way?

8. Looking back at your list of the ways Abraham and his son Isaac point to God the Father and his Son, Jesus, which one is especially meaningful to you?

9. If you were a Jewish person living at the time of Christ's crucifixion, how would reflecting on the story of Abraham being called to offer Isaac as a sacrifice help you to make sense of Christ's death on the cross?

Getting Personal

10. The big question of this week was, "How will you know that you are loved by God?" Did you grow up believing that God loves you, or did that become clear to you at some point later on? Do you ever doubt God's love for you? Why or when?

Getting How It Fits into the Big Picture

11. Throughout this study, we're trying to grasp how each section in Genesis fits into the bigger story of God's plan for redemption. How would everything about the Bible be different if God had not given Abraham and Sarah a son?

Week 8

Jacob

Genesis 25:19–35:21

Personal Bible Study

Jacob

GENESIS 25:19–35:21

If you've never read Jacob's story, or if you only know bits and pieces of it, consider reading all of Genesis 25:19–35:29 (skipping chapter 26) as you work through the questions below. Otherwise, you can read only the sections indicated.

1. Read Genesis 25:19–34 and Genesis 27. God told Rebekah what his plan was for her children (Gen. 25:22–23). What was it?

2. How did each person in Isaac's family fail in response to this clearly revealed plan of God for the Promised One to come through Jacob instead of through the firstborn, Esau? Note your answers in the chart below.

Isaac (Gen. 25:23, 28; 27:1–4)	
Rebekah (Gen. 25:28; 27:5–17, 42–46)	

Jacob (Gen. 25:29–34; 27:11–27)	
Esau (Gen. 25:29–34; 27:34, 38, 41)	

3. Read Genesis 28:10–22. While Jacob grew up hearing about God from his parents and grandparents, his first real experience with the God of his fathers occurred in a place he named Bethel, which means "house of God." List six promises God made to Jacob through his dream at Bethel (vv. 13–15):

1)

2)

3)

4)

5)

6)

4. Some see Jacob's response to God's promises as a good start, but still lacking. What positive signs do you see, and in what ways does Jacob still need to grow according to Genesis 28:16–22? Note your answers in the chart on page 207.

Signs That Jacob Is Beginning to Change	Signs of Jacob's Need for Further Growth
Gen. 28:16–17	
Gen. 28:18	
Gen. 28:20–21	
Gen. 28:22	

5. God's love was extended to this unlovely sinner at Bethel as he promised great things to Jacob, not because of the kind of person Jacob was but in spite of the person he was. The same love worked in Jacob's heart through many painful experiences over the next twenty years to make him more than he once was. While Moses provides us with a generous record of events and development in Jacob's life, we will not be able to cover it all in the Teaching Chapter to follow, such as Jacob's experience with Laban and his marriages to Rachel and Leah (Gen. 29:1–31:55). Read Genesis 29–31 with an eye toward how Jacob is still a work in progress even as God is at work in his life as evidenced in his response to various difficulties. What stands out to you in this account of Jacob's twenty years in Haran working for Laban that indicates that Jacob is still a work in progress, that God is at work to change him even though Jacob still has a way to go to be all that God intends for him to be?

6. Read Genesis 32:1–12. As Jacob prepared to see his brother Esau, not knowing if Esau would accept him or kill him, we witness Jacob not only making a plan but, for the first time in Moses's account of his life, bowing to pray. What does Jacob's prayer (Gen. 32:9–12) reveal about how God is at work in his life?

7. Read Genesis 32:22–31. In the dark, Jacob couldn't tell who his adversary was. In the beginning he is identified as a man, but by the time their contest ends, Jacob has become convinced that his opponent is God himself. According to the following verses, what leads Jacob to believe that he is actually wrestling against God, and how do we know this is who Jacob thinks he has wrestled with?

~ Genesis 32:25

~ Genesis 32:26

~ Genesis 32:28

~ Genesis 32:30

8. The touch of God to Jacob's hip brought a great deal of physical pain and left Jacob with a permanent limp. Why do you think God did this, and what do we learn from this?

9. Genesis 32:28 says that Jacob has "striven with God and with men," and has "prevailed" or "won." Does the picture of Jacob limping away

from this wrestling match seem like "prevailing" to you? Why might God say that Jacob has prevailed?

10. Think back to when Adam was instructed to name the animals, when Adam named Eve, and also about how God changed Abram to Abraham (Gen. 17:3–5) and Sarai to Sarah (Gen. 17:15–16). What is the significance of God giving Jacob the new name of "Israel" (Gen. 32:28)?

11. Read John 1:43–51. How does Jesus compare Nathanael to Jacob/Israel?

12. How does Jesus compare himself to the stairway that Jacob saw in his dream?

Teaching Chapter

"Unless You Bless Me"

Over my years of connecting with parents of dying children, there have been several times I have seen desperate parents give religion a try in an effort to get the miracle they seek. They've submitted to the ministrations of faith healers. One sweet friend began to read her Bible and did her best to pray. But when God did not deliver the blessing she sought, when the miracle did not come and her son's death came instead, she gave up on God for good. "I'm just not one of those people who can believe," she told me, to my great sorrow.

But Jill Kelly was different. My friendship with Jill began on the day her husband, Jim Kelly, former quarterback for the Buffalo Bills, handed her a newspaper with a story about the loss of two of my children to Zellweger Syndrome, saying, "I think you're going to want to read this." Jim and Jill were the parents of Hunter, who was five years old at the time, the oldest living child born with Krabbes disease, a disorder related to Zellweger Syndrome.

Soon we were in touch, trading e-mails and having long telephone conversations, often as she kept a watchful eye on Hunter, who had to be turned and suctioned throughout the night.

Jill was not a Christian when she had Hunter. But confident that this son of hers was going to go to heaven when he died, which she knew could be very soon, Jill wanted to make sure she went to heaven too. And so the day came when she got on her knees and prayed a desperate prayer to God to do something in her life.

Jill will tell you that at first she didn't really have much interest in

Jesus or any intention of allowing him to change her life. She had no real knowledge of her sin and her need for a savior. But what began as an arrangement to secure the blessing of heaven for herself so that she could one day be with her son transformed into a relationship in which she fell in love with the source of blessing and the essence of God's blessing: Jesus himself. "He took me from where I was in my self-ish desire for heaven to his Word, where he revealed my need for him because of my sin," Jill told me.

Many of us come to God initially and primarily for what we can get from him. We're savvy consumers, and we see God as the source of the many things we want but have been unable to get on our own. We think we have the system worked out—we are supposed to pray and go to church and try to be good—and that puts us in good stead with God so that he will be disposed—even obligated—to give us the things on our prayer list—good health for ourselves and those we love, freedom from the ache of need or the intense pain of loss, freedom from the frustra-tion of struggle.

And then the loss comes or the struggle ensues, and we begin to wonder what good there is in following God. It becomes obvious that we have really only been *using* God in hopes of gaining his blessings.

As we consider the story of Jacob, we see that his whole life was about the blessing of God—grasping for it, deceiving for it, working for it, dreaming of it, wrestling for it, and finally resting in it. In his story, we see what it looks like to begin as a person who wants to use God to obtain his blessings and then to be transformed into a person who is willing to do whatever it takes to know God personally and intimately in Jesus Christ, which is God's greatest blessing. We see what it means to be changed—changed from being a person defined by struggle to get things from God into a person whose identity flows out of submission and surrender to God.

Grasping His Brother's Heel

Jacob's life began with a struggle in more ways than one. First was his mother's struggle to become pregnant, which took twenty long years. Now, no pregnancy is easy, and certainly no pregnancy with twins is easy, but it seems Rebekah's pregnancy with twins was especially tumultuous. Genesis 25 says, "The children struggled together within her" (v. 22), and so she went to the Lord, asking why this was happening. God said:

> Two nations are in your womb, and two peoples from within you shall be divided; the one shall be stronger than the other, the older shall serve the younger. (Gen. 25:23)

This warfare in her womb would have far-reaching results. Without explanation or apology, God informed Rebekah that his plans and purposes for these boys and the nations they would each father had been set and would not run along the lines of cultural convention or natural order. The younger one would be the one through whom the Promised One would come.

When Rebekah finally gave birth (which, though she thought it would put an end to the struggle between these boys was really only the beginning), out came first the furry, fiery, red-headed Esau, whose foot was firmly in the grasp of his twin brother, Jacob, whose name means "heel-grabber" or "cheater."

These two boys were opposite to the extreme, and Mom and Dad each had a favorite. Picture the family Christmas-card photo when the boys are nine or ten. Isaac, his arm around Esau with his unkempt head of red hair, dirt behind his ears, a bow and arrow on his back, and holding the severed head of his latest conquest. Then there is Rebekah with her arm around the son she adores, Jacob, who is obviously less adventurous, perhaps more calm and calculating. This is not exactly the perfect family whose annual holiday letter will leave us envious. This family is deeply divided, and life is difficult in their tent.

Over the years Isaac became blind physically but perhaps even blinder spiritually. God had made it clear that Jacob, the younger, would be the son of promise instead of Esau, just as Isaac, the younger son of Abraham was the son of promise instead of the older Ishmael. But that went against what Isaac wanted, and he preferred to ignore it. He hoped to overrule it. And Jacob, not trusting God to provide it, schemed and deceived to take it.

One day Esau showed up at the family tent, famished from his latest hunting trip, and Jacob was ready for him, ready to pounce on his brother's moment of weakness. He's living up to his name, grabbing for what he can get.

> Jacob said, "Sell me your birthright now." Esau said, "I am about to die; of what use is a birthright to me?" Jacob said, "Swear to me now." So he swore to him and sold his birthright to Jacob. Then Jacob gave Esau bread and lentil stew, and he ate and drank and rose and went his way. Thus Esau despised his birthright. (Gen. 25:31–34)

What is happening here? What is a birthright? The firstborn received twice as much property as each of the other sons in a family, and, more importantly, the firstborn became the head of his family. With the birthright taken from Esau by trickery, Jacob was legally considered the firstborn. Refusing to trust that God would bring about what he had promised when he said, "The older will serve the younger," Jacob took it into his own hands to wrest the place of prominence and blessing in his family.

Jacob wanted the right things. His desire was for the blessing of being in the line of the Promised One. He wanted to inherit everything that God had promised to his grandfather Abraham and his father, Isaac. But there was no sign that he wanted God. There was no reaching out for God but only grabbing for God's blessings.

The fact that Jacob manipulated Esau to sell him his birthright must have become a longstanding source of irritation to Isaac as he grew older, matched only by Rebekah's constant reminders of which son had been chosen by God. Somewhere along the way Isaac had stopped listening to God. Now he seemed to listen only to his own appetites and preferences. About to die, he wanted to make sure his favorite son had the blessing of the firstborn, so he called Esau and told him to go hunt for some game, make him a big meal, and bring it to him so he could bless him.

Perhaps old man Isaac, with his poor eyesight, had also begun to talk with the volume of one whose hearing was fading. Or perhaps it was just the thin walls of tent living, but however it happened, Rebekah overheard Isaac making plans to give Esau the blessing that should have been reserved for Jacob. And she went into high gear.

When she suggested to Jacob that he cook up goat meat to taste like game stew and put on some goatskins to feel similar to hairy Esau, Jacob was afraid. It wasn't that he was offended morally by this suggested deception, as he should have been. He was just afraid that he would be found out and that his efforts to secure the blessing he so longed for from his father would backfire. He was afraid that if found out, his father would curse him rather than bless him.

In fact, Jacob had longed to hear words of blessing from his father his whole life. Instead Isaac seemed to have words of genuine blessing and affirmation only for Esau. There was a real void in Jacob's life and in his heart. Just once he wanted to feel his father's loving touch and hear him speak to him about his future the way that came so naturally when Isaac talked about Esau. So he butchered the goats, cooked up the stew, and donned the goatskins.[1]

If you have longed to hear words of encouragement, affirmation, and approval from your mom and dad your whole life but have heard only criticism or comparison, then you know how Jacob felt. You know about the empty place in his heart, which he did not trust God to fill but took into his own hands to fill.

Jacob played the part of Esau, smelly stew-fixer, with gusto. And it excited all of Isaac's senses, who said, from the depths of his soul:

> See, the smell of my son is as the smell of a field that the LORD has blessed! May God give you of the dew of heaven and of the fatness of the earth and plenty of grain and wine. Let peoples serve you, and nations bow down to you. Be lord over your brothers, and may your mother's sons bow down to you. Cursed be everyone who curses you, and blessed be everyone who blesses you! (Gen. 27:27–29)

Isaac blessed Jacob with the covenant mantle of fertile land, bountiful provision, a universal empire, and a shield of protection. But the joy of giving such a fervent blessing was short-lived. The real Esau returned

---

[1] I am indebted to Timothy J. Keller for this insight into Jacob's longing for his father's blessing from his sermon "The Problem of Blessing," October 28, 2001, in *The Gospel According to Jacob* sermon series, Redeemer Presbyterian Church, New York.

with genuinely gamey stew, asking for his father's blessing. We read that "Isaac trembled very violently" (Gen. 27:33). This was not a quaking with anger as we might expect, or an eruption of fury. This was a trembling before God, a recognition that his attempt to thwart the plan of God had been overruled. And now, even though his beloved Esau begged for the blessing with tears, Isaac said that the blessing he had given to Jacob would not be withdrawn.

Esau too received a word from his father, but it was more anti-blessing than blessing. Instead of the "dew" and "fatness" Jacob was promised, Esau will live "away" from that blessing. Instead of nations bowing down to him, he will live always fighting against other nations. And instead of lording it over his brother, he will bow down to his brother. What an insult. We understand when we read, "Now Esau hated Jacob." We feel the insult along with Esau.

And we see that this family—the family from which the Promised One is going to come—is really a mess. Everyone in the family sought the blessing of God without bending the knee to God.

But we also see our gracious God at work in the midst of this family and their failures. In spite of Isaac's opposition and Rebekah's manipulation, Jacob's deceitful imitation and Esau's indifference, God's word will be accomplished.

> *Blessing comes not through grasping, but through trusting and being willing to wait on God.*

Have you thought that perhaps God had a plan for your life but that you ruined it by your resistance, your crafty manipulation, your cunning deceitfulness, or your casual indifference? Can you see that nothing can hinder God's plan for your life—not your stubbornness or your self-centeredness or your scheming? "If we are faithless, he remains faithful—for he cannot deny himself" (2 Tim. 2:13). And we are all faithless, aren't we? The good news is that our lives and our futures are not determined by our faithlessness to God but by the faithfulness of God.

Genesis says that Esau "comforted himself" by planning to kill Jacob. We'd like to respond to that with unfamiliar horror, but we recognize this method of self-comforting, don't we? Maybe we're not plotting murder, but we certainly comfort ourselves with visions of how we might murder the reputation of someone who has hurt us by how we'll relate our version of the story. We comfort ourselves with planning how we will cut that person down to size with our cunning words and unanswerable arguments. Rather than seeking healing for the wound through forgiveness, we nurture the offense by plotting how we will make that person regret what he or she has done.

Esau's simmering rage made life dangerous for Jacob, and so he had to go. Rebekah sent him off toward her family home in Haran—alone, and certainly afraid that his brother might be murderously chasing after him. Worn out from the struggle, he came to the city called Luz and settled for a rock as a pillow and went to sleep. He was not looking for God, yet God, in grace, came to Jacob that night in a dream.

Dreaming of a Ladder

> And he dreamed, and behold, there was a ladder set up on the earth, and the top of it reached to heaven. And behold, the angels of God were ascending and descending on it! (Gen. 28:12)

Jacob dreamed of a ladder that reached from heaven down to earth. Unlike the tower built by the people of Babel, this was a ladder built by God. This was not a ladder on which men would make their way up to the gates of God but a ladder on which God would come down to man on this night, to a lonely, fearful, loved-by-God heel-grabber.

Jacob had every reason to fear that God was coming to curse him, but God came down not to curse but to bless Jacob, saying:

> I am the LORD, the God of Abraham your father and the God of Isaac. The land on which you lie I will give to you and to your offspring. Your offspring shall be like the dust of the earth, and you shall spread abroad to the west and to the east and to the north and to the south, and in you and your offspring shall all the families of the earth be blessed. (Gen. 28:13–14)

~ Jacob was a fugitive, but God promised to bring him back home. He will not be a fugitive forever.

~ Jacob had no wife or children, but God promised him offspring. He will not be childless forever.

~ Jacob was essentially impoverished, having left home with nothing, but God promised to give him the land on which he is lying. He will not be impoverished forever.

> *Blessing is not merely getting things from God, but experiencing the presence of God.*

~ Jacob had no reason to think he was someone God could use in the lives of others; he only knew how to look out for himself, but God promised that through him all the families of the earth would be blessed. His life will have impact forever.

~ God made it clear to Jacob that the blessing he longed for was indeed his. He would be the recipient of the promises first made to his grandfather Abraham. God also added a new and special promise: "Behold, I am with you and will keep you wherever you go, and will bring you back to this land. For I will not leave you until I have done what I have promised you" (Gen. 28:15).

~ Jacob was very alone, but God promised that he would no longer be alone. God will be with him wherever he goes.

Though Jacob had no future prospects at this point, God assured Jacob that these divine promises would shape his future, that his future would be full of God's blessing.

Jacob awakened from this dream in a state of stunned awe, saying:

> "Surely the LORD is in this place, and I did not know it." And he was afraid and said, "How awesome is this place! This is none other than the house of God, and this is the gate of heaven." (Gen. 28:16–17)

Jacob had heard his parents and grandparents talk about Yahweh, but Jacob had never personally met him. Now he has. God has begun a work in Jacob's life, but Jacob will long be a work in progress.

I know what it is like to be a work in progress, too. Do you? Aren't you grateful that God did not wait for you to figure it all out, to rid yourself of self, to center your desires on him before he came to you, revealed himself to you, and began to remake you? Instead, he sought you out, and, "I am sure of this, that he who began a good work in you will bring it to completion at the day of Jesus Christ" (Phil. 1:6).

Living Far from Home

Jacob left Bethel with his divine dream imprinted in his mind and implanted in his heart, growing in confidence of God's commitment to bless him and in valuing God's presence with him.

Jacob found his way to Haran. And over the coming years, Jacob the trickster will be tricked. He will work for seven years to marry Rachel only to discover the morning after the wedding that he has married Leah and will have to work another seven years for Rachel. Jacob the cheater will be cheated out of his rightful wages by his father-in-law, Laban.

After twenty years in Haran, far away from his family and the Promised Land, but confident of God's protective presence with him, we find that God is in the process of fulfilling his promises to Jacob. Jacob had a *people*—four wives (Rachel and Leah, as well as their two maidservants who also became his wives) and eleven children—from whom a whole nation will spring. He now had *possessions* as he became rich in flocks and herds. But he did not yet have a *place*—the place God promised to him.

> Then the LORD said to Jacob, "Return to the land of your fathers and to your kindred, and I will be with you." (Gen. 31:3)

Returning to His Brother

Jacob knew that he had something to take care of before he could settle back in Canaan. He had sorely wronged his brother, and he had to make it right. The deceiver had grown in grace, and his conscience would no longer allow him to sidestep an attempt at reconciliation.

I'm sure he would have preferred just to let it go, don't you think? He could have gone back and settled in Canaan without ever having to see his brother. It would have been easy for him to convince himself, "That was so long ago. Esau is doing fine now. What good could come from dredging up those old hurts?"

We can imagine him thinking that way, because we think that way. Many of us have someone we have wronged to whom we have never come clean, and frankly, we don't want to.

When I was a freshman in college, I roomed with a girl I knew from home. She was a year ahead of me and was the resident assistant on our dorm hall. One night another girl in the dorm tried to take her own life, and my roommate told me about the situation as I was heading out the door the next morning to go to class. I mentioned it to yet another girl in my class who lived on our hall. When I got back to our room, my roommate said with great intensity, "Be sure you don't tell anyone about what happened. *You haven't told anyone, have you?*"

And I said, "No."

But then, of course, she found out that this other girl from our dorm knew, and over the coming months she would bring it up in conversation, wondering aloud how this girl found out, while I stayed awkwardly and deceitfully silent.

I moved down the hall at the semester break to escape the tension in the room and then went home for the summer. But I was miserable. Every time I tried to pray, I sensed God nudging me to come clean. My deceit had become a barrier not only between me and my friend but also between me and God. So I drove to her house and told her. It was humiliating to confess my lie and continued cover-up and to learn that she and all the other leaders back at school knew all along anyway. But it was freeing and healing to come clean with how I had wronged her.

So often I want my relationship with God to be only about what goes on between him and me. But the truth is, my biggest breakthroughs in relationship with him have come when I've forgiven those who have hurt me and when I've asked for forgiveness from those whom I have hurt and offended.

We simply can't be right with God if we have not done everything in our power to make things right with other people. Perhaps there is someone you've avoided because you have so far been unwilling to humble yourself and admit, "I was wrong, and I hurt you. I can make excuses and lay out my reasons, but I don't want to. I just want to ask your forgiveness and start over." Don't wait twenty years to do it. Now is a good day to take the first step in that person's direction, while this image of Jacob humbling himself before Esau is fresh in your mind.

Jacob began making preparations to see Esau and sent ahead messengers to tell Esau he was coming with gifts of livestock and servants. Jacob obviously wanted to do more than say, "I'm sorry." He was set to make reparations for what he had stolen from Esau. But then the messengers returned with a report that had to be unnerving. Esau was on his way, and he had four hundred men with him—a small army—and Jacob was understandably afraid.

But it is here we see that God is blessing Jacob, not only by providing for him and protecting him but by changing him. Jacob is not running from his failure but facing up to it. He's not grabbing; he's about to give away much of his own wealth to his brother. And he's not making plans to get what he wants from God; he is turning to God in prayer. For the first time in the account of Jacob's life, we see Jacob bow the knee in prayer. This was no panic prayer telling God what to do. Jacob held on to God's promise to bless him and prayed in light of that promise with sincerity and humility:

> *Blessing is not God giving to me but God working in me, changing me into the image of Christ.*

And Jacob said, "O God of my father Abraham and God of my father Isaac, O LORD who said to me, 'Return to your country and to your kindred, that I may do you good,' I am not worthy of the least of all the deeds of steadfast love and all the faithfulness that you have shown to your servant, for with only my staff I crossed this Jordan, and now I have become two camps. Please deliver me from the hand of my brother, from the hand of Esau, for I fear him, that he may come and attack me, the mothers with the children. But you said, 'I will surely do you good, and make your offspring as the sand of the sea, which cannot be numbered for multitude.'" (Gen. 32:9–12)

Jacob's prayer was, *God, you have given me so much grace . . . give me more.*

After praying, Jacob gathered his wives and children and the rest of his possessions and sent them across the river in the dark of night. It was a dangerous and desperate move, and it left him alone on the far side of the river away from his brother, Esau. It must have been very quiet there all alone. He must have been exhausted from directing such a massive moving project. But there was no sleep ahead for Jacob. In the pitch-black darkness he felt a strong hand grip him, and a wrestling match ensued. This was no light-hearted tussle. It was an all-out, sweaty, strenuous, furious fight.

Wrestling in the Dark

The truth is, Jacob had been wrestling all his life. He had wrestled the birthright from his brother. He had wrestled the words of affirmation and blessing from his father. Then he wrestled the blessing of having Rachel as his wife from his father-in-law. Now he wrestled someone new. He just didn't know who—at least, not at first.

> And Jacob was left alone. And a man wrestled with him until the breaking of the day. When the man saw that he did not prevail against Jacob, he touched his hip socket, and Jacob's hip was put out of joint as he wrestled with him. (Gen. 32:24–25)

When his foe put his hip out of joint with just a touch, it began to dawn on Jacob that this was not just a man. Apparently his opponent was strong enough to have won the struggle at any moment but chose not to. As the dawn began to break, it began to dawn on Jacob just who his adversary was, especially when he said, "Let me go, for the day has broken" (Gen. 32:26). Jacob knew that no human can see the face of God and live (Ex. 33:20). And that convinced him. Jacob realized that his adversary was no mere man but God himself in human form—perhaps the pre-incarnate Christ.

> Jacob said, "I will not let you go unless you bless me." (Gen. 32:26)

If his opponent stayed and the sun rose so that Jacob could see his face, Jacob would not survive it. Jacob's life was in danger, yet Jacob begged him to stay. Why would he do that?

Jacob had come to the place where the blessing of God meant more to him than life itself. But Jacob was no longer willing to grasp and deceive and manipulate to get the blessings of God. He had become convinced that God would make good on those promises to him. Jacob wanted to do whatever it took—even if it cost him his life—to know the singular blessing that comes from knowing and being known by God himself.

Less concerned about getting all he wanted from God, Jacob wanted God to have all of him. And the way he will enter into that blessing is not only by coming clean with his brother about what he had done but also by coming clean before God about who he is.

> He said to him, "What is your name?" And he said, "Jacob." (Gen. 32:27)

This was a call for confession. It must have been painful just to say his own name, as at that moment it dripped with its original meaning and served as a confession of guilt. *I'm Jacob, the twister, the deceiver, the cheater. I have no right to any blessing.* But now God has gotten to the heart of the matter. And it is Jacob's heart that God has wanted. And God, in his grace, did not leave Jacob lingering in the pit of shame.

> Then he said, "Your name shall no longer be called Jacob, but Israel, for you have striven with God and with men, and have prevailed." (Gen. 32:28)

The name Israel literally means "God fights" or "God strives." God gave Jacob a new name, a new identity that defined him, not by his personal failure but by God's conquest of his heart, God's defeat of his old ways of deception, God's strength in his weakness. Jacob entered into a struggle with God, reminding God of his promises and begging him for his mercy, and it was Israel who emerged from it.

Walking with a Limp

To have Jacob's heart, God was prepared to dislocate Jacob's hip.[2] This was not a bone temporarily out of joint but a crippling injury. For the rest of his life, Jacob would walk with a limp, reminding him of this

---

[2]Numerous key insights and turns of phrases in this chapter come from Sinclair Ferguson's sermon series *The Life of Jacob*. This phrase comes from the sermon "All Night Wrestling," October 21, 2007, First Presbyterian Church, Colombia, SC.

long and difficult night. And yet we also read, "And there he blessed him." (Gen. 32:29). Is this what the blessing of God looks like, walking with a limp?

I remember sitting in a Bible study of Genesis a decade ago when the lecturer, Sue Johnson, said, "God wrenched his leg, and for the rest of his life Jacob walked with a limp." After class I raced to my car, full of emotion. Life at that point was a day-to-day struggle to manage my daughter's seizures. I knew that her life would soon be over and mine would never be the same. *I am going to walk with a limp for the rest of my life,* I said to myself through tears. I had always been strong. I had places to go and things to do. I didn't want a limp.

> *To be blessed is not to live free of struggle, but to cling to Christ in the midst of the struggle.*

I suppose there was a bit of a wrestling match going on between God and me as I sat there in the car. I knew that I could not overpower or manipulate God, and ultimately I realized I didn't want to get my own way anyway. What I wanted most was to be touched deeply by God in it, to see his face in it, to be changed by him through it.

I know I'm going to walk with a limp the rest of my life, I remember thinking as I put my head down on the steering wheel. *But I don't want that limp to remind me only of the struggle and the sorrow; I want it to remind me of a place of surrender, a place where God met me and blessed me through brokenness, a place of breakthrough into a deeper, more genuine relationship with God himself.*

For God to have our hearts sometimes requires the divine dislocation of whatever it is that makes us strong, so that Christ's strengths can shine through our weaknesses.[3] Jacob lost his wrestling match with God, but this loss was actually his greatest victory.

To be truly blessed by God is not to emerge from the struggles of life unscathed, but to emerge from them having been pressed more deeply into God, to have become more desperate for God, to have become convinced that having your identity flow from his victory in your life is

[3]Ibid.

worth more than walking away from the struggle with your health and position and lifestyle perfectly intact.

Have you ever become desperate enough for God, desperate enough for him to touch your life in a deep and permanent way, that you have been willing to risk everything to have him?

Becoming Israel

After Jacob dealt with Esau and entered into the Promised Land, for the first time in his life he built an altar to God, at Shechem, just as his grandfather Abraham had done before him (Gen. 12:7). Significantly, he called the altar "El-Elohe-Israel" (Gen. 33:20), that is, "God, the God of Israel." The God of his fathers was now Jacob's God.

Whereas before this his entire life had been characterized by his determination to seize the promises and blessings of God for himself, now he has realized that the fulfillment of the promises must be the work of God rather than the work of Jacob. He ceased struggling against God and was now able to receive from God.

It would be great if we could say that when we come to that place of open-handed surrender before God, then we can count on getting not only the blessing of God in that moment but also an assurance of ongoing blessings from God. But in Jacob's life we see that blessing does not mean a lack of struggle or sorrow.

It is a short time later that we find Jacob cradling a newborn baby as he sits beside the lifeless body of his beloved wife, Rachel. The love of Jacob's life has told him to name their son Ben-oni, which means "son of my sorrow." Of course, Jacob, named "deceiver" or "trickster" at his birth, knew firsthand the power of a name. So he refused Rachel's dying wish, and instead of calling him Ben-oni, Jacob named him *Benyamin*— "the son of my right hand."

Jacob had learned that God's greatest blessings sometimes come with great pain. And he was convinced that because God keeps his promises, even this great sorrow would be used in the hands of God for blessing his life. Notice what happens in Genesis 35:21:

Israel journeyed on and pitched his tent beyond the tower of Eder.

Did you catch it? It had been a long time since Jacob was renamed Israel, but this is the first time in the narrative of Jacob's life that he is actually called "Israel." For the first time, Jacob has *been* Israel. His confident faith in God's sure promise has overridden even his beloved wife's dying wish. Jacob has become Israel. He has put his hope in the God who has made and is keeping his promises to him.

Who is this God that Jacob has determined he can trust with even this heartbreaking sorrow? Jacob has put his hope in the God who will give the Son of his right hand to become the Son of his sorrow. This Son, Jesus, will one day stand in Samaria by what was called "Jacob's well," talking with a woman who will ask, "Are you greater than our father Jacob?"

And the answer is, *Oh yes, Jesus is far greater than Jacob!*

- While Jacob was full of greed and deceit, Jesus was full of grace and truth.
- While Jacob began grasping for the blessings of God, even from the day of his birth, Jesus's birth evidenced his refusal to grasp the blessings of God. "Though he was in the form of God, did not count equality with God a thing to be grasped, but made himself nothing" (Phil. 2:6–7). Jesus let go of the riches of heaven so that he might make us co-heirs with him of all he stands to inherit.
- While Jacob was given a vision of a ladder on which angels ascended and descended, Jesus made it clear that he *is* that ladder, the link between heaven and earth, saying, "No one comes to the Father except through me" (John 14:6).
- While Jacob wrestled alone on a dark night to gain a blessing for himself, Jesus wrestled alone on a dark night in the garden of Gethsemane to gain a blessing for you and me. Jesus knew he would not merely walk with a limp for the rest of his life but was about to offer up his life.
- While Jacob could not look on the face of his adversary and live, God has given to us "the light of the knowledge of the glory of God in the face of Jesus Christ" (2 Cor. 4:6).

Jacob asked the man who wrestled with him to tell him his name. To know a name is to have power. If he could know the name of God, he could call upon him for blessing at any time. On that dark night, while God blessed Jacob, he didn't tell him his name. But, my friend, what was denied to Jacob has been given to us! This is the name that is above every name, the name at which every knee will bow, the only name under heaven by which we must be saved. *Jesus is the sweetest name I know.*

Jesus himself is the greatest blessing God could ever give to you, and because he has given Christ for you and to you, you have everything you need. "He who did not spare his own Son but gave him up for us all, how will he not also with him graciously give us all things?" (Rom. 8:32). You don't have to grasp or grab; you need only to open your arms to receive.

> Blessed is he whose help is the God of Jacob,
> whose hope is in the LORD his God. (Ps. 146:5)

~~~~~~

How Genesis Points to What Is Yet to Come: They Will See His Face

As Jacob sent drove after drove of livestock in Esau's direction, he thought, "I may appease him with the present that goes ahead of me, and afterward I shall see his face. Perhaps he will accept me" (Gen. 32:20). Jacob knew he had deeply wronged his brother, and he did not know if he would see fury or forgiveness in his brother's face when they finally met again.

But it was another face that Jacob had to see first. An adversary whom Jacob first thought was a man came and took hold of him and wrestled with him throughout the night. Jacob asked the man to tell him his name, but he would not. His identity evidently became clear to Jacob, because we read that Jacob named the place Peniel, which means "face of God," saying, "For I have seen God face to face, and yet my life has been delivered" (Gen. 32:30). The face against which his own face had been pressed in the sweaty contest was none other than the face of God. God had promised and delivered his presence with Jacob wherever he went, but this was different. This was personal and intimate. This was transforming.

Jacob saw only the outline of the face of God through the dark of night. God withdrew at dawn to protect Jacob, because no man in his sinful state can see God's face and live (Ex. 33:20). In his holiness, God cannot look upon sin. Had Jacob, the deceiver, looked clearly into the face of God that night, he would not have been given the blessing he had done nothing to deserve but would have come under the curse he rightly deserved.

But the day is coming when Jacob and all redeemed rascals and sanctified schemers will see God face-to-face in the light and live. We will no longer "see in a mirror dimly, but then face to face" (1 Cor.13:12). On that day, the Spirit of God will have completed his work of sanctification in all who belong to him so that we will be able to look in the face of God without fear of being consumed or ashamed or rejected. This will be the day we have always longed for, the closeness and intimacy with God we've always wanted.

"Blessed are the pure in heart," Jesus said, "for they shall see God" (Matt. 5:8). Those who will one day look into the face of God are not naturally pure. This purity is a blessing from God. They are those who have come clean with God; they've confessed to him who they really are. But God has not left them that way. His Spirit has been at work purifying them, making them holy as he is holy.

John saw a vision of this coming day of reunion and revelation. "They will see his face," he wrote in Revelation 22:4. This will be the face that nestled to Mary's breast to nurse as a baby. It will be the face that looked with compassion on those who came to him for healing and was marked with tears at the death of his friend Lazarus (John 11:35). It will be the face that "shone like the sun" when he was transfigured on the mountain (Matt. 17:2). This is the face that was turned toward Jerusalem, knowing that going to Jerusalem meant going to the cross (Luke 9:51); the face that was pressed into the ground in agony as he wrestled with God on that dark night in Gethsemane (Matt. 26:39); the face that was spit on and struck by those for whom he died (Matt. 26:67). This is the face that was wrapped in cloth in the tomb (John 20:7) and the face that appeared to the disciples after the resurrection, saying to Thomas, "Have you believed because you have seen me? Blessed are those who have not seen and yet have believed" (John 20:29).

When John writes in Revelation 22 that we will "see his face," it is near the end of his description of his vision of the new heaven and new earth. And we realize that he has saved the best for last. While the beauty and abundance, the healing and the wholeness, of heaven will be more wonderful than we can fully grasp now, it will not be as wonderful as looking into the face of Jesus. What will truly make heaven, heaven, will be seeing the face of Christ and living in the light of his face for all eternity.

Jacob

GENESIS 25:19–35:21

Getting the Discussion Going

1. Take a minute to imagine the day-to-day reality of living in the home of Isaac and Rebekah along with Jacob and Esau. What do they talk about around the dinner table, and what topics do they avoid? What are the nagging issues and unresolved hurts? What is it like when Esau brings his Hittite wives home and after Jacob leaves home?

Getting to the Heart of It

2. Jacob's life was marked by struggle even before he was born, and throughout his life we saw him struggle. How was Jacob's whole life really a struggle with God to see who was in control?

3. God said that Jacob struggled with men and with God and "prevailed" or "won." In what way(s) did Jacob "win" in his struggle with God?

4. Over and over again in Genesis we are seeing that God does not choose whom he will use based on human custom or personal virtue. Why do you think that is, and on what does he base his choice? (Verses to consult include Rom. 9:6–16; Eph. 1:3–4, 11–12; 2 Tim. 1:9.)

5. Many people talk about wrestling with God, when they're really talking about rebelling against God or resisting God. We notice that it is God who initiated the wrestling match with Jacob, and it was certainly purposeful. How would you explain God's purpose in dealing with Jacob

in this way, and how is this vastly different from the way we might talk about our struggling with God's ways, God's Word, or God's plans as "wrestling with God"?

6. According to the Westminster Shorter Catechism (Q. 35), sanctification is "the work of God's free grace, whereby we are renewed in the whole man after the image of God, and are enabled more and more to die unto sin, and live unto righteousness." How does Jacob picture for us the process of sanctification in the life of a believer?

Getting Personal

7. This week we observed Jacob, who spent much of his life interested in getting God's blessings but not really that interested in knowing God himself or having the blessing of intimate relationship with God. In our consumerist culture it comes naturally to approach God looking for what we can get from him rather than seeking how we can get more of him. Can you see this in your own life, and would you be willing to share how God has been at work in you to help you to value him more than just his blessings?

Getting How It Fits into the Big Picture

8. Throughout this study, we're trying to grasp how some of these familiar stories fit into the bigger story of God's plan for redemption. How do we see God continuing and protecting his plan through Jacob's life for the promised offspring?

Joseph

Genesis 37–50

Personal Bible Study

Joseph

GENESIS 37-50

1. Read Genesis 37:1–11. What three reasons do you find in these verses for Joseph's brothers' hatred and jealousy toward him?

~ Genesis 37:2

~ Genesis 37:4

~ Genesis 37:5–11

2. Read Genesis 37:12–36. In what ways do Joseph's brothers show great callousness and cruelty?

3. Read Genesis 39:1–23. Although God never spoke directly to Joseph like he did to Abraham, Isaac, and Jacob, we read eight times in this chapter that "the LORD" (using the personal covenant name for God)

was with Joseph. Why might the narrator want to assure us that God was with Joseph in such a personal way?

4. Read Genesis 40:1–22. How must it have encouraged Joseph when his interpretations of the dreams of the chief baker and chief cupbearer proved true?

5. Read Genesis 41:1–45. How does it become obvious in this chapter that the Lord truly has been with Joseph?

6. Read Genesis 41:46–56. Note the names Joseph gave to his two sons born in Egypt. What do they reveal about how God has worked in him throughout his years of slavery and imprisonment?

～ Manasseh:

～ Ephraim:

7. While Joseph seems to have forgiven his brothers before they arrived in Egypt, he put them through a series of tests to see if they were still the same hardhearted men who sold him into slavery. What do the following verses reveal about changes in Joseph's brothers?

～ Genesis 42:18–28

～ Genesis 42:29–43:10

~ Genesis 43:11–34

~ Genesis 44:1–34

8. In Genesis 45:1–15, we see the climax of the story as Joseph re-vealed himself to his brothers. Note that Joseph repeated three times that God had sent him there. How could he say to his brothers, "You sold me here" (Gen. 45:5) and also, "It was not you who sent me here, but God" (Gen. 45:8)?

9. At the very end of Genesis, in 50:19–20, Joseph repeated the theme of God's sovereignty, which serves as a summary of his entire life, say-ing to his brothers, "Do not fear, for am I in the place of God? As for you, you meant evil against me, but God meant it for good, to bring it about that many people should be kept alive, as they are today." Explain in your own words what he means by this statement.

10. How does Joseph point to Christ? Look up the verses in the sec-ond column of the chart below, noting the ways Joseph foreshadowed Jesus.

Joseph	Christ
"Israel loved Joseph." (Gen. 37:3)	Matt. 3:17 *Just as Joseph was dearly loved by his father, so was Jesus his Father's beloved Son.*
"His brothers . . . hated him even more for his dreams and for his words." (Gen. 37:4, 8)	John 1:11; 5:18; 7:5

"His brothers were jealous of him." (Gen. 37:11)	Matt. 27:18
"They conspired against him to kill him." (Gen. 37:18)	Matt. 12:15
"They stripped him of his robe." (Gen. 37:23)	Matt. 27:28
"They . . . threw him into a pit. . . . They . . . lifted him out of the pit." (Gen. 37:24, 28)	Matt. 12:41; Mark 16:6
Joseph served as a slave. (Gen. 39:1)	Phil. 2:6–7
Joseph was falsely accused. (Gen. 39:14–18)	Matt. 26:59–60
Joseph's "feet were hurt with fetters; his neck was put in a collar of iron." (Ps. 105:18)	Matt. 27:28–30; John 19:1–2
Joseph was exalted over all Egypt. (Gen. 41:39, 40)	Phil. 2:9; 1 Pet. 3:22
"Pharaoh said to all the Egyptians, 'Go to Joseph.' . . . All the earth came to Egypt to Joseph to buy grain." (Gen. 41:55, 57)	John 1:16; 6:35; Acts 4:12
Joseph forgave his brothers for their cruelty to him. (Gen. 45:5)	Luke 23:34
Joseph said, "It was not you who sent me here, but God." (Gen. 45:8)	Isa. 53:4; Acts 2:23; 4:27–28

Can Anything Good Come out of This?

What pictures are stuck on the flannel-graph board of your memory from the story of Joseph? Many of us come to the story of Joseph fully stocked with Sunday school images and life lessons.

- We see Joseph excitedly telling his family about his dreams that suggest they will one day bow down to little brother, and we remember being taught that we should not brag.
- We see our multicolor crayon creation of Joseph's coat of many colors and remember being taught about avoiding the jealousy that led Joseph's brothers to plot his death.
- We see Joseph fleeing the aggressive advances of Potiphar's wife and remember being admonished to run away from temptation.
- We see Joseph rising to prominence in Potiphar's house, then in the prison, and later in Pharaoh's court, and we remember being taught about the rewards that come from being industrious and trust-worthy.
- We picture Joseph's brothers bowing down to him in his Egyptian garb, unaware of who he is, and we are inspired by his example to forgive those who have hurt us.

Certainly there are many life lessons to be learned from Joseph's godly example. And for some of us, this is the primary way we've read and understood the story of Joseph as well as the rest of the Old Testament. We've come again and again to the Bible's narrative looking

238 Week 9: Joseph

for the take-away of examples to follow, biblical principles for godly living. But is that the primary way we are to read Joseph's story and the rest of the Old Testament?

for the take-away of examples to follow, biblical principles for godly living. But is that the primary way we are to read Joseph's story and the rest of the Old Testament?

Consider that Moses gave us an account of the creation of the earth and all that is in it in two chapters and the story of the fall of humanity in one chapter. He took eleven chapters to introduce us to Abraham, the father of the people of God. Since then we've been following the line of the Promised One from Abraham to Isaac to Jacob. And if we look ahead, we realize that the Promised One is not going to come through Joseph but through his big brother Judah. So why did Moses dedicate one-third of the book of Genesis—thirteen chapters—to Joseph?

Perhaps Jesus can help us with this question. Remember where we started this study—with Jesus coming alongside the disciples who were walking to Emmaus. These disciples had thought Jesus was the Messiah, but when Jesus was crucified, they figured they must have been wrong about him—because surely God would not allow the Savior of the world to suffer in that way.

> And he said to them, "O foolish ones, and slow of heart to believe all that the prophets have spoken! Was it not necessary that the Christ should suffer these things and enter into his glory?" (Luke 24:25–26)

How should they have known it was "necessary" that the Christ should suffer?

The next verse says that "beginning with Moses and all the Prophets, he interpreted to them in all the Scriptures the things concerning himself" (Luke 24:27). As we try to imagine what Jesus might have said as he worked his way through Genesis, we have to ask, what did Jesus say to these disciples about the story of Joseph? Do you think he worked his way through Joseph's story, using it to reinforce lessons about humility and fleeing temptation and forgiveness? More likely, when he got to the account of Joseph's life in Genesis, that what he had just said, about its being necessary for the Christ to suffer before entering his glory, really began to make sense. When Jesus began to explain "the things concerning himself," perhaps it was when he got to Joseph's story that it first became clear to the disciples that they should not have been so surprised that when Messiah came, he was rejected by his own people and put to death. If they had understood that the Old Testament had given them pictures and pointers of who Messiah would be, what he would do, and how he would accomplish his work, they would have known that the savior God sent would certainly suffer before he was exalted.

Joseph was the first of many deliverers God sent who would picture and point to the greater deliverer God would send in his own Son. Joseph's story pictured for all the generations of the people of God how this Savior-Son would accomplish his saving work—suffering before glory, rejection before acceptance, humiliation leading to exaltation, descending into the lowest pit before being raised to the highest pinnacle.

When Jesus opened the minds of the disciples to understand the Scriptures, perhaps he pointed to Joseph and said something like, "Remember how Joseph was rejected by the sons of Jacob? So was I. Remember how Joseph's brothers wouldn't listen to what he said and conspired to kill him? So did my Jewish brothers refuse to listen to me and conspire to kill me. Remember how Joseph left his home of privilege with the father who loved him and became a slave in Egypt? That's what happened to me when I left my Father's home in heaven and came to this world, taking the form of a servant. Remember how Joseph was eventually exalted to the king's right hand and his brothers came and bowed down to him? That is what is ahead for me. Shortly I will ascend to my Father's right hand, and the day will come when every knee is going to bow and every tongue is going to confess that I am Lord."

Joseph's life was a preview of the saving work of God that would ultimately be accomplished in Jesus Christ. And if we want to see how God will accomplish the salvation of his people, we will explore Joseph's story not primarily to learn from Joseph's example but so that we might see the greater Savior to whom Joseph points.

Beloved Son

By the time Joseph arrived in Jacob's family, there was already a houseful of siblings. From the very beginning of his story we are told that "Israel loved Joseph more than any other of his sons, because he was the son of his old age" (Gen. 37:3). The intensity of the love Jacob had for his son Joseph was matched only by the intensity of the hatred Joseph's brothers had for him. Genesis 37:4 says, "When his brothers saw that their father loved him more than all his brothers, they hated him and could not speak peacefully to him." (Can't you just feel the tension?) The antagonism of Joseph's brothers toward this favored son was only exacerbated when Joseph told them about his dreams:

> He said to them, "Hear this dream that I have dreamed: Behold, we were binding sheaves in the field, and behold, my sheaf arose and stood upright. And behold, your sheaves gathered around it and bowed down to my sheaf." His brothers said to him, "Are you indeed to reign over us? Or are you indeed to rule over us?" So they hated him even more for his dreams and for his words. Then he dreamed another dream and told it to his brothers and said, "Behold, I have dreamed another dream. Behold, the sun, the moon, and eleven stars were bowing down to me." But when he told it to his father and to his brothers, his father rebuked him and said to him, "What is this dream that you have dreamed? Shall I and your mother and your brothers indeed come to bow ourselves to the ground before you?" And his brothers were jealous of him, but his father kept the saying in mind. (Gen. 37:6–11)

Understandably, Joseph's brothers were offended by the suggestion that God had given him a vision of the future in which they would one day bow down to him. They already resented him for being their father's clear favorite, and this just added more logs to that fire.

In a culture in which elders were reverenced by the younger, Jacob was understandably taken aback too, yet he was not quick to condemn his young son's dream. He must have thought back to that night when God clearly spoke to him through a dream in which he saw angels ascending and descending on a ladder that went up into heaven. Jacob knew the power of a dream from God.

Jacob should also have remembered the pain inflicted upon him by a father who obviously favored his brother, Esau, and been determined not to inflict the pain of parental favoritism on his own sons. But evidently he didn't. And when his oldest son, Reuben, slept with Jacob's concubine, Bilhah (Gen. 35:22), it gave Jacob an excuse to give the status of the firstborn to another son—his favorite son, Joseph. That was the significance of the colorful robe he gave to Joseph. This was not a working man's garment but the royal robe of one who would one day rule as head of the family.

Sometimes, because we grew up hearing a sanitized, kid-friendly version of this story, we can be unmoved by the horror and harshness of what happened to Joseph. But now that we are grown-ups, let's allow ourselves to see it for what it is. When we read that his brothers "stripped" his robe from him, this is the same word as would be used for skinning an animal. This was a violent attack. The term for throwing him into the dry cistern is the term used for discarding a dead body. Joseph lay bruised and bleeding on the rocky floor of the dried-out cistern where his brothers intended to let him starve to death. And as he begged his brothers to spare his life, they were callous enough to sit down to supper and simply ignore his agonized cries (Gen. 42:21). While their original plan was to let him die, one brother got the idea of making a little money on the deal, so they ended up selling Joseph off as a slave.

Perhaps Joseph spent his first weeks and months in Egypt looking for his father to show up and rescue him. He didn't know his father thought he was dead. There had to have been long nights sobbing in the darkness, longing for his own bed, his own home, his own people. Yet somehow, in the painful darkness of the pit, in the confines of the slave quarters, and later in prison, Joseph

> *Because God meant my suffering for good, I know he is with me in the darkest of times.*

not only knew that God was with him but also was confident in God's plan to use him. That confidence gave him peace as he waited for God to work out his plan, even as that plan brought him pain.

Joseph held on to the revelation from God of his future exaltation. His memory of this vivid dream, and his confidence that it was a vision from God of the future God would bring about, enabled him to endure the violent attack of his brothers, the humiliation of standing naked before heathen slave traders, being carried off to Egypt, and so much more.

242   Week 9: Joseph

It reminds me of what the writer to the Hebrews says about Jesus, "who for the joy that was set before him endured the cross, despising the shame, and is seated at the right hand of the throne of God" (Heb. 12:2). Jesus, too, was confident in the plan of God to use him to save his brothers who hated him. He too was stripped of his clothing and descended into the pit of death. He too cried out with tears "to him who was able to save him from death" (Heb. 5:7) and was not saved. His confidence in what was ahead when he would be exalted in heaven at the right hand of God, surrounded by a great multitude of his brothers empowered Jesus to endure the cross.

One day Joseph lived in the comfortable home of his father where he enjoyed the privileges of the being the chosen heir—and the next he was targeted, attacked, and humiliated—ending up as a common slave in a foreign country. What a picture this provides to us of the humiliation of God's beloved Son, Jesus, who was not an unwilling victim like Joseph but willingly offered himself up to be treated this way.

> Christ Jesus . . . though he was in the form of God, did not count equality with God a thing to be grasped, but made himself nothing, taking the form of a servant, being born in the likeness of men. And being found in human form, he humbled himself by becoming obedient to the point of death, even death on a cross. (Phil. 2:5–8)

Joseph's emergence from the pit of death and eventual ascension to the right hand of Pharaoh also provides to us a picture of the resurrection and glorification of God's beloved Son, Jesus.

> Therefore God has highly exalted him and bestowed on him the name that is above every name, so that at the name of Jesus every knee should bow, in heaven and on earth and under the earth, and every tongue confess that Jesus Christ is Lord, to the glory of God the Father. (Phil. 2:9–11)

Just as Jacob's sons one day bowed before Joseph, as God had told him in his dream, so the day is coming when all will bow before Jacob's greater Son, Jesus.

Fruitful Sufferer

At the very beginning of his covenant relationship with his chosen people, God predicted tremendous suffering ahead for his people:

> The LORD said to Abram, "Know for certain that your offspring will be sojourners in a land that is not theirs and will be servants there, and *they will be afflicted for four hundred years.* But I will bring judgment on the nation that they serve, and afterward they shall come out with great possessions." (Gen. 15:13–14)

God's people would suffer. But it would not be wasted, meaningless suffering. It would be fruitful suffering. They would emerge from Egypt with great wealth and great in number, preserved as a race rather than intermarried with the Canaanites. How would they become "strangers in a foreign land"? Through the suffering and salvation of Joseph.

After dreaming his dreams, it is certain that spending years as a slave and then years in a foreign prison was not the trajectory Joseph anticipated for his life. This was not the pathway to becoming the exalted leader of his family that Joseph had expected. Certainly Joseph must have wondered at times if something had gone terribly wrong with God's plan for his future and the future of his family. Yet when we hear Joseph speak during his years of captivity, it is not complaint or self-pity or rage that we hear. Over and over again, we hear him speak of God in great submission and confidence.

When Potiphar's wife tried to seduce him, he said, "How then can I do this great wickedness and sin against God?" (Gen. 39:9). No one from his family was around to see his sin, and certainly no one in this culture would have blinked an eye, since sexual promiscuity was a daily part of all slaveholding households. But Joseph knew that God was with him and that God would see, so it was unthinkable to him. When he interpreted dreams in prison and for Pharaoh he said, "It is not in me; God will give Pharaoh a favorable answer" (Gen. 41:16). Joseph not only knew God was with him, but he also knew God was at work in him, working through him. Joseph did not assume that his suffering was a sign that God had forgotten him or abandoned him. Over and over again in his story we read that "the LORD was with him. And whatever he did, the LORD made it succeed" (Gen. 39:23).

How different Joseph was from the way we are. We are so quick to assume that if God is with us, there will be no pit, no pain. When the unthinkable happens to us, we accuse God of abandoning us, not caring about us, not loving us. Because we think it is God's job to hover around us ensuring our comfort, whenever we find ourselves in a hard and dark place, we think God has somehow fallen down on the job.

Far from complaining or becoming embittered about his suffering, Joseph emerged from prison celebrating what God was doing through his life by means of the suffering.

> Before the year of famine came, two sons were born to Joseph. Asenath, the daughter of Potiphera priest of On, bore them to him. Joseph called the name of the firstborn Manasseh. "For," he said, "God has made me forget all my hardship and all my father's house." The name of the second he called Ephraim, "For God has made me fruitful in the land of my affliction." (Gen. 41:50–52)

Born to him in Egypt by an Egyptian wife, Joseph gave his sons Hebrew names, confident that God was not finished working through him on behalf of his people. The names were in fact songs of praise to God both for the work God had done *in* Joseph to keep him from becoming bitter toward his brothers for their cruelty and for the work God had done *through* Joseph to bless the people of Egypt. Joseph had eyes to see that his suffering had not gone to waste; it was not random or meaningless but fruitful. Joseph didn't turn his attention to being fruitful only after the season of suffering was over. In the land of his affliction, in the middle of the struggle, in the heart of the darkness, Joseph was confident that God was at work.

Because God meant my suffering for good, I will not let it be wasted.

But was there ever a more fruitful sufferer than Jesus? Surely the fruitfulness of Joseph's suffering was a foreshadowing of the eternally abundant fruitfulness of the suffering of Christ:

Although he was a son, he learned obedience through what he suffered. And being made perfect, he became the source of eternal salvation to all who obey him. (Heb. 5:8–9)

If you have turned to Christ in faith, you are part of the great harvest of fruit produced through the suffering of Christ.

Exalted Savior

One day, Joseph was at the very bottom. How could one have sunk any lower than to be a Hebrew slave in an Egyptian prison? But in just one day, Joseph went from the very bottom to the very top. In one day he went from the pit of prison to the palace of Pharaoh. Joseph interpreted Pharaoh's dream, which predicted a coming famine. And when Joseph outlined a plan to Pharaoh for preparing for the famine, Pharaoh not only accepted the plan but also put Joseph in charge, making him prime minister of all Egypt.

[Joseph] gathered up all the food of these seven years, which occurred in the land of Egypt, and put the food in the cities. He put in every city the food from the fields around it. And Joseph stored up grain in great abundance, like the sand of the sea, until he ceased to measure it, for it could not be measured. (Gen. 41:48–49)

Seven years later, when the time of famine came and the hungry came to Egypt after hearing about the storehouses of grain Joseph had laid up, Pharaoh sent them to Joseph:

Pharaoh said to all the Egyptians, "Go to Joseph. What he says to you, do." So when the famine had spread over all the land, Joseph opened all the storehouses and sold to the Egyptians, for the famine was severe in the land of Egypt. Moreover, all the earth came to Egypt to Joseph to buy grain, because the famine was severe over all the earth. (Gen. 41:55–57)

Here, as in so many other ways, Joseph points us to the heart of the ministry of Jesus—the one who said, "I am the bread of life; whoever comes to me shall not hunger" (John 6:35). Just as Joseph was the one to whom the whole world came to be fed, just as he became the savior of the world in his day, so Jesus is the one to whom the whole world must come.

"There is salvation in no one else, for there is no other name under heaven given among men by which we must be saved" (Acts 4:12).

It must have been that day, when Joseph's brothers first showed up in Egypt and bowed themselves before him with their faces to the ground (Gen. 42:6), that everything finally clicked into place for Joseph. Just as he had dreamed so many years ago, his brothers were bowing before him. God had given him the dream, and God had brought it about. His recognition of God's invisible hand at work in his circumstances—even in the cruelty of his brothers—left no room for bitterness.

From this vantage point he could see that in all of his suffering—all the humiliations of slavery, all the discomforts of prison, all the years of longing for the kindness of his father and the comforts of home—God had been at work to put him in place to provide for his family when the famine came. This was not just any family that needed to be saved. This was the family from whom the Promised One would come. These were the people God had called out from all the people of the world for himself who were destined to live in the land God had promised to them, where they would produce the Son who would be the great Savior. As the children of Israel read Joseph's story as they prepared to enter the Promised Land, they must have grown in confidence that God would continue to provide for them and guide them in his providence.

Joseph knew it was the evil done to him by his brothers that had set the whole chain of events in motion and brought him to where he was— evil they were responsible for. But he also knew their evil actions were in fact part of God's sovereign plan to bless his people. This enabled him to say to his brothers:

> As for you, you meant evil against me, but God meant it for good, to bring it about that many people should be kept alive, as they are today. (Gen. 50:20)

Surely Jesus could have said the same thing to those who conspired against him, lied about him, beat him, and nailed him to the cross: "You intended to harm me, but God intended it all for good. You think this was all your plan, but it is God who has brought me to this place so that I can accomplish a great and good purpose, so that I can give life to all those who will come to me."

This was the theme of Joseph's life, the climax of his story. And this was the theme of Jesus's life, the climax of his story. And I have to ask you, is this resounding truth and confidence anywhere in *your* story? It is anywhere in your perspective about the circumstances that have shaped your life? What in your life would change everything about your life if you were to write across it, "You meant it for evil, but God meant it for good"?

~ That man who touched you and took your innocence and dignity from you—he meant evil against you. Are you open to considering that God wants to use it for something good?

~ That coworker who maligned you or that boss who refused to advance you—she meant evil against you. Can you begin to believe that God has intended all along to use it for good?

~ The organization that used you and then forgot you, the spouse who betrayed you, the sibling who stole from you—in their selfishness they meant evil against you, but are you ready to see what God wants you to see from Joseph's life and from Jesus's death, which is that God intends to use it for good in your life and in the lives of others?

What circumstance in your life have you seen as a tragedy or injustice that took you off the course of blessing God had in mind for your life? Can you see that nothing and no one—not even you—can derail God's plan for your life? Can you see that God did not abandon you but that he has been there with you in the pit, planning to use it to accomplish something good in your life?

It is this truth about God's sovereignty over every aspect of my life that has made all the difference in the lowest places of my life.

David and I had never heard of Zellweger syndrome before our daughter, Hope, was born with the fatal genetic disorder and lived a short six months. But once we had a child with Zellweger, we knew that we are both carriers of the recessive gene trait for the syndrome. That means that whenever we have a child, that child has a 25 percent of having the fatal syndrome.

Most losses are not singular but rather a series of losses that come like waves. And for a while after Hope died, I grieved her death, her absence from me. Then I grieved her life, the limitations of it and the suffering in it. And then I began to grieve our loss of potential. Because after having Hope, we felt that the wisest thing was not to have any more children, and so David had a vasectomy.

It was a year and a half after Hope died that I lay in bed one morning thinking about getting up, when my thoughts turned to remembering that I still had not started my period. And as I did the mental calculation I realized that I was not just late—I was really late. I could not hide the flicker of fear from David. "That's *impossible*," I told him. But after dropping him off at work I went directly to the drugstore to buy a pregnancy test. I wanted to take the test, rule it out, and get on with my day. But there were quickly and clearly two blue lines.

My heart began to pound as I hopped in my car and drove up to David's office. I just shook my head *yes* when I saw him. Then we sat there shaking our heads together, wondering how this had happened, discussing how we had both wished at times that David had not had that vasectomy, and assuming that God had overruled our actions. We felt a cautious sense of joy that we might have another healthy child to raise and enjoy—something we wanted but had not expected. But we also felt afraid—afraid that we might have another child we would love and lose.

David feared I would blame him; I feared he would blame me. Then I remembered the words Joseph had said to his brothers, and they seemed to apply. That's when I told David, "It wasn't you who sent me here, but God." I wasn't suggesting that God had done something outside the bounds of the natural order but that he is Lord over the natural order. This pregnancy was no accident that happened outside of God's sovereign plan for our lives. In fact, the confidence that God was in it paved the way for us to accept it, even welcome it, even when we learned that this child, our son Gabriel, also had the fatal syndrome.

Recognizing God's sovereignty over our circumstances and embracing a confidence that God would use even this for good made all the difference as we faced loving and losing another child. Instead of wanting to avoid the suffering, I begged God to make me fruitful in the suffering. Instead of accusing God of abandoning me, I wanted to experience him like never before in the darkness of the days to come. Knowing that we were not the victims of incredible odds but the beloved children of God, held in the sovereign hands of God, meant that this was not something that had slipped through the cracks apart from God's notice, but something that was written in the book of our lives and Gabriel's life even before our lives began.

> You saw me before I was born. Every day of my life was recorded in your book. Every moment was laid out before a single day had passed. (Ps. 139:16 NLT)

Most of us may be willing to say that God allows suffering into our lives, but we are certain that he would never initiate it, send it, or be in any way behind it. We know that God does not *do* evil, so it is hard for us to grasp that he could in any way be involved with anything in this world that brings us pain. That just doesn't seem right.

Certainly it is true that God *allows* suffering. We see that over and over in Scripture. And so while it is not inaccurate to say that God *allows* evil and suffering, it is inadequate, and perhaps misleading, to limit defining God's involvement in suffering to this word, suggesting that he only passively (and, we hope, perhaps reluctantly) gives permission for pain to invade a believer's life. We need only read the psalmist's commentary on Joseph's story to have some serious holes poked in our "God only allows" argument:

> When he summoned a famine on the land
>> and broke all supply of bread,
> he had sent a man ahead of them,
>> Joseph, who was sold as a slave.
> His feet were hurt with fetters;
>> his neck was put in a collar of iron;
> until what he had said came to pass,
>> the word of the LORD tested him. (Ps. 105:16–19)

As we take Scripture at face value, we see that God did not merely allow the famine; he summoned it. He did not merely allow Joseph's brothers to sell him as a slave; he sent him to Egypt. Joseph was put to the test of suffering by God's decree. God ordained all the circumstances that brought Joseph so much pain.

Obviously Joseph understood this. Joseph did not say, "You *meant* evil against me, but God *used* it for good," as if God runs along behind circumstances outside of his control, coming up with ways to make something good out of the mess after the fact. God is no passive observer who finally becomes involved only after disaster strikes, saying optimistically, "I'm sure I can figure out how to turn this into something good!" He has a purpose and design in what is happening to us from the beginning, and even though what is happening to us might not *be* good, God intends it all for our ultimate good.

When I've found the truth—that God is sovereign over the suffering in my life and intends to use it for good—not only hard to understand but difficult to believe, and difficult to swallow, what has helped me most is to look at the one Joseph was always meant to point us to— our Savior Jesus Christ. Only when I turn my gaze to the cross of Christ can I begin to believe that God really can use something desperately evil and painful for incredible good. When we look at the cross, we see the most innocent victim, the most immense suffering, the greatest injustice, the most hurtful betrayal, the greatest physical and emotional agony. Surely putting the pure Son of God on the cross was the greatest evil of all time.

> *I know God intends to use my suffering for good, even when I can't see what that good is.*

But was it not also the greatest good ever accomplished? Because of the cross, guilty sinners like you and me don't get what we deserve— punishment. Instead, we get what we don't deserve—the mercy and forgiveness of God. When we look at the cross, it fills us with confidence that God is sovereign over everything—including evil and suffering. And if he can intend the evil and suffering of the cross of Christ for such amazing good, we can begin to believe that he can and will use what is evil and may seem senseless in our lives for good.

Joseph could look back over his life and see that God intended to use his suffering to put him in place to save his family when the famine came. But the truth is, we may not be as fortunate as Joseph was to be able to look back at our suffering and point to the clear purpose God had in it. We may never see in this life exactly how God is using our loss for good. But just because we can't see or articulate clearly his purpose in our suffering doesn't mean he doesn't have one.

The question is not about whether God will use the suffering in your life for good. That question has been settled in the life of Joseph and far more in the life and death of Jesus. Paul wrote of this as a settled issue when he wrote, "*We know* that for those who love God all things work together for good" (Rom. 8:28). The question is, do *you* know this? Has this issue been settled deep in *your* soul? Is the reality of God's sovereign providence shaping your perspective about the painful places in your life?

I don't know how God is going to use what you've experienced for good, but I know he will. Your suffering will one day give way to great glory. This is the God-given dream that Joseph held onto in the dark. This is the joy set before Christ that enabled him to endure the cross. This, too, is your sure and certain hope that can enable you to endure whatever your future may hold.

> For I consider that the sufferings of this present time are not worth comparing with the glory that is to be revealed to us. (Rom. 8:18)

How Genesis Points to What Is Yet to Come: When His Glory Is Revealed

What kept Joseph going all of those years spent as a slave in a foreign country and as a prisoner in a foreign jail? It was the dream that God had given to him about the future and his confidence that it would come to pass. God had given him a vision of the future in which he was exalted, and that strengthened Joseph to face the present in which he was suffering.

The same is true for Jesus. The writer of Hebrews tells us it was "for the joy that was set before him" that Jesus "endured the cross, despising the shame, and is seated at the right hand of the throne of God" (Heb.

12:2). What strengthened Jesus for the suffering and humiliation of the cross was his confidence in the glory to come.

How can we, like Joseph and like Jesus, endure the suffering inherent in living life in this broken world? It is as we fix our gaze on the glory that is to come that we are strengthened to endure the suffering we face today. Our confidence in the glory ahead for us, and our valuing the glory ahead for us, shape our perspective about our current struggles. Paul tells us how:

> So we do not lose heart. Though our outer self is wasting away, our inner self is being renewed day by day. For this light momentary affliction is preparing for us an eternal weight of glory beyond all comparison, as we look not to the things that are seen but to the things that are unseen. For the things that are seen are transient, but the things that are unseen are eternal. (2 Cor. 4:16–18)

When we read Paul describe his troubles as "light" and "momentary," we wonder if he really knew what it is like to suffer. But the truth is that Paul's suffering included being imprisoned, beaten, stoned, shipwrecked, robbed, hungry, thirsty, cold, and naked—none of which we would describe as insignificant or brief. For Paul it was a matter of comparison and perspective. Paul saw the suffering of this life through the lens of eternity, in light of the glory to come.

Paul saw a set of balance scales. On one side of the scales is the suffering of this life—the temporary pains and short-term losses. On the other side of the scales is the glory we will experience in heaven—the satisfying joy of being with Jesus, the overflowing inheritance of our eternal reward, the radiant newness of our glorified bodies, and the unending pleasure of living in the presence of God with no shame, no sorrow, and no suffering. When Paul said his trials were light, he didn't mean they were easy or painless. He meant that compared with what was coming they were small and insignificant. All our hard times now are like feathers on one side of the scales compared to the weight of glory ahead for us.

Joseph was confident that his suffering was purposeful and the promise of glory was sure. So was Jesus. And so can we be confident that there is the purpose and promise for all who are willing to share in the suffering of Christ—"we suffer with him in order that we may also be glorified with him" (Rom. 8:17). Just as the sufferings of Joseph were purposeful in the plan of God, which was to put him in the place to be a savior of the world in his time, and just as the sufferings of Christ were purposeful to make him the great Savior of the world for all time, so can "we rejoice in our sufferings, knowing that suffering produces endurance, and endurance produces character, and character produces hope" (Rom. 5:3–4). "We rejoice in hope of the glory of God" (Rom. 5:2).

What will enable you to suffer patiently and purposefully is your confidence in what is to come, your sure hope that "after you have suffered a little while, the God of all grace, who has called you to his eternal glory in Christ, will himself restore, confirm, strengthen, and establish you. To him be the dominion forever and ever. Amen" (1 Pet. 5:10–11).

Discussion Guide

Joseph

GENESIS 37-50

Getting the Discussion Going

1. Dreams play a significant part in Joseph's story. There are three sets of two dreams: Joseph's two dreams, the chief cupbearer's and the chief baker's dreams, and Pharaoh's dreams. Have you ever had a powerful dream? Are you able to remember your dreams and relate them to other people?

Getting to the Heart of It

2. Joseph's story in Genesis 37 begins with Joseph having two dreams that he tells his family about. Why do you think God gave Joseph those dreams, and what purposes did they serve in his life?

3. How were the dreams of Joseph, his fellow prisoners, and Pharaoh different from the kinds of dreams we have today? What do we have today that Joseph did not have that provides us with insight and even certainty about what is coming in the future?

4. We'd like to believe that if we belong to God and we are living lives that are pleasing to God, then his presence in our lives will protect us from significant suffering. We have to wonder if Joseph thought to himself, "I believed in that dream you gave me; I ran from temptation. Is this how you reward those who serve you, Lord?" What aspects of Joseph's experience, as well as that of other people in the Bible, help us to see that obeying God does not necessarily protect us from suffering?

5. How would you respond to someone who said that Joseph was just really unlucky at times and at other times really lucky?

6. The God of the Bible is so great that he not only breaks through the natural order to do miracles but is also involved concurrently and confluently in all that occurs in this world without violating the natural order. In other words, God is involved in our world in non-miraculous ways, directing all things toward his foreordained ends for the good of his people. Which do you find more challenging to believe—that God does miracles to accomplish his purposes or that God works through ordinary occurrences to bring about his intended ends?

Getting Personal

7. The theme of Joseph's story is found in his words, "It was not you who sent me here, but God" (Gen. 45:8), as well as, "You meant evil against me, but God meant it for good, to bring it about that many people should be kept alive, as they are today" (Gen. 50:20). Are there any experiences in your life that, although painful or hurtful, you can already see God using for good in your life?

Getting How It Fits into the Big Picture

8. Throughout this study, we have been seeking to grasp how the passage we're studying fits into the bigger story of God's plan for redemption. And while we see a principle we can apply in our own lives from Joseph's words, "You meant evil against me, but God meant it for good, to bring it about that many people should be kept alive, as they are today," why was it important for those for whom Moses originally wrote Genesis, the children of Israel, to understand specifically what God's purpose was for the suffering in Joseph's life?

The Sons of Jacob

Genesis 29–30; 34–35; 38–39; 48–49

Personal Bible Study

The Sons of Jacob

GENESIS 29–30; 34–35; 38–39; 48–49

1. Read Genesis 29:31–30:24. What do you see in the earliest days of Jacob's family that are seeds of future heartache and conflict in the family?

2. Read Genesis 34. Remembering that Moses wrote Genesis for the children of Israel as they prepared to enter the Promised Land, where they would need to drive out the Canaanites who were living there, what warnings should they have received from this terrible episode?

3. Read Genesis 35:21–26. How was Reuben's action likely more than simply a sexual matter, and how was Jacob's response less than adequate?

4. The story of Judah's sinfulness in Canaan, recorded in Genesis 38, is a stark contrast to Joseph's righteous acts in Egypt, recorded in Genesis

39. In the chart below, compare and contrast similar elements in these accounts:

Judah's Sexual Sin with Tamar	Joseph's Refusal to Sin Sexually with Potiphar's Wife
Gen. 38:1	Gen. 39:1
Gen. 38:16	Gen. 39: 7, 10
Gen. 38:18, 25	Gen. 39: 12–13, 16–18
Gen. 38:26	Gen. 39:19–20

5. Read 38:27–30. Over and over again in Genesis, God has surprised us by choosing the one we didn't expect, proving that he is the one who determines who is esteemed in his sight. How is this the case with Judah and with his sons, Zerah and Perez? (Be sure to include the insight gained from Matt. 1:3 or Luke 3:33.)

6. Read Genesis 48. Whereas Joseph was born in Canaan and spent his early years in the Patriarch's tents, Joseph's sons were born in Egypt and grew up in the opulence and opportunities of Pharaoh's courts. Their mother was the daughter of an Egyptian priest of sun worship. With this in mind, why would it have been important to Jacob to adopt these boys as his own and bless them?

7. Read Genesis 49:1–28. How is each aspect of the prophecy for Judah and his tribe fulfilled by Christ? In the chart below, read the specific prophecy Jacob spoke and note in the second column how it is fulfilled by Christ.

Prophesied to Judah	Fulfilled by Christ
Praise: "Judah, your brothers shall praise you . . . bow down before you." (Gen. 49:8)	Phil. 2:9–10
Power: "Your hand shall be on the neck of your enemies. . . . Judah is a lion's cub." (Gen. 49:8–9)	Rev. 5:5, 11:16–18
Preeminence: "The scepter shall not depart from Judah, nor the ruler's staff from between his feet." (Gen. 49:10)	Rev. 19:14–16
Prosperity: "The choice vine . . . washed his garments in wine. . . . Teeth whiter than milk." (Gen. 49:11–12)	John 2:1–11; Eph. 1:18; 2:7

8. Genesis has provided us with a history on the origins of the people of God—the people God has called to himself and covenanted with. The rest of the Bible is not a general history of the world but the history of God's people, and the Bible ends with a picture of the future of God's people. What key truth do we learn about those God calls "my people" from each of the following verses:

∿ Genesis 17:7–8

∿ Exodus 3:10

∼ Ruth 1:16

∼ Isaiah 19:21–25

∼ Jeremiah 24:7

∼ Ezekiel 37:12–14

∼ Zechariah 2:10–12

∼ Romans 9:25–27

∼ Galatians 3:27–29

∼ Revelation 21:7

They Say You Can't Choose Your Family

In the classic *To Kill a Mockingbird* by Harper Lee, Jem says, "Atticus says you can choose your friends but you sho' can't choose your family, an' they're still kin to you no matter whether you acknowledge 'em or not, and it makes you look right silly when you don't."[1]

I suppose Atticus has a point. We don't get to choose the family we were born to though some of us are certain that if we could have, we would certainly have made a far superior choice. If you could have chosen your family, what would you have chosen? Would you have chosen people who were more refined and socially connected or more relaxed and unconventional? Would you have chosen relatives who had a different set of values than your family or a different family culture than the one you grew up in? Do you ever look around at your friends and at times feel a little envious of the family they came from, thinking to yourself, "Why wasn't I born into a family with a summer home in the mountains or a legacy of foreign mission work or a history of higher education or business acumen? Why wasn't I born into a family with grandparents who taught their children and grandchildren how to can peaches or how to make sales or how to pray? Why didn't I get a dad who would have passed along his good athletic genes or a mom who would have passed along her genes for thin thighs and smooth skin?"

But none of us got to choose, did we? We didn't get to choose where we were born, when we were born, or into what family we were born.

But God did.

---

[1] Harper Lee, *To Kill a Mockingbird* (New York: Harper Collins, 1960), 371.

That's what we've seen in Genesis—God calling and forming the family he would one day be born into. God called Abraham away from his own family to establish a new family—a new family that God would uniquely call "my people." His intention was that the descendants of Abraham through Isaac, and the descendants of Isaac through Jacob, and the descendants of the twelve sons of Jacob would form a new family, a new people, a new nation—and not just any family or people or nation but uniquely the one God would call "my people." This would be the family into whom the Promised One would be born. One day God would enfold himself into a virgin's womb, a woman who was a descendant of this family.

So since God got to choose the family he was born into, what kind of family did he choose? Most of us might think we could have chosen better for him too. No effort has been made by the biblical writer to sanitize the portrait of this family in Genesis. Does it not add to the credibility of the Bible that there's no effort to hide the embarrassing flaws and failures of the family God calls "my people"? Aren't there some things about your family, some episodes in your history, that you don't put out there for everyone to know about, things that are embarrassing or even shameful or shocking? If we were giving God advice, surely we would tell him to be a bit more discrete in hanging out the family laundry.

As we come to the end of Genesis, Jacob and his sons, a contingent of seventy people in all, have gathered in Egypt. This is a polygamous family marked by manipulation, incest, prostitution, jealousy, murder, rape, sibling rivalry, idolatry, deceit, and estrangement. As we've gotten to know them better, we want to say to God, "Are you sure that *these* are the people you want to give your name to, the ones to whom you want to entrust the future of your salvation plan, the ones you want to claim as your own treasured possession?" These are not exactly the kind of people who inspire confidence for putting God's name on display in the world. They do not seem to be in any way worthy of this honor.

> *God chose me in Christ not because I'm good, but to give me his goodness.*

If you want to get a feel for the family I was born into, one of the simplest ways to do it is to look at the album I have in my living room of nearly fifty years' worth of my parents' photo Christmas cards. You will see the one taken on the front porch of their first little house with my older sister and my skinny daddy and pregnant mother, and you'll know how they got their start. Later you'll see the picture taken with all of us standing in front of my dad's four-seater airplane we traveled in throughout my growing up, and you'll know that we were a family who enjoyed adventure. You'll see the picture with all of us making a fuss over my little brother, Tom, the year he was adopted. A couple of years ago the photo card was a picture of my parents with me and my brother and sister and our children on a fiftieth anniversary cruise to Alaska, and in that picture you'll see who our family has become.

I'm quite sure Jacob's family didn't take a Christmas card photo every year and send it along with a newsy letter about all the developments and activities and travels of the family that year, but what do you think we would have seen in those family photos and what would we have read in that family letter if they had? Go with me on this, using your imagination with me if you will, as we open up their family album to get a feel for this family God calls "my people," the family God chose to be born into.

A Picture of Family Failure

Imagine that first family photo Jacob sent out when he finally had a wife of his own. No, wait a minute, there are two wives in the picture—the pretty one, Rachel, on the right, and he has his arm around her, and her not-so-pretty older sister, Leah, on the left. There's plenty of space between these two, almost as if Jacob wishes she wasn't in the picture. But while Rachel stands in Jacob's embrace with no children, Leah is surrounded by a brood of children—six sons and a daughter. Jacob's firstborn son, Reuben, is nestled between him and his mother, Leah, with Simeon, Levi, Judah, Issachar, Zebulun, and Dinah filling in all around. The accompanying letter might read:

Dear Friends,

　　We're living here in Haran where I continue to watch over the flocks of my uncle Laban. During the time I've been here, the flocks and herds have grown plenty, making Uncle Laban very wealthy. But I'm still just a hired hand. So I'm planning to ask Uncle Laban to release me soon so I can come home to my own country. When we come, we'll be a big group. In addition to my children with Leah, I will also bring the children born to me by Leah and Rachel's maid-servants—Dan, Naphtali, Gad, and Asher. But our big news is that we will also be bringing a baby! After all these years, God has finally answered Rachel's prayers, and she is pregnant! We can hardly wait! [Genesis 29–30].

Perhaps the next family photo is taken as they hastily prepared to leave Haran, sneaking away while Laban was out shearing sheep. Leah and Rachel along with Jacob's concubine wives, Bilhah and Zilpah, are mounted on top of camels with their children around them and all of their belongings stuffed in packs hanging from the saddles. The letter reads:

We're on our way home! We had to slip away secretly because Laban seems to have grown increasingly resentful toward me, even though I've only increased all of his wealth. But we had to go. Actually the Lord spoke to me (I know that is hard for all of you who only remember me as a schemer and a cheater to believe, but it's true). God told me to return to the land of my father and grand-father. And he promised to be with me. But I have an important stop to make first. I have to make things right with Esau. If you don't hear from me next year, you'll know that didn't go so well. [Genesis 30–31]

Jacob's reunion with his brother, Esau, went far better than he expected or deserved. And as they said good-bye, Jacob told his brother that he would meet him in Sier. But really he had no intention of that. And sadly he didn't go to Bethel either, as God had instructed, but set-tled in Shechem, which, though it was within the land of Canaan, was only halfway obedience.

It was only after Jacob's family was forced to leave Shechem in shame that they went on to Bethel. There are no smiles in the next fam-ily photo. Dinah, his daughter, had been raped by the son of the local prince. And while Jacob seemed to barely care, Dinah's brothers Simeon and Levi were furious and took it upon themselves to slaughter every male in the town and help themselves to their possessions. This family photo is taken in Bethel as they all gathered around the altar Jacob built as he renewed his vow of wholehearted devotion to God. The letter might have read:

> I hardly know where to start. It's been a very difficult year. We've left Shechem, and we've come to Bethel, where I should have settled long ago as God told me to. And we're making a fresh start of things. We've gotten rid of all the pagan idols that were in our tents. I buried them under the great tree near Shechem. And God has met with me again here at Bethel. In fact, he has given me a new name, a name that gives me hope that he is not finished with me, and so I sign this with that new name—Israel—which means "God fights." [Genesis 34–35]

It is Jacob and his brother Esau gathered around their father, Isaac's, bed in the next photo. Conveniently, none of the wives or grandchildren are around for this picture. The love of Jacob's life, Rachel, had died in childbirth, and there is just not as much joy taking a family photo without her. And then there is the awkwardness of Reuben, who, in an act of sedition, slept with Bilhah, one of his father's concubines, the mother of his brothers Dan and Naphtali. As a result, Reuben was stripped of his firstborn status and inheritance and really doesn't like being around Jacob much anymore. In the letter, Jacob may have written:

> It is hard to take up my pen to write, as I still don't feel like doing much of anything since Rachel died. Burying my father has only added to my sorrow. It was good to be there with him and Esau around his bed when Dad took his last breath, but I still feel like an outsider when I'm with the two of them. Benjamin, the son of my right hand, is always here to cheer me up as he toddles around the tent. But ever since I transferred the firstborn status from Reuben to Joseph and gave him a special robe to wear as a sign of his place in the family, there is constant tension in the tents. Let's just say that I'm not sure everyone is coming home for a big family dinner this year. [Genesis 35]

Then, a few years later there are only two people in the picture—a darkened, slump-shouldered Jacob with his young son Benjamin:

Friends,

It is only me and Benjamin in the picture this year. Ever since Joseph was killed by a wild animal when I sent him into the fields to check on his brothers, I don't go out much, and the rest of the boys always seem to have some reason to be somewhere else. As you remember, Judah moved away to live in Adullam a while ago, where he married a Canaanite woman and had two sons, Er and Onan, who died, and another son Shelah, who is promised to Er's widow, Tamar. But it looks like that is not going to happen now, since Judah slept with Tamar himself, thinking she was a prostitute, and now she is pregnant with his child (I mean children, since it looks like it will be twins). Sometimes I wonder what God is going to have to do to accomplish everything he has promised to do through our family, because it is so hard to live here separately among the Canaanites and not be absorbed by them and their ways. We're praying for rain here, as we haven't had any for quite a while now and food is becoming scarce. I'm thinking about sending the older boys over to Egypt because we've heard there is grain being distributed there to anyone who is hungry. [Genesis 37–38]

Then, years later, those on Jacob's list get a dramatically different picture and report from Jacob. Squeezed into the photo are all seventy members of Jacob's family, and there in the background you can see the pyramids of Egypt! Jacob hardly knows where to start in giving his friends the unbelievably good news:

I don't need any gifts this year. I've been given the most incredible gift I could ever imagine. But, honestly, I never even imagined it. As you can see, I'm in Egypt, and would you believe that I am surrounded by all of my sons and their wives and my grandchildren? And when I say "all of my sons," I mean all of them. I know the big, strong, tall one standing by me looks like an Egyptian, but that is my son Joseph—the son I've spent so many years mourning! I thought he was dead all those years, but it ends up God had sent him ahead of us to Egypt so that he would be in a place to provide for us when the famine came. Remember that dream he had so many years ago that caused so much discord in the family? It came true! Now we know for sure it wasn't his ambitious imagination; it was from God. All the boys are here, and they bowed down before Joseph just like he dreamed, because he is the prime minister of Egypt. What is most amazing is that Joseph is not a bitter man. He is a tender man, a godly man, a wise man. He has forgiven his brothers because he's convinced that God has been in this all along. And he is taking care of us. Pharaoh himself has welcomed us to make ourselves at home. In fact we've been assigned the best land of Egypt. We live in the Goshen region, separate from all the Egyptians, because they're not real keen on shepherds. We have land, we have food, and we have each other, and there's only one thing more I want. I've made Joseph swear to me that they will not bury me in Egypt but will take my body out of Egypt and bury me with my ancestors in Canaan. While we may be settled here now, I know my family will not be here forever. God marked out the boundaries of the land of Canaan for my grandfather Abraham, and he promised the entire territory would one day belong to his descendants. And I know God will make good on his promise. [Genesis 46–47]

A Picture of the Family's Future

This brings us to Jacob's final family photo and letter, sent out after his death. Taken at the blessing of Joseph's two sons, Manasseh and Ephraim, the photo shows Jacob with his hands crossed, his right hand on the younger son, Ephraim, and his left on the head of Manasseh, elevating Joseph's sons as coheirs with his other sons.

Dear friends of our father, Jacob,

We want to let you know that shortly after we took this photo, our father drew his feet into the bed, breathed his last, and joined our grandfather Isaac and great-grandfather Abraham in death. When the period of mourning is over, we'll be bringing his body back to the land of Canaan for burial as he made us promise we would. In fact, right before he died he reminded Joseph of the time God Almighty appeared to him at Luz and said, "I will make you fruitful, and I will multiply your descendants. I will make you a multitude of nations. And I will give this land of Canaan to your descendants after you as an everlasting possession." We know God has made our father fruitful. There are more grandkids around here these days than we can keep count of. But, honestly, it is hard for us to understand how God is going to accomplish his promise to give us the land of Canaan as an everlasting possession. As you know, all we own now is the plot of land on which we will bury our father beside his father. And for now, we've got it good here in Goshen.

Father gathered all of us together around his bed right before he died, and he spoke to each of us, telling us what will happen to us in the days to come. It was clear to us that he was speaking to us not as Jacob but as Israel, as a true prophet of God. And while it was all a blessing, since all of us are blessed just to be in this family set apart by God for his purposes, some of what he had to say was hard to hear. We know that many of us are going to have to face the consequences of what we've done in the past. There's plenty we could tell you about what he said but we don't want this to be one of those long, boring family letters with too much information, so we'll limit it to just one son's blessing, since it was so surprising.

Now, you probably think we want to tell you about Joseph's blessing. Certainly he has become the star of the family. But while our father's blessing on Joseph was generous, and while we fully anticipate Ephraim and Manasseh's tribes will become large and powerful, it is not Joseph's blessing we must tell you about.

You know about Judah. You know that he's the one who suggested we sell off Joseph to the slave traders and deceive our dad by dipping Joseph's coat in goat's blood. And you know that he left home a long time ago and moved to Adullam, and that two of his sons died because they were so evil, and that Judah ended up conceiving a child with his daughter-in-law Tamar. But hopefully you also know that when he was confronted with that, he acknowledged his sin. All of us who knew him recognized that something was happening in his life. This was humbling to him, and he began to change. Since then, Tamar has given birth to twins named Shelah and Perez, and it looks like once again in our family, the younger is going to be the one to watch.

A few years ago, when we first got here to Egypt, before Joseph revealed himself to us, we all saw the greatest evidence that God was working in Judah's life. Standing in front of the brother he had sold into slavery, he said, "God has found out the guilt of your servants." He wasn't trying to cover it up anymore. Then Judah went into this long speech, pleading with Joseph to put him into prison instead of keeping Benjamin. The same guy who was once so jealous of his favored brother Joseph, that he was willing to sell him off as a foreign slave, was now willing to offer himself to be put in prison in place of his favored brother Benjamin. The same guy who had callously let his father believe for twenty years that his son was dead could not bear the thought that his father would grieve the loss of another favorite son.

Judah is well aware of what he deserves because of how he has lived most of his life. That's why, as our father, Jacob, was working his way through his sons in birth order, telling them of what was to come, Judah was standing there shaking in his sandals. He heard what our father said to Reuben, Simeon, and Levi, and, honestly, what God said to them seemed more like a curse than a blessing. Judah knew that he deserved no less than what they received, based on the evil things he has done. So that's why we were all surprised by dad's blessing for Judah. Here's what he said:

> Judah, your brothers will praise you.
>> You will grasp your enemies by the neck.
>> All your relatives will bow before you.

> Judah, my son, is a young lion
>> that has finished eating its prey.
> Like a lion he crouches and lies down;
>> like a lioness—who dares to rouse him?
> The scepter will not depart from Judah,
>> nor the ruler's staff from his descendants,
> until the coming of the one to whom it belongs,
>> the one whom all nations will honor.
> He ties his foal to a grapevine,
>> the colt of his donkey to a choice vine.
> He washes his clothes in wine,
>> his robes in the blood of grapes.
> His eyes are darker than wine,
>> and his teeth are whiter than milk. (Gen. 49:8–12 NLT)

To be honest, there's a lot about this blessing that we simply don't under-stand at this point. We do know that our father's words are really more about our descendants than about us, since we are old. In fact, we're beginning to wonder if Judah's blessing is really about one particular descendant. When we think through what Dad said, the only way we can make sense of it is if the offspring God promised in the day of Adam and Eve will be born to one of Judah's descendants. If the Promised One comes through Judah's descendants, it makes sense that all of our descendants will praise him and bow down before him and that he will be powerful like a lion, a ruler whom all nations will honor, an heir who will live in the abundance of all our God's good gifts.

In the middle of all the blessings, our father said something inter-esting that we simply cannot forget. He said, "I wait for your salvation, O LORD" (Gen. 49:18). And when he said it, we realized that he wasn't talking about an experience but about a person. Our father, Jacob, put his hope in the God who saves, Yeshua. And that's what we intend to do too.

While there is so much we don't understand, like our father before us and his father before him and his father before him, we have heard God's call to be his people, and we are holding on to his promises. We too wait for God's salvation, for Yeshua.

Signed,
Reuben, Simeon, Levi, Judah, Issachar, Zebulun, Gad, Asher, Joseph, Benjamin, Manasseh, Ephraim, Dan, and Naphtali

P.S. Come see us sometime in Goshen. We probably won't be here long. [see Genesis 48–49]

But, of course, they would be there for four hundred years before God brought them out of Egypt and into the Promised Land. Over the years to come many sons of Judah would rule over them as kings, just as Jacob had prophesied, including Israel's greatest king, David, who established a kingly dynasty that continued through Solomon, Asa, Jehoshaphat, Azariah, Jotham, and Josiah. But the sons of Jacob continued to wait and look for the one to whom the scepter belongs, the one whom all nations will honor, the king whose kingdom will never end.

A Picture of Fulfillment

And it wasn't just sons of Jacob who watched and waited. Years later, magi from the east came to Jerusalem and asked, "Where is he who has been born king of the Jews? For we saw his star when it rose and have come to worship him" (Matt. 2:2). He had finally come, the king whom all nations will honor, the one to whom the scepter belongs. The chief priests and scribes were summoned by Herod to find out where the Christ whom his Israelite subjects had been waiting for was supposed to be born.

> They told him, "In Bethlehem of Judea, for so it is written by the prophet:
> 'And you, O Bethlehem, in the land of Judah,
>   are by no means least among the rulers of Judah;
> for from you shall come a ruler
>   who will shepherd my people Israel.'" (Matt. 2:5–6)

When one of those who had been waiting and watching, Simeon, came into the temple and saw the baby Jesus held in his mother's arms, he realized that this was the salvation Jacob had put his hope in. The waiting of all the sons of Jacob was over, and he said:

> Lord, now you are letting your servant depart in peace,
>   according to your word;
> for my eyes have seen your salvation
>   that you have prepared in the presence of all peoples,
> a light for revelation to the Gentiles,
>   and for glory to your people Israel. (Luke 2:29–32)

Interestingly Simeon understood something that most Jewish people of his day did not—that the coming of Messiah was not solely
for Israel. Ever since God had prom-
ised Abraham that his descendants
would be a blessing to all the families of the earth, it was clear that the
Promised One was coming to bless
the whole world, not just the children of Israel.

> *God chose me in Christ
> not because I am
> beautiful, but to make
> me beautiful.*

The people of God began as a family called out of the rest of
humanity. Then, under Moses, the people of God became a nation,
and God instituted special civil and ceremonial laws to separate his
national people from the Gentile pagans around them. This separation
was what Paul was talking about when he wrote to Gentile believers,
"You were at that time separated from Christ, alienated from the com-
monwealth of Israel and strangers to the covenants of promise, having
no hope and without God in the world" (Eph. 2:12).

But when Christ came, he made a way for God to accomplish the
greater plan that he had intended from the very beginning—that those
"who once were far off" might be "brought near" (Eph. 2:13).

When Jesus launched his ministry, he chose twelve men as his
disciples. And just as Jacob's sons seemed an unlikely lot to represent
God and do the work of God in the world, so did these twelve men—
fishermen, a revolutionary, a sell-out to the Romans, a thief and betrayer.
They made an unimpressive group.

Do you think it was just a coincidence that he chose twelve? Of
course not. Jesus was signaling to all those who thought the promises
of Abraham were only for Abraham's physical descendants that he was
establishing a new people for God, "a chosen race, a royal priesthood,
a holy nation, a people for his own possession" (1 Pet. 2:9). Belonging
in this family would not come based on the blood that flows through a
person's veins but by the belief that transforms a person's heart—not by
birth but by rebirth. Just as Jacob's sons were made into the people of
God only by God's mercy, so are all people made into the people of God
only by God's mercy (1 Pet. 2:10). Just as Abraham established a new

family for God by responding to the call of God, so did these disciples establish this new family for God, the church, by responding to the call of Jesus when he said to them, "Follow me."

They followed him, all the way to the cross. But after that, they wondered if it had all been a mistake. How could Jesus have been the lion of the tribe of Judah? He was a lamb who was slaughtered. Rather than a king taking his throne, he was a servant who suffered.

It was not the first time Jesus came that he fulfilled all that Jacob prophesied regarding Judah's great descendant. If we want to see the complete fulfillment of Jacob's prophecy concerning Judah, we need some assistance from the apostle John. John provides us not with a family photo from the past but with a picture of the future of the people of God, a picture drawn with words in the book of Revelation. Revelation is not a story or instruction; it is a series of pictures, which is why John says, "I saw," thirty-three times. Think of it as a family photo from the future, a picture of the family of God gathered around the throne of God—a family made up of people like Jacob and his sons who determined to wait for the salvation of the Lord. It is a family photo of people like Peter and John and Matthew and Thomas, who were blessed to see Yeshua and walk with him, and people like you and me who look back in faith at the salvation of the Lord, who came in the person of Jesus, and look forward to his coming again.

At first, the picture painted for us seems to be a hopeless and sorrowful scene:

> And I saw a strong angel proclaiming with a loud voice, "Who is worthy to open the scroll and break its seals?" And no one in heaven or on earth or under the earth was able to open the scroll or to look into it, and I began to weep loudly because no one was found worthy to open the scroll or to look into it. (Rev. 5:2–4)

In this heavenly drama, the search is on for someone who is worthy to open the scroll that contains God's sovereign plans for history—someone who is pure enough to be worthy, someone who is wise enough to be worthy, someone who is loving enough to bring God's plan for his people to its glorious fulfillment. We need only look back at the lives of the sons of Jacob, at the failures of the twelve apostles, and at our own reflections to understand this sad scene of rampant unworthiness. But we haven't yet seen the whole picture.

> One of the elders said to me, "Weep no more; behold, the Lion of the tribe of Judah, the Root of David, has conquered, so that he can open the scroll and its seven seals." (Rev. 5:5)

Finally, there he is, the Lion of the tribe of Judah! He is worthy! He has conquered his enemies just like Jacob said he would. All of God's people, everyone in his family, are bowing down to him. And they are singing:

> Worthy are you to take the scroll
>> and to open its seals,
> for you were slain, and by your blood you ransomed people for God
>> from every tribe and language and people and nation,
> and you have made them a kingdom and priests to our God,
>> and they shall reign on the earth. (Rev. 5:9–10)

In fact, the Lion of the tribe of Judah is the Lamb who was slain! And he is taking his throne, surrounded by song. It is not the angels who sing this song. They have no need to be ransomed. The people who sing this song are unworthy on their own to be made into the people of God, yet God has adopted them and given them his name. These are the ones who never would have chosen him if left on their own, yet, in mercy, he chose them, called them, and drew them to himself. "Once you were not a people, but now you are God's people," and "he chose us in him before the foundation of the world, that we should be holy and blameless before him. In love he predestined us for adoption as sons through Jesus Christ" (1 Pet. 2:10; Eph. 1:4–5).

Have you sometimes wondered if, when the truth about you is revealed, it will disqualify you from being included in the people of God? Have you been afraid that when it comes down to it, God will be ashamed to name you as his own? Look at the twelve sons of Jacob. Look at the twelve apostles. And see that Jesus is populating his family, his church, with imperfect but repentant people, flagrant but forgiven sinners. We bring nothing to the table that makes us worthy to be claimed by Christ. It is the Lamb who was slain who has made us worthy. The Lion of the tribe of Judah has invited us to reign with him over his kingdom, the Promised Land God has always intended his people to live in—the new heaven and new earth.

> *God chose me in Christ not because I am strong, but because he wants to be the strength of my life.*

Seeing Jesus throughout Genesis has made us want to join in the song of praise around the throne, hasn't it?

> Lion of the tribe of Judah, who reigns from your throne;
>   Savior of the world who feeds our hungry souls;
>   Israel of God, who has shown us the face of God;
>   beloved Son, from whom the knife was not spared;
>   our shield, our very great reward;
>   Lord of the nations;
>   ark of God, who protects us from the judgment we deserve;
>   second Adam, who gained for us more than the first Adam took from us,
>   living Word and light of the world—
>   we have seen you throughout the pages of Genesis, and it has
>   made us love you more and long for you more.
>   You are the Promised One who came, and you will come again.
>   Like Jacob and his sons, we wait for your salvation, O Lord.

How Genesis Points to What Is Yet to Come: Seated on Twelve Thrones

Jesus told his twelve disciples, "Truly, I say to you, in the new world, when the Son of Man will sit on his glorious throne, you who have followed me will also sit on twelve thrones, judging the twelve tribes of Israel" (Matt. 19:28). In other words, Jesus's apostles would be the leaders of the true remnant of God's people made up of Jews and Gentiles, who, by embracing

Jesus, would bring judgment to all who had the advantages of having the promises of God and yet rejected Christ.

Revelation 7 describes the new world Jesus spoke of, in which there will be those from every tribe of the sons of Israel (v. 5). But it is not just sons of Israel who are there. There will be "a great multitude that no one could number, from every nation, from all tribes and peoples and languages, standing before the throne and before the Lamb, clothed in white robes, with palm branches in their hands, and crying out with a loud voice, 'Salvation belongs to our God who sits on the throne, and to the Lamb'" (Rev. 7:9–10.) The joy of all those around the throne who have descended from the twelve tribes will result from how God used the Jews' rejection of Christ to bring in the Gentiles (Rom. 11:11–12). All will stand together as one before the throne. Revelation 21 describes the city where the people of God, made up of Old and New Testament saints who put their hope in the Promised One, will live:

> And he carried me away in the Spirit to a great, high mountain, and showed me the holy city Jerusalem coming down out of heaven from God, having the glory of God, its radiance like a most rare jewel, like a jasper, clear as crystal. It had a great, high wall, with twelve gates, and at the gates twelve angels, and on the gates the names of the twelve tribes of the sons of Israel were inscribed—on the east three gates, on the north three gates, on the south three gates, and on the west three gates. And the wall of the city had twelve foundations, and on them were the twelve names of the twelve apostles of the Lamb. (Rev. 21:10–14)

The gates that lead into this city have the names of the twelve tribes. The twelve tribes were led by those who at one point turned away from God's provision, joined themselves with the world around them, and did very wicked things. But they were chosen by God, blessed by God, and changed by God as his grace worked in them and enabled them to put their hope in the Promised One. If their names are written above the gates, then there is hope for those of us who have turned away from God's provision, joined ourselves to the world around us, done very wicked things, and then turned toward God in repentance and faith. The names of the twelve tribes on the gates give us confidence that we, too, will be welcomed into this city.

The foundation of the walls around this city bear the names of the twelve apostles. Once again these twelve men were profoundly flawed people. Yet they were so transformed by their experience with Jesus Christ that they spent the rest of their lives witnessing to the world around them that Jesus was the Promised One sent from God. If the foundation of the walls of the city of God has the names of the twelve apostles, we know it is the message they proclaimed—that Jesus was the true Israel of God and must be believed in—that is the foundation of our security. Forever we will be encircled in the city of God by the testimony of the twelve apostles: "Jesus is the stone that was rejected by you, the builders, which has become the cornerstone. And there is salvation in no one else, for there is no other name under heaven given among men by which we must be saved" (Acts 4:11–12).

Into eternity, the people of God—those who have been chosen by God, chastised by God, changed by God, cherished by God—will enjoy the salvation of God.

Discussion Guide

The Sons of Jacob

GENESIS 29–30; 34–35; 38–39; 48–49

Getting the Discussion Going

1. At the beginning of the chapter, there was a quote from the classic *To Kill a Mockingbird* in which Jem says, "Atticus says you can choose your friends but you sho' can't choose your family, an' they're still kin to you no matter whether you acknowledge 'em or not, and it makes you look right silly when you don't." What kinds of things would most of us be looking for if we could choose our own family?

Getting to the Heart of It

2. This week we've been focused on the sons of Jacob, the leaders of the twelve tribes who will make up the nation of Israel. What stands out to you about these twelve sons and about God's choosing them to be his people?

3. Read Deuteronomy 7:7–9 and 1 Corinthians 1:27–29. What do these verses reveal about how God chooses who will belong to him?

4. In the Old Testament, the people of God weren't synonymous with the physical descendants of Abraham, Isaac, and Jacob but most often with the "true sons of Abraham," who put their faith in God's promise of an offspring who would save his people from their sins and therefore bless them. In the same way, the people of God in the New Testament era are those who have put their faith in Jesus as the promised offspring through whom salvation and blessings flow. So, the people of God are those in both the Old and New Testament eras who responded to God

by faith and whose spiritual origin rests exclusively in God's grace. Look back at the notes you made in the final Personal Bible Study question about those God called "my people." What stood out to you? Did anything change, challenge, or expand on whom you've always understood to be the people of God?

5. Many of us come to the Bible with an individualistic view of Christianity. While God certainly cares for us and interacts with us as individuals, and his purposes for us are personal, we have to balance that perspective with the truth that the heart of the story of the Bible is God's dealings not with individuals but with a people—a people he has called to himself from all the peoples of the earth. So while there is a great deal we can learn from Genesis about how we can expect God to deal with us as individuals, we cannot miss the context, which is that God's purposes are not primarily about individuals but about his chosen people. What does this mean for the person who says, "I love Jesus, but I don't need the church"?

Getting Personal

6. In the blessings Jacob gave to his sons, we see the judgment and mercy of God at work. Several of them would have to live with some natural consequences of their past actions. Yet all of them were blessed by being part of God's chosen people. As you think about your own past failures, the consequences you've lived with because of past sins, how does it encourage you to see God's choice of these sons of Jacob as his special possession?

Getting How It Fits into the Big Picture

7. Throughout this study, we have been seeking to grasp how the passage we're studying fits into the bigger story of God's plan for redemption. Both Genesis and Revelation end on a similar note—waiting for the one to whom the scepter belongs, the salvation of the Lord (Gen. 49:10, 18). Revelation ends with the cry, "Come, Lord Jesus!" (22:20). How is our waiting for God's salvation like that of the sons of Jacob, and how is it different?

Bibliography

Atkinson, David. *The Message of Genesis 1–11*. Downers Grove, IL: InterVarsity, 1990.

Boice, James Montgomery. *Genesis: An Expositional Commentary*. 3 vols. Grand Rapids, MI: Zondervan, 1987.

Carson, D. A. "That First Temptation: Sin and the Fall." Sermon, European Leadership Forum, 2003.

Clowney, Edmund P. *The Unfolding Mystery: Discovering Christ in the Old Testament*. Phillipsburg, NJ: P&R, 1988.

Clowney, Edmund P., and Timothy J. Keller. "Preaching Christ in a Postmodern World." Audio recording. Reformed Theological Seminary, Jackson, MS, n.d.

De Graaf, S. G. *Promise and Deliverance: From Creation to the Conquest of Canaan*. Vol. 1. St. Catherines, Ontario: Paideia Press, 1979.

Duguid, Iain M. *Living in the Gap Between Promise and Reality*. Phillipsburg, NJ: P&R, 1999.

———. *Living in the Grip of Relentless Grace*. Phillipsburg, NJ: P&R, 2002.

Ferguson, Sinclair B. *The Life of Jacob*. Sermon series. First Presbyterian Church, Columbia, SC, 2007.

Genesis. LifeChange Series. Colorado Springs, CO: NavPress, 1987.

Greidanus, Sidney. *Preaching Christ from Genesis*. Grand Rapids, MI: Eerdmans, 2007.

Hughes, R. Kent. *Genesis: Beginning and Blessing*. Preaching the Word. Wheaton, IL: Crossway, 2004.

Keller, Timothy J. Sermon series. *Bible: The Whole Story—Creation and Fall* (2009); *The Gospel According to Abraham* (2001); *The Gospel According to Jacob* (2001). Redeemer Presbyterian Church, New York.

Lucas, Dick. *Joseph*. Sermon series. St. Helen's Church, Bishopsgate, UK, 1986.

Pink, Arthur W. *Gleanings in Genesis*. Chicago, IL: Moody, 1922.

Williams, Michael D. *Far as the Curse Is Found: The Covenant Story of Redemption*. Phillipsburg, NJ: P&R, 2005.

For additional content, downloads,
and resources for leaders, please visit:

www.SeeingJesusInTheOldTestament.com

Also Available in the
Seeing Jesus in the Old Testament Series

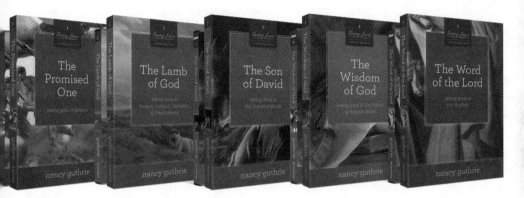

The Promised One: *Seeing Jesus in Genesis*

The Lamb of God: *Seeing Jesus in Exodus, Leviticus, Numbers, and Deuteronomy*

The Son of David: *Seeing Jesus in the Historical Books*

The Wisdom of God: *Seeing Jesus in the Psalms and Wisdom Books*

The Word of the Lord: *Seeing Jesus in the Prophets*

A companion DVD is also available for each study.